God's Gangs

God's Gangs

BARRIO MINISTRY, MASCULINITY, AND GANG RECOVERY

Edward Orozco Flores

NEW YORK UNIVERSITY PRESS

New York and London

NEW YORK UNIVERSITY PRESS
New York and London
www.nyupress.org

References to Internet websites (URLs) were accurate at the time of writing.
Neither the author nor New York University Press is responsible for URLs that
may have expired or changed since the manuscript was prepared.

LIBRARY OF CONGRESS CATALOGING-IN-PUBLICATION DATA
Flores, Edward Orozco.
God's gangs : barrio ministry, masculinity, and gang recovery / Edward Orozco Flores.
pages cm
Includes bibliographical references and index.
ISBN 978-1-4798-5009-9 (hardback) — ISBN 978-1-4798-7812-3 (paper)
1. Hispanic American gangs—California—Los Angeles. 2. Ex-gang members—
Rehabilitation—California—Los Angeles. 3. Ex-gang members—Services for—California—
Los Angeles. 4. Church work with Hispanic Americans—California—Los Angeles.
5. Church and social problems—California—Los Angeles. 6. Hispanic American men—
California—Los Angeles—Social conditions. I. Title.
HV6439.U7L725 2013
261.8'3310660979494—dc23
                        2013020339

Manufactured in the United States of America
10 9 8 7 6 5 4 3 2 1

Also available as an ebook.

For Ana

CONTENTS

LIST OF TABLES AND FIGURES

TABLES

FIGURES

ACKNOWLEDGMENTS

This book could not have been possible without a great deal of personal and professional support from family, friends, and colleagues, all the way from California to Chicago. This book was a labor of love, each phase bringing me closer not only to academic truths, but also to the beauty that is found in having an ideal writing environment.

I will forever carry the memory of Victory Outreach and Homeboy Industries' inspirational efforts. I was privileged to have been let into my respondents' lives, and I wish there was some way to reciprocate and show my deepest appreciation. Over shared meals and small visits, they taught me how to be grateful for the most minimal of life's gifts: homemade food, a simple prayer, or a big, warm handshake. These experiences blessed me with peace and joy as I engaged in the arduous, tedious, and tiring process of conducting research and writing. I was fortunate enough to have experienced a path of spiritual growth through academe.

I want to give thanks to several persons at the University of Southern California (USC). Immense gratitude goes to Pierrette Hondagneu-Sotelo, who provided unwavering support, as well as expeditious and instructive feedback. In addition, Hernan Ramirez, Glenda Marisol Flores, Lata Murti, and Emir Estrada provided a lively and inclusive environment in which to entertain core ideas that now form this book. I am also thankful to Kristen Barber, for her insightful feedback, which helped me to develop more nuanced analyses of Latino masculinity. And lastly, I would like to thank the John Randolph and Dora Haynes Foundation for a doctoral dissertation fellowship that allowed me to engage in data collection.

Just before the great leap from California to Chicago, I was met with an unexpected surprise. Dowell Myers, director of the Population Dynamics Research Group (PDRG) at USC, asked me to be his project manager for the summer. Little did I know that the work would not only be challenging, but exciting and rewarding, and that at the end of it I would have large U.S. Census and American Community Survey datasets ready and waiting to be used for this book's demographic analysis. For this, I give thanks to Linda Lou, Hyojung Lee, and Anthony Guardado, fellow researchers at PDRG, for having helped with the construction of the data files.

I want to give thanks to colleagues at the Department of Sociology at Loyola University Chicago, as well. My department chair, Rhys Williams, structured a plan that worked well to help me finish a book as a new assistant professor. Several colleagues also provided an intellectually stimulating environment, critically examining a range of issues of inequality that made me much more ambitious in my aims: Tal Wright, David Embrick, and Kelly Moore. The religion working group, consisting of Rhys, Elfriede Wedam, Courtney Irby, Todd Fuist, Thomas Josephsohn, and Beth Dougherty, offered invaluable feedback concerning the themes embedded in this book's focus on religion. As with all writing, however, any mistakes in this book are solely attributable to the author.

Endless thanks go to my immediate family for their social support. My parents, Maria Elena Orozco and Alberto Jiménez Flores, hail from *la Sierra*—a rural, mountainous range in west-central Mexico that holds the substance from which myths are made. Their immense passion for learning and penchant for always finding new family stories to tell gave me the ideal background with which to enter into a Ph.D. program. They have an inexhaustible reservoir of oral history that always spills out at the dinner table, and as a result, I have been motivated to seek no other career but one dedicated to the pursuit of knowledge. They have a Ph.D. in our family's history, and mine is in sociology.

I want to thank my siblings, Judy, Josh, and Hazel, who have given me a great deal of support throughout my life. Judy has shared her wisdom as the first to go to college, Josh has a talent for making my visits home seem like just any other day, and Hazel gives me joy when she says it is her goal to follow in my footsteps. And, I would also like to acknowledge the Padillas. The Padillas are known for finding great ways to celebrate, and they were the first to celebrate my book contract. Grandma Ramona, Grandpa Ed, Maggie, Jesus, Yolanda, Michael, Jesse,

Krystal, Kiko, Kenya, Jamie, and Caroline all created a lively environment in which to take a break from work.

My final words of gratitude are reserved for my partner, Ana Maria Padilla. Ana shares a keen interest in social justice issues, and in the short span of a few years I have received much more fulfillment than I could have dreamed. We never tire of talking about her expertise (organizing and research) or of mine, of inspiring stories, or of our daily frustrations. Ana has supported me, immeasurably contributing to the development of this book, by enduring the most noble of all sacrifices: moving with an academic to a cold, far-away state. For this Ana, I owe you my support. In the words of a Mario Benedetti poem, you are *mi amor mi cómplice y todo*.

Introduction

I visited Sergio, a twenty-five-year-old former Chicano gang member, one bright, sunny Saturday at a small home he was renting near an East Los Angeles cemetery.[1] As I stood on the porch of his house knocking on the front door, I noticed a couple of plants in clay pots and a cluttered mess: weights and a rusty weight machine, cartons and candy wrappers, two lawn chairs with light cigarette ash, and ants creeping around the cracked paint of his porch's thin pillars. Sergio greeted me, shirtless, in his loud, boisterous voice, with a firm handshake that pulled me in to a half-embrace. He invited me inside, offered me a glass of water, and shouted to his son and girlfriend in the next room that I had come to visit.

As we sat down, I noticed that he had two fresh tattoos in green writing: one in block letters above his chest that bore the name of his two-year-old son, Benito, and another that rested on his left shoulder blade with the words "Golden Brown" in cursive. I spotted them just before his son crawled up on a chair and slammed a case of dominos down on the wooden dining table where we were seated. Sergio asked his son in an eager tone, "Wanna play dominos, Benito?"

Sergio quickly turned to me and asked if I knew how to play dominos. He explained that he had learned when he was incarcerated years before and that he would show me if I didn't already know. As his son fumbled with our pieces, I asked Sergio about the origin of the second tattoo. He revealed that "Golden Brown" was a phrase that an artist from Homeboy Industries fashioned, referring to "people who come from a street background, and don't want to feel proud about it" but at the same time "don't feel ashamed of it" and are now focused on "being family men and supporting their family." He identified with this group. This book conceptualizes this expression of masculinity, in which Sergio distanced himself from past Chicano gang involvement and embraced domesticity, as *reformed barrio masculinity*.

This book investigates a growing feature of contemporary urban social life: recovery from gang life. Sergio, who had spent eighteen months in Juvenile Hall and experienced drugs and gang violence, was content to have left gang life behind. He was now trying to earn a steady income and "be there" for his girlfriend and child, like several other male recovering gang members we will meet in this volume. Yet in the course of Sergio's path stood several obstacles, such as a criminal record, lack of education, and a drug addiction problem. However, Homeboy Industries, a nonprofit organization founded by a Jesuit priest, provided a place where he could work and receive individual and group therapy. Although his old habits, such as drug use and getting into fights, were hard to break, Sergio used spiritual practices and new definitions of masculinity he learned at Homeboy Industries to make the shift from gang activity to domestic life as a single father.[2]

Los Angeles is the epicenter of the American gang problem. In 2000, the U.S. Department of Justice's National Drug Intelligence Center estimated that there were 152,000 documented gang members in Los Angeles County, the largest gang population in the United States. According to recent estimates, gangs account for more than half of all homicides in the city (Howell et al. 2011). And the gang problem is hardly restricted to Los Angeles alone. Gangs have proliferated across the United States in the past three decades. Criminal gang activity has been reported by law enforcement personnel in states such as Oregon, Iowa, Nevada, and North Carolina—states with little or no gang activity prior to 1980 (Klein 1995). Rituals and customs from Los Angeles's Eastside gangs, such as hand signals, graffiti, and clothing styles, have spread to small towns and big cities alike. Drawing from interview data with hundreds of local law enforcement agencies nationwide, gang scholar Malcolm Klein (1995, 97) found that 94 percent of small cities (<10,000 population) and 56 percent of big cities (>100,000 population) that had no gang activity prior to 1980 had reported gang activity in 1992. However, gang members generally commit little crime (Klein 1995). Historically, many have often "matured out" of the gang lifestyle through employment and parenthood as they have reached adulthood (Vigil 1988, 108).

The Federal Bureau of Investigation (FBI) and local law enforcement agencies around the country have reacted aggressively, assuming that gangs are highly organized, violent, and proliferating due to internal migration (Klein 1995). They have pursued mass-arrest "suppression" tactics and promoted legislation aimed at deterring gang crime through intimidation. In California, as in many other states, these measures have included "gang injunction" laws that prevent gang members from congregating in public spaces, "gang enhancement" laws that enhance sentencing for violent crimes, and "three strikes" laws that mandate life sentences for third-felony convictions. These stiff measures have been shaped by, but have also helped to shape, the public perception that gang members are career criminals and that they must be prosecuted more forcefully and subjected to lengthier sentences to protect the public. Sergio recounted that, while he was incarcerated, he observed corrections officers mock inmates as they were released, declaring that most of them would be back behind bars again.

The suppression approach, which has assumed gang members to be violent and incapable of rehabilitation, is severely misguided; research on gangs suggests that most gang members do not commit serious crimes of violence (Klein 2004). However, through the escalated threat that the police pose to gang members, the suppression approach unintentionally compounds cohesiveness and organization in gangs and escalates criminal activity (Klein 2004). Rather than assume gang members cannot be rehabilitated, gang scholars have argued that gang activity is a product of social environment and suggested that efforts to address the gang problem would be best aimed at ameliorating the social conditions that give rise to gangs (Horowitz 1983; Klein 1995; Moore 1978; Rios 2011; Vigil 2007). For example, gangs tend to flourish in low-income, highly segregated urban neighborhoods that are severely marginalized and socioeconomically disadvantaged (Klein 1995). Gang members are typically black and Latino men who have experienced strained relations and violence at home, on the streets, and with police (Vigil 1988; Vigil 2007). Socioeconomic disadvantage and marginalization obstruct low-income black and Latino men's access to resources through which they might fulfill conventional expressions of manhood, such as education and employment (Horowitz 1983; Rios 2011).

To compensate for lack of access to conventional expressions of manhood, low-income black and Latino men attempt to exert control and dominance over women (Anderson 1990; Baca Zinn 1982). Marginalized black and Latino men seek areas outside of conventional, mainstream spheres (i.e., school or work), such as the streets, for the development of masculine expression (Ferguson 2000; Lopez 2003; Majors and Billson 1992; Rios 2011). Gang activity, in particular, compensates for the absence of stable employment by allowing men to symbolically create and access alternative expressions of masculine dominance through behavior, dress, and language (Lay 2004; Majors and Billson 1992; Messerschmidt 2005; Rios 2011). Describing the streets as the key setting for drug deals, fights, and love affairs, Richard Majors and Janet Billson (1992, 85) have suggested, "The streets become the community living room, the sports arena, the recreation hall." Harsh police tactics that target disadvantaged and marginalized black and Latino men further emasculate gang members and make hypermasculine performances all the more salient (Rios 2009).

Immigration further refracts the issues of race and class that give rise to gang membership. Second-generation immigrants often suffer strained relationships both with their parents' ethnic community and mainstream society, and, as a result, are particularly vulnerable to urban poverty, marginality, and gang membership (Thrasher 1927; Vigil 1988; Smith 2006). Sons of Latino immigrants often discover that their fathers' homeland "ranchero" culture may not suffice as a masculine badge of dignity or protection on the streets, and they may turn to gangs and drug dealing as masculine badges of honor, income, status, and protection (Bourgois 1995; Smith 2006). Among second- and later-generation Latinos, masculine status becomes embedded in a community code of honor, and dishonor is experienced as a loss of manhood (Horowitz 1987; Horowitz and Schwartz 1974). As a result, Chicano gang members develop aggressive, hypermasculine stances to cope with the tenuous nature of self-esteem and honor on the streets (Horowitz 1983). Chicano gang members adapt to high levels of interpersonal violence on the streets and in the criminal justice pipeline with more violence (Rios 2009). Thus, gang membership can provide protection on the streets, group loyalty, and a feeling of family belonging, but it can also encompass violent, self-destructive behavior (Hunt and Joe-Laidler 2001; Moore 1991; Vigil 2007).

Whereas the formation of coethnic communities and return visits to the native homeland help keep masculinity contests and violence among immigrants' sons in check (Smith 2006), the hostile legal reception of undocumented Latino immigrants further exacerbates disadvantage, preventing immigrants from returning home for religious and family celebrations, and stifling the formation of an immigrant coethnic community. In light of the factors that give rise to social marginality, compensatory masculinity, and gang activity, the hostile policing method of suppression is counterproductive, exacerbating the very elements that allow gangs and violence to flourish.

Amid the tide of increasingly punitive gang ordinances, support has simultaneously grown for community-based social programs that humanize gang members and attempt to meet their needs. In 1986, Father Gregory Boyle began mentoring gang members through Dolores Mission Catholic Church. Soon after, he started the Jobs For a Future (JFF) program, which sought to link gang members with employment opportunities. *Los Angeles Times* journalist Celeste Fremon (2004[1995]) beautifully captured the early years of Father Greg's outreach, which operated on the idea that labor market integration would help gang members leave gang life, in her book *G-Dog and the Homeboys*. Father Greg subsequently started the Homeboy Bakery in 1992, offering local gang members employment. In 2001, it gave rise to Homeboy Industries, serving both gang men and women.

With substantial public support and donations, Homeboy Industries moved into a large, modern $8.5 million building in downtown

Los Angeles in October 2007 (Homeboy Industries 2008). By 2010, Homeboy Industries had expanded to offer not just job training and work, but also counseling, educational programs, legal assistance, and tattoo removal. It claimed to be the largest gang intervention program in the nation, operating on a $9.8 million budget, employing roughly five hundred recovering gang members, and giving assistance to twelve thousand persons annually (Homeboy Industries 2010; Becerra 2010; Rutten 2010).[3] Antonio Villaraigosa, mayor of the City of Los Angeles, publicly hailed Homeboy Industries' efforts at the 2007 opening of their new facility, and in the following year he implemented coordinated gang prevention and intervention strategies through contracts with several local organizations.[4] For example, the City of Los Angeles began to host Summer Night Lights programs in several community parks, at which nonprofits and community groups provided recreational activities until midnight.

The rising popularity of community-based social programs has stirred a debate over restrictive versus reformist crime policy. On the one hand, proponents of "tough on crime" measures have rallied behind the restrictive "suppression" approach, advocating mass arrests and incarceration. This is reflected in public support for measures such as gang injunction laws, gang enhancement laws, and three strikes laws. On the other hand, activists and community leaders have often favored addressing gang prevention and intervention through social reform— public investment in social programs. Examples of this include the famed L.A. Bridges program, established in 1997 in response to the riots that took place in the city five years earlier, as well as the Gang Reduction and Youth Development (GRYD) program, created by Villaraigosa to succeed L.A. Bridges. Yet another example is Operation Ceasefire, a youth gun-violence intervention strategy that was first implemented in Boston in 1996 and spread to other cities such as Chicago, Pittsburgh, and Los Angeles.[5]

The debate over crime policy has been further fueled by the immigration reform debate, recasting decades-long concerns with public safety through the post-9/11 concern over "national security." In addition to mass arrest and incarceration, the federal immigration acts of 2003, 2005, and 2006 strengthened the 1996 Illegal Immigration Reform and Immigrant Responsibility Act (IIRIRA), "cross-deputizing" local law

Figure I.1. Father Greg in his office with a Homeboy (courtesy of Homeboy Industries)

enforcement officials as federal immigration agents (Marrow 2009, 770). Local officers can screen for undocumented immigrants and turn over suspects to immigration authorities through two programs: 287(g) and Secure Communities. These measures have been widely contested by activists and community leaders, who claim that restrictive immigration policies deepen inequalities in racially segregated neighborhoods. As the Obama administration has detained and deported record numbers of Latino immigrants, critics have pointed out that under 287(g) and Secure Communities many Latinos are deported for minor offenses—or for merely reporting offenses. Former Los Angeles Police Department (LAPD) chief William Bratton (2009) even wrote an op-ed piece for the *Los Angeles Times* defending "Special Order 40," which prevents the LAPD from cooperating with measures such as 287(g). Bratton defended the immigrant community, explaining that crime increases when immigrants are afraid to come forward as witnesses.

Recent online *Los Angeles Times* articles about gangs have revealed how the hot debate over gangs and crime policy has become tinged by xenophobic hostility toward undocumented immigrants. Three major gang sweeps occurred during the period in which fieldwork was conducted for the present study. In one case, the *Los Angeles Times* reported, twelve hundred law enforcement personnel, including several SWAT teams, were deployed with assault weapons and military vehicles, arresting seventy-eight members of the Avenues gang (see Rubin 2009). Responding to online coverage of the raids, several *Los Angeles Times* readers posted comments that reflected hostility toward gang members, the poor, and immigrants. One remarked, "They don't get deported and we taxpayers have to support them." Another wrote, "This FILTH'S parents should have NEVER been allowed in this country. If they hadn't been we wouldn't have this problem!!!!" (Surprisingly, the readers failed to take note that the article mentioned federal immigration officials were present, and that none of the arrested were undocumented.) Although these comments might easily be discounted as coming from a few extremists on the fringe of the immigration reform debate, analysis of mainstream media coverage of Latino immigration has suggested that extremist views play a formative role in shaping anti-immigration rhetoric (Chavez 2008). The failure to address gang crime has driven a deep wedge into crime policy debates and compounded the heated rhetoric on the issue of adjusting undocumented immigrants' legal status.

Segmented assimilation scholars, such as Alejandro Portes and Ruben Rumbaut, have taken note of the nativist, anti-immigrant backlash directed at Latinos, as well as the decline of employment prospects and rise of youth gangs in inner-city neighborhoods, and have predicted that many immigrants today will experience "downward assimilation" into the urban underclass of juvenile delinquency, gangs, and drugs (Portes and Rumbaut 2001). Portes and Rumbaut, in particular, have suggested that a hostile "context of reception" in the U.S. (as typified, for instance, by California's Proposition 187 movement) leaves

Figure I.2. Law enforcement just before the Avenues raid (courtesy of *Los Angeles Times*)

some children of immigrants vulnerable to assimilation into "oppositional," reactive ethnicities—such as Chicano or African American identity—that are associated with a rejection of mainstream American values, such as education, formal employment, and upward mobility. Segmented assimilation theory predicts disturbing outcomes based on these trends: given a hostile context of reception for immigrants, their children and subsequent generations will form reactive racial identities and experience downward assimilation (Portes and Rumbaut 2001).[6]

As dire as the fate of children of Latino immigrants in the U.S. may indeed seem, segmented assimilation theory offers overly pessimistic and deterministic predictions. It has missed the subtle demographic changes that have occurred within the Latino community. Census-based demographic analyses have suggested that, at least on a national level, Latinos are modestly moving up within the labor market (Park and Myers 2010). As posited by segmented assimilation theory, race relations between whites and Mexican Americans are highly contextual, profoundly shaped by salient public policy debates and the extremist views that color those debates. However, in contrast to segmented assimilation theory, this study suggests that racial identity is not crystallized across adulthood. Rather, in adulthood, formerly delinquent Latino men recede from the locus of gang life, and begin to take on conventional aspirations. As Latino men leave gang life, a transition that gang scholars have noted is common, they distance themselves from Chicano gang masculinity and embrace the warm, nurturing characteristics of conventional fatherhood. This process of exit from gang life is herein termed *gang recovery*, and the masculine expressions that characterize recovery from gang life are termed *reformed barrio masculinity*. Reformed barrio masculinity is by no means an oppositional, reactive ethnicity; rather, recovering gang members' day-to-day lives are much more conventional, focusing on the transition away from street life and into domesticity.

Drawing from participant observation and interviews with adult male former or current Chicano gang members, mostly of immigrant origin, this volume shows that such men are not trapped in a path of downward assimilation into the urban underclass. Rather, Chicano gang members experience social reintegration against a backdrop that is characterized by exclusion and marginality, but also modest social reintegration and mobility. This volume argues that urban street ministries facilitate recovery from gang life through religious practices such as worship services or group therapy, and that discursive and embodied masculine negotiations reorient Chicano gang members away from the street and toward the household.

The first street ministry discussed is Homeboy Industries, a nondenominational, nonprofit organization founded by Father Greg, the Jesuit priest. Homeboy Industries has become a model for gang intervention programs across the nation.[7] The second is Victory Outreach, a highly spiritual evangelical-Pentecostal church. According to its website, Victory Outreach specializes in urban ministry and has grown to over six hundred chapters worldwide in thirty countries.[8] These organizations both originated in Los Angeles's Eastside, in the Boyle Heights neighborhood, and continue to operate in the area. Los Angeles is characterized by hyperconcentrations of capital and deep pockets of marginalization and poverty, and gang membership has flourished in this ethnically diverse, postindustrial setting of social inequality. The city, reflective of many other "global cities" (Sassen 1998), is thus the perfect setting for an examination of faith-based social programs addressing the gang problem.

Recovering Gang Members in Los Angeles:
Street Gangs, Religion, and Masculinity
Gangs, Crime, and Desistance

The study of urban life, street gangs and crime dates back to the early-twentieth-century Chicago School of sociology. Led by Robert Park and Ernest Burgess, the Chicago School was the first to hypothesize a link between crime and pockets of concentrated poverty (e.g., Asbury 1928; Thrasher 1927; Whyte 1943). Through the end of the twentieth century and the turn of the twenty-first, gangs grew and so did the application of the Chicago School approach (e.g., Horowitz and Schwartz 1974; Padilla 1992; Venkatesh 2008). Chicago-trained University of Southern California (USC) professor Emory Bogardus transplanted the Chicago School approach to the study of gangs in Los Angeles (e.g., Bogardus 1926; Bogardus 1943), and later, renowned USC gang researchers drew upon the Chicago school's assertions concerning marginality and crime (e.g., Moore 1978; Vigil 1988).

More recent scholarship influenced by the Chicago School, as well as research on Chicago gangs, has suggested that gang activity thrives in a context of drug markets and a lack of social controls (e.g., Fagan 1996; Hagedorn 1998; Padilla 1992; Taylor 1990; Venkatesh 1996; Venkatesh 1997). Likewise, other scholars have emphasized that gangs are rooted in institutionalized racism, poverty, and urban marginality, and that gang life is fundamentally an expression of marginalized masculinity (Majors and Billson 1992; Horowitz 1983; Rios 2011; Vigil 2007; Yablonsky 1997). The long-standing assumption undergirding the Chicago School approach, and much sociological research on gangs, has been that gang membership and activity would decrease if underlying structural factors were to be addressed.

Yet there has not been much social science research on gang recovery programs, programs that facilitate desistance from gang violence and substance abuse. Examining the process of exit from gang life has been challenging for sociologists, and very little research exists on gang desistance (Klein 1971; Decker and Lauritsen 1996). Canonical works in urban sociology have extensively analyzed how low-income men become socialized into street life, while devoting much less attention to how men become socialized *out* of street life. If anything, ethnographers have sometimes attached short epilogues to new editions of urban classics, documenting research subjects' exit from street life—though only long after the researchers were themselves in the field (e.g., Bourgois 1995[1987]; Macleod 1995; Venkatesh 2008). These epilogues tend to suggest that there is a deep disjuncture between the nature of street life and the demands of domestic adulthood. The reorientation from street life to conventional life is presented as either banal (Venkatesh 2008) or as an existential crisis in adulthood around the meaning of manhood (Bourgois 1995[1987]).

Scholars associated with the Chicago School have noted that strong family ties and stable employment are associated with socialization out of the gang (e.g., Horowitz 1983; Vigil 1988; Moore 1991; Vigil 2007). Likewise, other scholars have described the process of leaving the gang or a delinquent lifestyle as one of "maturing out" (e.g., Matza 1964, 22–26; Skolnick 1988; Vigil 1988). However, contradictions remain in the study of gangs and gang exit. Gang membership and formal employment frequently coexist, indicating that formal employment alone does not necessarily facilitate exit from gang life (Hagedorn 1994; Jankowski 1991).

Complicating the issue of gang exit is the simple question, "What constitutes a gang?" Ethnographers have notoriously struggled with trying to pin down gang membership and territoriality as a singular construct; it may instead arise from highly fluid, contextualized interactions (Garot 2007; Garot 2010; Garot and Katz 2003). Furthermore, researchers have found that gang behavior can be an expression against the racializing and exclusionary tendencies of modernization (Brotherton 2008; Hagedorn 2008; McDonald 2008). For example, the Almighty Latin King and Queen Nation (ALKQN) upholds a charter that emphasizes community empowerment (Brotherton and Barrios 2004).

The context for this study is Los Angeles's Eastside, where Chicano gangs inhabit the space of the street differently than their gang counterparts in Chicago or New York. Chicano gang life in Los Angeles is characterized by expressions of "*locura*," or wild, destructive behavior, as well as heavy consumption of alcohol and illicit drugs (Vigil 2007, 63). This contrasts with some notable Chicago and New York gangs that do not promote heavy drinking or drug use. Conversations with former gang members during fieldwork at a few national Victory Outreach events suggested regional differences in gang social dynamics: members discussed how some gangs call themselves "organizations," operate with a corporate structure, and sell drugs but prohibit their members from using them. In addition, researchers have even found that at least one major New York gang, ALKQN, offers Alcoholics Anonymous and Narcotics Anonymous programs (Brotherton and Barrios 2004).

By contrast, Chicano gangs in Los Angeles inhabit a space that incorporates drug use but not drug recovery. This dichotomy opens up a third space, between gangs and mainstream society, for community organizations to operate within. This volume investigates that which could not have been investigated in a different urban street gang context: how faith-based programs operate between gangs and the broader community to facilitate recovery from gang life. Given that a large majority of respondents were immigrants or of immigrant parentage, the issue of faith-based recovery is intimately tied to that of immigrant integration herein. Ultimately, this book argues that Catholic and Pentecostal religious practices facilitate Chicano gang recovery by reorienting masculine expressions away from the street and toward conventional social spheres, such as the church, household, and workplace.

Immigration and Religion

Religious institutions have played a large role in the ongoing history of immigrant America (e.g., Hirschman 2004; Sanchez-Walsh 2003; Espinosa et al. 2005; Badillo 2006). Dating back to the wave of early-twentieth-century European immigration, religious institutions have competed for immigrants' membership by providing resources to assist with integration. Protestants such as Jane Addams engaged in philanthropic missions to help disenfranchised immigrants, while the Catholic Church countered the spread of Protestantism and the Americanization of new arrivals with programs to aid homeless and alcoholic immigrants (Moloney 2002), and resources such as parochial schools and healthcare (Lopez 2009). The nature of immigrant-community integration and its relationship to religion has also had a gang component. Second-generation European Americans, especially the children of Italian and Irish immigrants, were prone to gang membership

(Thrasher 1927; Whyte 1943), and Italian parents often sent their boys to Catholic school for disciplinary purposes (Gans 1962). Religion has thus historically been an integrative mechanism sheltering immigrant children from the underlying causes of gangs: poverty and marginalization.

America is a competitive religious marketplace; one-third to one-half of Americans have switched religious affiliation at some point in their lives (Hadaway and Marler 1991; Roof and McKinney 1987, 165, cited in Warner 1993, 1075). This point is particularly helpful in underscoring Latino religiosity. Pentecostalism has made the biggest inroads into the Latino community, both in Latin America and among immigrants in the United States. In the U.S., for every one Latino who has converted to Catholicism, four have converted away from it (Espinosa 2006). Storefront Pentecostalism has been the fastest growing phenomenon in U.S. Latino religiosity, serving "socially and culturally homophilous" congregations of marginalized immigrants (Stohlman 2007, 62). Just as with earlier European immigrants, today's Latino and Asian immigrants have settled into low-income, marginalized communities, but they have also experienced religion as an integrating force. Immigrants have used religion to construct meaning from the experience of being uprooted (Warner and Wittner 1998; Levitt 2001; Ebaugh and Chafetz 2000; Chafetz and Ebaugh 2002; Leonard 2005; Chen 2008). Immigrants have relied on religious communities for both social and material benefits, such as the building of social capital (Ebaugh and Chafetz 2000; Davalos 2002), and to participate in politics and other forms of civic engagement (Menjivar 2003; Pardo 2005; Hondagneu-Sotelo 2007; Levitt 2008; Hondagneu-Sotelo 2008). Victory Outreach and Homeboy Industries address a distinct and growing demand in the American religious marketplace: exit from gang life.

The use of Pentecostal conversion to facilitate gang recovery has been documented locally, as well as abroad (Brenneman 2011; Vigil 1982; León 1998; Sanchez-Walsh 2003; Vásquez, Marquardt and Gómez 2003; Wolseth 2010). In one of James Diego Vigil's (1982) earliest anthropological accounts of Latino life on Los Angeles's Eastside, Vigil found that Chicano gang members lived in a context of acculturation, but were marginalized from both mainstream American society and the traditional Mexican community. However, through religious conversion at Victory Outreach, gang members experienced human revitalization, exiting gangs and socially reintegrating into the Mexican American community. Luis León (2004) also conducted research on Victory Outreach in Los Angeles's Eastside. He found that Victory Outreach strategically made use of Catholic imagery to make religious worship among Chicanos much more effervescent. For example, Victory Outreach presented women on stage as chorus singers who embodied mannerisms associated with the Virgen de Guadalupe.[9] These accounts of religious conversion and gang recovery illustrate the salient features of the religious marketplace in America: it is characterized by dynamic and voluntaristic religious participation (Warner 1993). Stephen Warner (1993, 1076), in his landmark article that contested the secularization thesis and called for a "new paradigm" in the sociology of religion, claimed that, in the American religious marketplace, "[t]aken-for-granted, traditional religion is passé. Born-again, return-to-the-fold neotraditional religion is all the rage." This volume examines gang recovery as an example of religion as "all the rage," in order to fill the gap in scholarly literature on gang exit.

Immigrant Assimilation

Segmented assimilation scholars argue that a pronounced level of anti-immigrant animosity has created a hostile context of reception for black and Latino immigrants. The risks include assimilation into reactive ethnicities and the urban underclass (Portes and Rumbaut 2001; Portes and Zhou 1993). Analysis of the largest study on immigrant assimilation, the Children of Immigrants Longitudinal Study (CILS), corroborated this, revealing that one-fifth of black and Latino second-generation immigrants had experienced incarceration by age twenty-four (Portes and Rumbaut 2006[1990], 280). However, other immigration scholars have protested the idea that contemporary black and Latino immigrants experience a uniquely hostile context of reception, arguing that xenophobic tendencies have always targeted immigrants (Alba 2003; Perlmann 2005; Kasinitz et al. 2004; Kasinitz et al. 2008; Waldinger 2001). The early-twentieth-century eugenics movement asserted that Southern and Eastern European immigrants were biologically inferior, and that their immigration and reproduction threatened the health of the nation (Jacobson 1999).

In immigration studies, the segmented assimilation canon—which has theorized multiple trajectories of immigrant assimilation—extends our understanding of Latino gangs and recovery by slowly integrating the field of religion and immigration with the Chicago School's focus on immigration, marginalization, and delinquency. Segmented assimilation theory has contrasted immigrants' experiences with gangs, as well as the empowering potential of religion to shelter immigrant youth from gangs (Portes and Zhou 1993; Zhou and Bankston 1998; Portes and Rumbaut 2001). Research has suggested that 1.5- and second-generation immigrants exposed to adolescent countercultures are vulnerable to dissonant acculturation and downward assimilation into gangs and street life (Zhou and Bankston 1998; Portes and Rumbaut 2001; Lay 2004; Vigil et al. 2004; Smith 2006).[10] Conversely, parents can leverage an immigrant community's resources to foster socioeconomic mobility through selective acculturation, a blending of American educational practices through traditional immigrant values. However, these studies have typically focused on middle-class youth or upwardly mobile working-class youth. A theoretical gap still exists in understanding how religion can empower previously delinquent youth in early adulthood, the focus of this book.

Segmented assimilation scholars' first line of inquiry dealt with "linear religion" (Portes and Rumbaut 2006[1990], 330), religious worship among immigrants who practiced the same religion as they had back home (i.e., Zhou and Bankston 1998; Zhou et al 2002). This line of inquiry slowly expanded to encompass religious worship among immigrants who converted after immigration and settlement, "reactive religion" (Portes and Rumbaut 2006[1990], 328). However, this too was often situated in the coethnic church (Chong 1998; Ng 2002; Kim 2004; Cao 2005). Only recently has segmented assimilation literature begun to examine how low-income, downwardly assimilated second-generation immigrants experience reactive religion. Extremely high religiosity, through Wicca, Rastafarianism, and evangelical Christianity, has been found to follow after downward assimilation in adulthood (Portes and Rumbaut 2006[1990]; Fernandez-Kelly 2007). The examination of faith-based gang recovery in this book departs from an understanding of American religion as dynamic and voluntaristic, in which "neotraditional religion is all the rage." This volume examines how adult Latino recovering gang members use religion in dynamic and voluntaristic ways, experiencing recovery from gang life and bucking predictions of downward assimilation.

Religious Voluntarism

Recent sociology of religion literature has offered a much more caustic response toward the issue of religious voluntarism. Research on religious congregations has suggested that the voluntaristic facets of American religious participation may actually create "particularistic spaces of sociability" (Ammerman 1997, 355). In these particularistic spaces, congregations are formed and reinforced along preexisting divisions in race, class, and nationality. Thus, voluntarism may *undermine* social integration.

As described in his book *Streets of Glory*, Omar McRoberts (2003) found this to be the case in Boston's Four Corners religious district. Cheap rents in Four Corners created a religious ecology that drew churches serving middle-class suburbanites. These churches were not neighborhood organizations, and their congregants kept local residents at an arm's length. More troubling, McRoberts found that religious particularism actually undermined neighborhood activism that could have potentially created sustainable change.

In a report published by the Urban Institute, McRoberts (2002) extended the problematic of religious ecology, particularism, and neighborhood activism to the field of ex-offender reentry. He reasoned that the assumption driving federal initiatives to direct resources to churches, in order to guide faith-based reentry, were fundamentally flawed. Anticipating observations he would make in *Streets of Glory*, McRoberts suggested that, because they are not rooted in their respective, surrounding neighborhoods, and because they are often characterized by particularism, churches and faith-based organizations do very little to facilitate ex-offender reintegration into the local community. This book examines the issue of faith-based gang recovery, with a keen eye on the issues of particularism that may arise through efforts to facilitate social reintegration.

Doing Latino Masculinity

In reviewing the research on Victory Outreach, the only gang recovery program studied by U.S. social scientists thus far, one finds that recovery from gang life has been facilitated through the construction of Latino masculinities. Luis León (1998) suggested that Victory Outreach integrates elements of immigrant Latino culture and masculinity, through a patriarchal church structure that promises the American Dream to marginalized immigrants. Victory Outreach codes masculinity in notions of honor: abstinence, economic stability, and nurturing relationships with women and children (Flores 2009; León 1998; Sanchez-Walsh 2003).

Similarly, anthropologist Elizabeth Brusco, in her study of Colombian evangelicalism, suggested that Latino masculinity was constructed against a dichotomy of "macho masculinity" and "machista masculinity" (1995, 78). Macho masculinity, based upon traditional notions of honor, is a closer fit with the model of European-based patriarchy, which had been previously institutionalized through colonization. Machista masculinity sharply contrasts with macho masculinity; it is characterized by absence from the household and cold, distant, and egoistic behavior. I previously found that recovery from street life and substance abuse reconstructed Latino masculinity around the binary of macho and machista masculinity; reformed gang members expressed macho masculinity through participation in the household and labor market, which I termed "reformed barrio masculinity" (Flores 2009, 1004). This study examines Homeboy Industries as a case in comparison to further deepen understandings of gang recovery and Latino masculinity.

To better understand the contests and shifts in Latino masculinities that occur along the path of recovery, this book draws from Candace West and Don Zimmerman's (1987) understanding of gender: gender is constructed *through* social interaction, as people develop gendered actions as a form of accountability—in relation to expectations based on gendered norms. This "doing gender" approach has been used to analyze how men use every day practices to position and reposition themselves in relation to women and other men, though most of this research has focused on middle-class or white men (i.e., Barber 2008; Dellinger 2004; Pyke 1996). The "doing gender" approach has been applied to the study of masculinities and crime by few scholars (Messerschmidt 2000; Messerschmidt 2004; Rios 2009; Rios 2011). James Messerschmidt (2004), through his analysis of life histories, found that marginal boys used interpersonal violence as a gendered strategy to compensate for lack of institutional male privilege. Victor Rios (2009), a former gang member–turned–academic, conducted research on delinquency among black and Latino street youth, and suggested that aggressive masculine displays have been constructed as compensatory responses to structural disadvantages in the gender order. Rios (2011) claimed that "the criminal justice system encourages expressions of hypermasculinity by threatening and confusing young men's masculinity," as police, probation officers, and juvenile detention guards regularly harassed black and Latino street youth with emasculating threats. He reasoned, "This, in turn, leads them to rely on domination through violence, crime, and a school and criminal justice counterculture" (Rios 2011, 130). He claimed that youth felt only two types of masculine expression were available, both of which led to violence: "play out a masculinity battle," or submit to the authority of the police and then take out their aggression on each other (Rios 2011, 131).

However, interpersonal violence is highly contextual, as males alternate between subordinate and dominant expressions of manhood when in different environments. In some cases, males use violence only at school but not home, while in other cases they use violence on the streets (Messerschmidt 2004). This volume similarly departs from the "doing gender" approach, exploring how social forces help to reintegrate adult men with gang pasts. Building upon Rios's research on street gangs and delinquency, this book unpacks how recovering gang members negotiate and affirm Chicano masculinity in order to escape the prison pipeline. Through the examples of Victory Outreach and Homeboy Industries, it examines how religious practices reorient masculine expressions from the street to the household, thereby empowering disadvantaged Latino men with gang pasts to leave gang life behind.

Embodiment

Lastly, this book investigates how men in gang recovery negotiate Chicano masculinity through the body and through the acquisition of new bodily practices. Raewyn Connell and James Messerschmidt have asserted, "Bodies are both objects of social practice and agents in social practice" (2005, 851). Similarly, masculine gang embodiment is both an object and an agent of gang and street masculinity. Men use the body to deepen gang affiliation and activity; they tattoo themselves with their gang's name or identifying symbols, flash hand signals, walk in distinctive ways, dress in oversized clothes, display distinctive colors, and groom their hair in particular styles (i.e., Vigil 1988; Major and Billson 1992; Brotherton 2008; Ferrell et al. 2008; Garot 2010).

The scant literature on gang recovery and embodiment has suggested that the body is also important in reformulating gang masculinity. Bodily practices help to position conventional masculinity over gang masculinity, and to socially integrate men into the site of recovery. Robert Brenneman (2009) and Stanley Brandes (2002) have both found that negotiating the meaning of crying helps men facilitate recovery, from alcoholism or gang life, by advancing new meanings of manhood. In addition, León has observed that in ecstatic Pentecostal worship, "[T]he experience of the body is central to worship and to the construction of a social body that coheres with other male bodies; men's bodies are ritually, emotionally, spiritually, and physically connected to one another" (2004, 238). This volume examines how embodied religious practices facilitate gang recovery, arguing that religious practices contest and negotiate Chicano gang masculinity by redirecting and reshaping the body and bodily practices.

Getting To Know Recovering Gang Members

This book is founded on eighteen months of fieldwork, conducted between June 2008 to December 2009, spent observing recovery from gang life at Homeboy Industries, a Jesuit-founded, nondenominational nonprofit in Downtown Los Angeles, and the evangelical-Pentecostal Victory Outreach, located in Eastside (an area that encompasses Northeast Los Angeles, Boyle Heights, and the unincorporated area of East Los Angeles).[11] I shadowed male subjects in their everyday lives, and conducted interviews with thirty-four persons who were or who had been gang members.[12] Of the thirty-four interview respondents, eighteen were from Homeboy Industries, fourteen were from Victory

Outreach, and two were members of both organizations. There were staff leaders in the sample: five were leaders at Homeboy Industries, and five were leaders at Victory Outreach. All of the respondents were male and Mexican or of Mexican origin, except for one who was of Guatemalan descent. Nine were "1.5 generation," which means that they were born in Mexico but brought to the U.S. before the age of thirteen; seven of these respondents were undocumented. Fourteen were second generation, of which many had been born to at least one undocumented parent. Eleven were third-plus generation.

Homeboy Industries and Victory Outreach both grew out of the Boyle Heights neighborhood. In fact, both grew out of the Pico Gardens and Aliso Village housing projects, built in 1942, which were—until the demise of the latter in 1999—the largest public housing projects west of the Mississippi River (Vigil 2007, 41). Pastor Sonny Arguinzoni, the founder of Victory Outreach, was a Puerto Rican from New York and an ex–drug addict who reformed through David Wilkerson's evangelical program Teen Challenge, under its director, Nicky Cruz, a former gang leader who had converted to Christianity. After Teen Challenge, Arguinzoni moved to Los Angeles from New York to attend the Latin American Bible Institute. There he met his future wife, Julie, and housed recovering heroin addicts in his one-bedroom apartment on Gless Street. Through the years, Pastor Sonny and Julie hosted gang members and heroin addicts in their home, offering to serve pancakes and small scraps of food that they claimed multiplied like the five-loaves-and-two-fish-miracle that fed five thousand persons in the Gospel (Arguinzoni 1991). After gaining wide popularity in the local community for helping to save gang members through faith in Jesus, Sonny and Julie Arguinzoni founded the first Victory Outreach church in Boyle Heights in 1967. They followed up this effort by starting a second Victory Outreach church in the Southeast Los Angeles County suburb of Pico Rivera, then expanding to the rest of Los Angeles County and northern California. Eventually, Victory Outreach started chapters in other states and abroad, and by 2010, it had over 600 churches worldwide. By recent count, 113 are located in California, most in the southern part of the state and in urban areas, including ten within Los Angeles City limits. Some of these storefront churches also run men's recovery homes and women's recovery homes. The Victory Outreach–Eastside men's recovery home was located in Chinatown, only a few blocks up the street from Homeboy Industries, in a tightly congested residential neighborhood, sloping down on a steep hill next to Dodger Stadium.

Unlike Sonny Arguinzoni, Father Greg, the founder of Homeboy Industries, did not have a gang past. He was born in Los Angeles to a third-generation Irish dairy-owning family. After graduating from a local Catholic school, he went on to receive several undergraduate and graduate degrees from private universities. Father Greg then worked in Cochabamba, Bolivia, as a missionary, where he learned the skill of community organizing through Christian Base Communities.[13] Following his return to the U.S., he dedicated himself to Dolores Mission Catholic Church, serving the poorest parish in the nation. From Dolores Mission—located, like the original Victory Outreach church, on Gless Street—Father Greg reached out to gang members and organized residents through Christian Base Communities. Father Greg started by offering wages to gang members at Dolores Mission for day labor work, such as painting or sweeping, and expanded by creating the employment outreach programs mentioned previously—JFF, Homeboy Bakery, and Homeboy Industries. By the time fieldwork for this book began, Homeboy Industries had developed a model that gang outreach organizations across the country were emulating, such as Light of the Village in Pritchard, Alabama. However, by 2010, Father Greg was encountering great difficulty in raising the five million dollars from donors and foundations needed to keep Homeboy Industries running on the massive scale to which it had grown.

The following descriptions derive directly from the observations I made during my fieldwork, which concluded in 2009. Both organizations had outreach ministries designed to help gang members transition out from gang life. Whereas the evangelical-Pentecostal Victory Outreach drew from a larger network of evangelical Christianity for music, film, and literature, the nondenominational Homeboy Industries offered group therapy classes similar to Alcoholics Anonymous and spiritual classes that drew upon Eastern and Native American spirituality. Other differences between the groups were suggested by their respective mission statements. Victory Outreach's mission statement emphasized a tightly knit, cohesive community and declared that it "inspires and instills within people the desire to fulfill their potential in life with a sense of dignity, belonging, and destiny." Homeboy Industries' mission statement emphasized a porous community and declared, "Jobs Not Jails: Homeboy Industries assists at-risk and formerly gang-involved youth to become positive and contributing members of society through job placement, training and education." In light of these differences between Victory Outreach's mission, to build a tightly-knit community among recovering gang members, and Homeboy Industries, to socially reintegrate recovering gang members into broader society, the most striking difference between the two organizations was the amount of time leaders expected members to commit. Homeboy Industries offered work and therapy, sending members home after work, whereas Victory Outreach urged members to spend evenings, weekends, and holidays at the church. Homeboy Industries sought to successfully reintegrate members *into* their local communities, whereas Victory Outreach sought to segregate members *from* their local communities.

Homeboy Industries was organized through a top-down hierarchy, in which few members could rise to the very top. Men in recovery advanced largely through education and work experience obtained outside of Homeboy Industries. In the nonprofit division of Homeboy Industries, about eighty recovering gang members washed windows, about ten served as clerical assistants, a few were supervisors or case managers, and only one was a drug counselor. Few of the men in gang recovery sat in meetings with "senior staff," a category composed largely of white-collar, middle-class professionals. In contrast, Victory Outreach was organized through a small, tight-knit hierarchy, where members advanced by starting at the bottom. Ascension through the ranks of Victory Outreach was dependent upon commitment rather than job experience or education. All of the church's pastors had been gang members or drug addicts, and had been residents at the men's recovery home. Victory Outreach did not solicit outside help from professionals or religious leaders.[14] In fact, no member of Victory Outreach Eastside had a college degree besides the pastor, who had been educated at the unaccredited Victory Outreach Education Training Institute (VETI) and Facultad, a partnering Protestant school of higher education.

Nonetheless, at both sites, barrio symbols were visible on flyers and posters, with airbrush artwork and images of lowriders promoting events. Most male members groomed themselves and wore clothes in accord with barrio style, including thick mustaches, shaved heads, old tattoos, oversized clothes and white sneakers. Men at both sites used East Los Angeles barrio slang, terms such as *heina* (girlfriend), *homeboy* (close male friend), or *ranking out* (deciding to not participate in something after committing to it). Leaders at both sites drew upon life in the barrio for examples in the lessons they taught.

Explaining the purpose of this project to the study participants, I said that I was seeking to learn more about the meaning of faith-based outreach to (ex–)gang members. I asked some male subjects if they were willing to be interviewed. Although I am not an ex–drug addict or ex–gang member, there appeared to be little discomfort for either me or my subjects when I conducted observations or interviews. At both Homeboy Industries and Victory Outreach, members dedicated much of their free time to meeting new persons. Homeboy Industries survived on public fundraising efforts, and one of Victory Outreach's main goals was to proselytize Christianity. Both organizations had received significant public exposure through television reports, newspaper articles, and books.

They were as eager to know about me, a Latino from a working-class immigrant family enrolled in a Ph.D. program, as I was to know about them. I was even recruited to teach at Homeboy Industries by a case manager, Mario. After drinking a few beers at his apartment and talking about the problems with suppression policing, racism, and immigration, Mario asked me to teach a class that would encourage recovering gang members (men and women) to think about college. I tried this for a few months, leading a one-hour class called College 101 once a week. The class usually had three to six participants, though the same people rarely came in consecutive weeks. While I frequently avoided taking fieldnotes in this class, as minors often participated, it did help me to build better relationships with a couple subjects, as our reading materials became a means to connect with and learn about the men.

I was also encouraged by Victory Outreach leaders to stay at the men's recovery home, just as any recovering drug addict or gang member would. I failed miserably at this. After three days, I found myself physically, mentally, and emotionally drained. The constant, loud Christian rock music, the frequent prayer groups, and the seemingly endless cleanup around the church gave me the greatest writer's block I have ever experienced. Rick, the home's director, begged me to try to stay and write fieldnotes despite these obstacles. When I went in to see him, Rick gave me a quotation from Scripture, 2 Corinthians 12:9–10, which he said was about finding "strength in weakness." I left, feeling like an abysmal failure, unable to find the strength to write fieldnotes. Fortuitously, the "strength in weakness" concept paralleled previous anthropological research on masculinity and recovery (e.g., Brandes 2002), and turned out to be centrally relevant to this book. It now anchors my analysis of Latino masculinity in the fifth chapter.

This book draws upon qualitative data collection and analysis, following the extended case method (Burawoy et al. 1991). The purpose of this method is to integrate the experiences of respondents who hailed from immigrant backgrounds and had been in gangs into segmented assimilation theory, which has focused largely on downward assimilation among Latinos. Chapter 2 draws from decennial census and American Community Survey (ACS) data to contextualize the demographic changes (age, poverty, and geographic mobility) occurring in the high-gang-activity neighborhoods from which the respondents came. The theoretical impetus to examine cases of young adult "recovering gang members" and frame the context of gang recovery against broad demographic changes across age cohorts in Los Angeles followed from Gans's (2007) call to expand the concept of immigrant acculturation to encompass third- and fourth-generation immigrants, as well as to theorize acculturation over the adult life-course.

Goals and Purpose of Book

This book demonstrates how recovery from gang life is centrally organized by religion and gender, arguing that religious practices shape the discursive and embodied negotiations that reformulate Chicano gang masculinity and socially reintegrate men away from the street and into the household. As noted above, "tough-on-crime" approaches, fueled by heated rhetoric over crime and anti-immigrant backlash, construct what I term the *Latino crime threat*: racist/sexist depictions of male Latino gang members as undocumented immigrants, career criminals, and terrorists. Recovery reconfigures Chicano gang masculinity to fit with dominant masculine displays, such as the "family man" or "man of God," contesting the Latino crime threat and facilitating social reintegration. Masculinity is reformulated from the self-destructive expressions of Chicano gang masculinity—such as gangs, drugs, and uncommitted romantic affairs—to the warm, nurturing "breadwinner" expressions of reformed barrio masculinity.

In addition, whereas segmented assimilation has made grim predictions about the fate of Mexican immigrants' children—that they will experience downward assimilation as a result of a hostile context of reception, gangs, and incarceration—I contend that these claims are largely overstated. The book shows that Latinos do experience integration and socioeconomic mobility in adulthood, and that Latinos with gang pasts do not necessarily crystallize a reactive ethnicity. Through urban ministry, and the shifts in masculine orientations that urban ministries help inspire and sustain, Latino recovering gang members avoid cyclical, entrenched poverty and marginality.

Chapter 1 investigates how poverty, marginality, and gangs have been long-standing features of Los Angeles's Eastside barrios. It argues that Latino marginality, despite being a concern of early social reformers, persisted due to the racialized nature of public policies and political platforms. Early-twentieth-century social policy eased integration for Southern and Eastern European immigrants, but left Latinos deeply marginalized. The Civil Rights Movement followed, but so did white resistance against it, centrally expressed through the rise of coded, antiminority suppression tactics aimed at blacks and Latinos. I examine how crime policy debates gave rise to notions of street criminals as lacking the ability to reform, and how this disproportionately targeted blacks and Latinos through the wars on drugs, crime, and terrorism. In the post-9/11 era, the discourse over gang crime has become aligned with the trope of national security and terrorism, further deepening the marginality experienced by disadvantaged Latinos. Sustained anticrime and anti-immigration rhetoric has been a central feature of the late modern era, and it has systematically constructed marginal Latinos as threats to the state.

Chapter 2 employs census and ACS data to evaluate the fitness of Los Angeles as a case study in segmented assimilation theory. Many elements of segmented assimilation theory hold up, such as increases in immigration and the nonwhite population, as well as high poverty rates. Further analysis, though, reveals that respondents' inner-city neighborhoods were characterized not just by high poverty rates, but also by demographic dynamism—moving up and out. Over time, age cohorts in the respondents' high-gang-activity neighborhoods experienced less poverty and residents were more likely to relocate elsewhere. These demographic trends set a different backdrop for this study on gang recovery, one in which gradual, limited socioeconomic mobility exists in adulthood—rather than the overly dim underclass portrait painted by segmented assimilation scholars.

Chapter 3 builds upon the growing body of literature on segmented assimilation and religion by examining how two urban American ministries facilitated immigrant-origin Latino recovery from gangs in the first decade of the twenty-first century. Despite declining middle-class work opportunities, religion provided gang members the social support and resources necessary to leave gang life behind. Two contrasting models of social reintegration sheltered recovering gang members from gang life, and encouraged them to achieve conventional markers of success, such as employment, home ownership, and marriage. While Victory Outreach facilitated gang recovery by creating rigid social boundaries between the church and the broader local community, Homeboy Industries facilitated gang recovery by maintaining and rearticulating porous boundaries between itself and the community. In examining the two faith-based approaches to gang recovery, this book builds on Omar McRoberts's (2003) *Streets of Glory*, as well as an Urban Institute report by McRoberts (2002). The two faith-based sites in this book socially reintegrate Chicano gang members by shaping the meanings of gang life and recovery, distancing Chicano gang members from the street, and thereby demonstrating that religious voluntarism does not necessarily lead to particularism or undermine ex-offender social reintegration.

Chapter 4 examines how recovering gang members described recovery from gangs, where they saw themselves in five years, and who they admired and tried to emulate. I contend that faith-based gang recovery took shape through reformulated notions of manhood. In faith-based recovery, recovering Chicano gang members contrasted masculine expressions: Chicano gang masculinity and reformed barrio masculinity. Whereas gang members rooted their sense of manhood in gang activities, such as drug use and gang violence, recovering gang members rooted their sense of manhood in domestic activities, such as being emotionally supportive husbands, fathers, and sons.

Chapter 5 examines how platforms for public speaking, such as group therapy or Bible studies, offered recovering gang members opportunities to experience reform from gang life, as well as to earn legitimacy for being reformed. The public talk of gang recovery invited situated performances that rearticulated Chicano masculinity. Recovering gang members used public talk to advance "redemption scripts" (i.e., Maruna 2001) and construct reformed barrio masculinity, facilitating recovery from gang life and social reintegration.

Chapter 6 examines how these gendered displays also involved the body and bodily practices, for example through dress codes, tattoo removal, and prayer. These gendered displays and bodily practices illustrated "the politics of performance" (Conquergood 1991, 190), as reformed barrio masculinity was used as a performance to challenge dominant ideas about Latinos such as the Latino crime threat. Men in recovery constructed reformed barrio masculinity by shaping malleable facets of Chicano gang masculinity (i.e., hair, dress style), as well as by reshaping and redirecting less malleable facets of Chicano gang masculinity (i.e., speech, cadence, posture).

The conclusion revisits the book's argument—that faith-based masculine negotiations facilitate recovery from gang life—and telescopes out to examine the implications. While critical criminologists and sociologists have celebrated the resistant nature of gangs to modernizing forces, Homeboy Industries and Victory Outreach show only seeds of resistance. This book instead urges a conceptualization of recovery from gang life as a process of turning inward to cope with racism. The conclusion reiterates the key findings in this volume: that, in spite of gang pasts and declining inner-city job opportunities, Latino recovering gang members seek to cut ties with gang life, build relationships with family members, and land well-paying, formal employment. The conclusion also reexamines how recovery rearticulates Chicano masculinity, from the self-destructive expressions of Chicano gang masculinity to the warm, nurturing characteristics of fatherhood, and how assumptions embedded in such gendered processes may be problematic for challenging hegemonic masculinity. Nonetheless, as Latinos contest racist/sexist images—admiring and trying to emulate faith leaders in their communities—we must remain open to the transformative possibilities that may lie dormant within recovery.

In closing, this volume brings to bear findings on recovery from gang life to the concept most central to the segmented assimilation paradigm: downward assimilation. As described in chapter 2 and revisited in conclusion, demographic trends indicate that Latinos are slowly, gradually moving up and out of Los Angeles's low-income barrios. The ethnographic findings on faith-based recovery presented herein similarly reject the trope of downward assimilation: Latinos do not embrace a reactive ethnicity nor do they become entrenched in cyclical poverty and marginality. Instead, Latino recovering gang members seek to achieve the American Dream by becoming "family men" or "men of God" who can provide for their families. A closer look at recovery from gang life reveals that while Latinos in the inner city do not follow the clean trajectory of classical assimilation, neither are they doomed to the tragedy of downward assimilation.

1

The Latino Crime Threat

A Century of Race, Marginality, and Public Policy in Los Angeles

arly in the morning of September 22, 2009, I went online to read the *Los Angeles Times*. I was struck by a headlines of a major, developing story: "Massive Police Raid Targets Brutal L.A. Gang." The subheading mentioned the Avenues gang, which the mayor and police chief two years previously had targeted in an "aggressive suppression strategy" against the city's eleven "most violent gangs"; this was the same gang that had earlier been connected to a case of a murdered Los Angeles County sheriff's deputy. I immediately felt tense and worried.

The previous week, Matthew, a twenty-year-old member of Homeboy Industries, and of the Avenues gang, had asked me if I knew of any vocational programs that could lead to stable employment. He said he had recently called a well-known vocational school, but that they were reluctant to answer his questions after they found out he had two felonies on his record. As I scoured the article for details, I feared that Matthew had been picked up in the gang sweep. The *Los Times* provided gripping photos of twelve hundred law enforcement officials and federal agents, armored with assault rifles and military-style vehicles, taking in these Latino men in the predawn hours. I scanned through photos of men who looked like Matthew—adult Latinos with shaved heads and white T-shirts, sitting on curbs with their hands cuffed behind their backs or stretched out on police cars as they were searched. The images looked like something out of the Iraq War. They were meant to send a clear message: we should fear urban gang members, and it is law enforcement that is protecting us from them.

I rushed to Homeboy Industries to collect details about the raid and find out if Matthew had been taken in. As I saw the chair where he normally sat occupied by someone else, a sinking feeling overtook me. The next day, I spoke with Matthew's supervisor, Valerie, a Latina with a college degree and very professional demeanor, who told me in a concerned tone that he had been arrested in the sweep. The FBI was working hard to build a case against the Avenues, drawing charges against the gang based on the Racketeer Influenced and Corrupt Organizations (RICO) Act. However, the FBI wiretaps linking Matthew to his gang were four to five years old, and predated his entrance into Homeboy Industries. Matthew was not involved in the death of the murdered deputy, but, according to Valerie, he was threatened with a life sentence and offered a plea bargain of ten years in prison for having carried a gun during drug deals several years ago. I was crushed, thinking of the excessive severity of the sentencing laws that he faced. The next day was the anniversary of President George W. Bush's nationally televised address on the greatest financial crisis since the Great Depression, and I couldn't help but think of the corporate executives that escaped prosecution for the events that led to the Great Recession. Matthew was released after Homeboy Industries staff members gave character testimony on his behalf in court, but he nonetheless lost three years waiting behind bars.

In his critical analysis of post-Depression American crime policies, law professor and sociologist John Hagan (2010) has argued that, following the 1970s, America's prevailing concerns with safety shifted from the international to the domestic realm. This played out through two shifts in crime policy: a realignment of law enforcement's focus from white-collar crime (i.e., "suite crime") to drug, property, and violent crimes (i.e., "street crime"), as well as through a shift in responsibility of prosecution from local and state governments to the federal government. In the "Age of Roosevelt" (1933–1973), politicians, policy makers, and academics focused on structural factors linked to crime, introducing solutions based on concepts of social reform (Hagan 2010, 67). However, President Ronald Reagan and other influential politicians subsequently shifted the focus away from social reforms and toward incarceration. They skillfully enflamed popular fear of crime with the myth of the career criminal, supposedly emboldened by society's weak punishments for violent crime. This shift led to increasingly severe sentencing for street crimes, exacerbating punishment for those perceived to be career criminals in the interest of national security.

As I read the *Los Angeles Times* article on the Avenues sweep, which mentioned law enforcement officials' intentions to prosecute gang members under the RICO Act, it certainly seemed to me as if not only the paper's imagery, but our federal policies and priorities were focused on sending a message that, as a nation, we should fear urban gang members. Remarks from an interview with an arresting gang officer scorned gang members who tried to reform but failed, implying that they were indeed career criminals and had to be imprisoned. Most notably, although the story did not mention nationality or class, those became the salient topics raised by angry readers online. As I scrolled down the page, through the dozens of comments laden with racist messages targeting Latinos, the most prominent theme seemed to be a concern with undocumented immigration (e.g., "Illegal immigration is the root of most gang problems here in CA").

Accompanied on occasion by virulently racist outbursts, several *Times* readers proposed racially oppressive tactics to address the problem of crime, including the following:

- Deportation (e.g., "Boot them out of the country")
- Militarization of the streets (e.g., "Reroute the 10,000 troops that are scheduled to go to Afghanistan")
- Militarization of the border (e.g., "[C]lose the border")
- Tougher sentences (e.g., "Only life sentences and the death penalty will cure the gang cancer destroying our country")

Shockingly, a few even advocated for sterilization of immigrants (e.g., "If you castrate them, then they won't be able to have kids that will grow up to be just like their parents").

Not every commentator shared those xenophobic tendencies. However, anthropologist Leo Chavez, in his analysis of media coverage of Latino immigration, suggested that mainstream news reports often provide sufficient commentary and imagery to facilitate sustained anti-immigration rhetoric. Racist, anti-Latino discourse creates a "Latino threat narrative" that centers on the themes of "invasion," "reconquest," and "separatism" (Chavez 2008, 29). It is this volume's contention that anti-Latino discourse concerned with gangs, crime, and national security is a crime-focused variation of the Latino threat narrative, what is termed the Latino crime threat in the introduction. The *Los Angeles Times'* coverage of the Avenue sweeps fostered development of the Latino crime threat by providing images of the militarized raid, as well as an online comment board on which readers could interpret those images. Restrictive crime policy and the Latino crime threat have developed in tandem; local law enforcement agencies have adopted oppressive policing tactics that draw from—as well as build on—misinformed stereotypes of urban street gangs as violent and organized (Klein 1995).

Sociologists and critical criminologists place post-1970s economic decline in advanced industrial nations at the core of their analysis of racism, marginality, and crime control (Bauman 2004; Wacquant 2009[1999]; Young 2011). The contemporary hegemonic project of the "security state" manages "the risks posed by social disintegration" by exercising social control through crime control, and by criminalizing social policy (Hallsworth and Lea 2011, 142–144). However, although they have noted the rise of mass incarceration and state surveillance targeting immigrants and persons of color, critical sociologists have failed to conceptualize race as an unstable category, socially constructed through political struggle. How did the late-twentieth-century tide of rising incarceration sweep across racial lines? How did Latinos remain marginalized, vulnerable to the state's surveillance, while earlier cohorts of Southern and Eastern European immigrants seemingly assimilated into the mythical "melting pot"?" Although European immigrants escaped the issues of immigrant poverty, marginality, and crime, these issues have now become much more acute among blacks and Latinos.

The early-twentieth-century Chicago School of sociology sought to combat the racist eugenics movement, which asserted that Southern and Eastern European immigrants' involvement in poverty and crime was a function of biology (e.g., Park, Burgess, and McKenzie 1925; Thrasher 1927; Whyte 1943). Building on the use of language from the hard sciences, the Chicago School instead emphasized that social ecology—structural factors such as urban development or social marginality—was the basis for immigrants' higher association with crime. This line of reasoning had a profound influence in the 1930s on the development of U.S. public policy and the way in which crime was addressed. Under Franklin Delano Roosevelt's administration, social policy took shape through a reformist-inspired agenda that sought to address crime by addressing its root causes: poverty and marginalization. For example, Roosevelt's Works Progress Administration (WPA) attempted to ameliorate social problems by addressing the issue of substandard housing conditions. However, in the struggle for progressive social policy, Chicago School–inspired reformers articulated claims that rested on racist and sexist depictions that further marginalized Los Angeles's Latino population.

In the post–Civil Rights Movement era, notions of black/Latino gendered pathologies, such as the "welfare queen" or the streetwise career criminal, have set the stage for the state's retreat from social programs and simultaneous increasing surveillance over marginalized populations. Law professor Dorothy Roberts (2012) captured this in her work on black mothers' relationship with social services, which in the years following the Civil Rights Movement has evolved from material assistance uplifting poor families to enforced surveillance and the threatened removal of black children from their families. Whereas prior to the Civil Rights Movement, racism in many places took the form of an overt "Jim Crow" regime, latter-day racism is characterized by much more subtle, "coded" form. Guided by neoliberal "blame the victim" ideologies and "race-neutral" policies that reinforce racial inequality, "colorblind racism" has emerged as the new racist hegemony of the post–Civil Rights Movement era (Bonilla-Silva 2003). Crime control, as a facet of the late modern state, has enabled racism to persist against blacks and Latinos (i.e., Gilmore 2007; Wacquant 2009[1999]; Western 2007).

The turn-of-the-century Latino crime threat—what *Los Angeles Times* readers viscerally responded to in the story about the Avenues sweep—evolved across a century of white racial domination and tumultuous racial conflict. The Latino crime threat was fashioned through the early-twentieth-century struggle for social reform, and was refashioned through white resistance against civil rights gains. The post-1970s rearticulation of white racial hegemony set the backdrop for modern crime control efforts, and has catapulted American racism into the twenty-first century through the post-9/11 War on Terror. It thus shortchanges our understanding of Latino urban marginality, gangs, and faith-based social programs to simply say that such processes have been shaped by restrictive crime policy. A more accurate analysis of the mass incarceration of Latinos and its undergirding logic, the Latino crime threat, accounts for the racialized and gendered nature of modernizing, state-sponsored policies and reforms.

The Myth of the Melting Pot: Race and Reform in Early-Twentieth-Century Los Angeles
Immigration and Backlash

The period between 1900 and 1920 saw the greatest growth in immigration in U.S. history. Waves of Southern and Eastern European immigrants washed ashore at Ellis Island and other entry points, and fanned out across America, gravitating toward large cities such as New York and Chicago. American immigration was at its highest peak in 1910, when 14.8 percent of the U.S. population was foreign born (see figure 1.1). Los Angeles remained relatively unaffected, as statistics show that the city's rate of foreign-born residents (19.9 percent) was only slightly higher than the national average in 1910 and during most of the century's first immigration wave.

Since its early history, Los Angeles has been a city of both utopia and dystopia (Davis 1990). In the early twentieth century, Los Angeles's Westside had a largely middle-class, native-born, white Protestant population. Many Angelenos were internal migrants who originally hailed from the Midwest and held socially conservative, antiunion values

(Milkman 2006). City ordinances in 1909 made western Los Angeles the first exclusively residential urban area in the United States (Spalding 1992). Conversely, Los Angeles's Eastside, especially Boyle Heights, was populated by a veritable diversity of ethnic groups: Jews, Russians, Mexicans, Japanese, Slavonians, and Chinese. Industrial development and dilapidated housing made the Eastside a destination for a large number of immigrants (Spalding 1992).

Major influxes of Russians, Jews, and Mexicans arrived in Boyle Heights at different times, but overlapping in a way that reinforced multiculturalism rather than ethnic succession. A large group of Russian Molokans, a Christian sect that had broken from the Russian Orthodox Church, migrated to Los Angeles between 1905 and 1910, and settled in Boyle Heights (Spalding 1992). "Russian Town," located along "the Flats" on 1st Street, was the largest Molokan enclave in the United States. The Russian Flats covered a large portion of Boyle Heights: bounded on the east by Lorena Street, on the west by the Los Angeles River, on the south by Olympic Boulevard, and on the north by Mission Road (Vigil 2007).

The early twentieth century marked a period in Boyle Heights' development when reformers managed to directly influence changes in social policies that shaped life in the neighborhood (i.e., Spalding 1992; Lewthwaite 2009). After the Los Angeles Housing Commission was established in 1907, commissioners investigated the 1st Street Flats that were home to the area's Russian and Mexican populations (Spalding 1992). Compared to the extensive tenement districts in East Coast cities, the population density in Los Angeles was relatively low. Nonetheless, slum housing like that along 1st Street still characterized much of Boyle Heights. A 1910 report by the commission stressed overcrowding and unsanitary conditions, as well as lack of sufficient water supply, toilet facilities, and drainage (Spalding 1992). More poignantly, the report stated that "Jacob Riis, when he went through our congested districts, said that he had seen larger slums, but never any worse" (Los Angeles Municipal Housing Commission 1910, cited in Spalding 1992, 108). In the 1920s, cheaper housing drew still more immigrants, including Mexicans. It was during this period that Mexicans began to build shacks in Boyle Heights' ravines and hollows (Gustafson, 1940, cited in Moore 1991, 11).

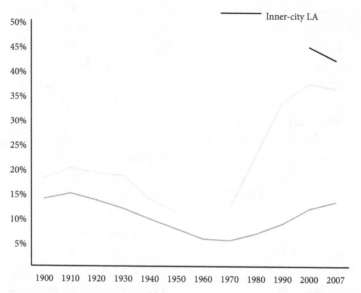

Figure 1.1. Percent Immigrant Population, by Year
Source: Census 1900–2000; American Community Survey 2005–2009.

Contrary to contemporary romantic perceptions of early-twentieth-century America as an inclusive "melting pot" for immigrants of European origin, many Americans responded to the rapid rise of Southern and Eastern European immigration with xenophobia. Eugenicists, who proclaimed that immigrants' genetic propensity led to involvement in crime, pressed for the Johnson Act, which effectively closed the U.S. to Southern and Eastern European immigration after 1924 (Jacobson 1999) (see figure 1.1). The eugenic stance was countered by the Chicago School sociologists, who contended that social problems in urban immigrant communities were rooted in social disorganization (Park, Burgess, and McKenzie 1925; Thomas and Znaniecki 1918; Thrasher 1927; Young 1929). The Chicago School argued that industrialization and urbanization created unsupervised, "interstitial" areas where boys could play, but that could also lead to petty theft and introduction to the criminal underworld (e.g., Thrasher 1927, 20). Immigrants tended to reside in lower-income neighborhoods, in a "zone of transition" (Park, Burgess, and McKenzie 1925, 148), where interstitial areas were abundant and second-generation immigrant boys were especially vulnerable to delinquency.

Pauline Young (1929) extended the social disorganization perspective to Boyle Heights' 1st Street Flats, which had pockets of marginalized poverty that yielded unsupervised territory for boys to play in. It was in this context that several Chicano gangs first emerged in Boyle Heights (Vigil 2007). Three persist as major Los Angeles gangs today: Cuatro Flats, Primera Flats, and White Fence (Vigil 2007, 40). However, oral histories archived with the Boyle Heights Historical Society (2011) have suggested that gang violence was not salient at the time. In addition, research on Chicano prisoners has suggested that, although White Fence was the first Eastside gang to start carrying guns—in the 1940s—there were no gang wars at the time (Vigil 2007). Nonetheless, anthropologist Diego Vigil has traced the roots of Los Angeles gangs to this era, suggesting that "gangs became so deeply rooted because of enduring social isolation and neglect of marginalized populations" (2007, 43).

The Paradox of Social Reform

During the 1930s, Franklin D. Roosevelt's New Deal ushered in an era of social reform across the nation. The Wagner-Steagall Act of 1937 established the United States Housing Authority (USHA), which spurred local governments to establish their own housing authorities in order to receive funding for slum clearance and public housing. The push for social reform through housing development advanced the Chicago School perspective on immigration, poverty, social disorganization, and crime. In Los Angeles, the racialized contests over public housing were disproportionately waged on the Eastside—Boyle Heights in particular.

William Burk's 1937 "Juvenile Delinquency and Poor Housing in the Los Angeles Metropolitan Area" was among a number of surveys and reports funded by the WPA during the era (Spalding 1992, 113). Burk found that the Flats had an "extraordinary" juvenile delinquency rate of 62.8 per 1,000 juveniles and a 60 percent repeat offense rate (Spalding 1992, 113). In 1938, the City of Los Angeles created the Housing Authority of the City of Los Angeles (HACLA), and together with the WPA, applied for funding under the Wagner-Steagall Act (Lefthwaite 2009). HACLA hired a photographer to document the case for public housing (Spalding 1992).

As American studies scholar Stephanie Lefthwaite noted in her analysis of race and social reform among Mexicans in early-twentieth-century Los Angeles, the push for social reform deepened racial divisions and exacerbated ethnic marginalization:

> A generation of reformers experimented with a variety of policies in health, housing, education, and labor: Progressive-era settlement work and housing reform; Americanization; segregation and repatriation. . . . Beneath these varied agendas, however, lay the patterning of racial, ethnic, and cultural differences. Reformers challenged yet supported the inequalities that circumscribed Mexican lives by promoting acculturation and racialization. (2009, 1)

Lefthwaite argued that, despite resistance from Mexicans, reformers built the case for their efforts through racist/sexist depictions of Mexicans. Photos of Mexican households suggested the absence of parental authority—that Mexican mothers were either negligent or did not meet middle class standards of domesticity—as well as the prevalence of delinquency. As a result, the photos used in reformers' reports rationalized paternalistic white–Mexican relations.

Mexican Americans engaged with the public housing debate on two contradictory fronts, arguing that Mexican communities "were indeed 'good communities' in need of rehabilitation rather than removal," while also affirming HACLA's motto of a "decent home" as an "American right" (Lefthwaite 2009, 202). Several Mexican American civic associations supported public housing, while one civic association, El Congreso, supported Bert Corona, of the Los Angeles County Health Department, in pushing for housing reform on the grounds of congestion and disease (Lefthwaite 2009). However, concerns over Mexicans' substandard living circumstances were later co-opted. The most notable example was Los Angeles City's purchase of the Chavez Ravine neighborhood from HACLA; the predominantly Mexican area was cleared for development in what would later become Dodger Stadium (Lefthwaite 2009). Social reform in Los Angeles thus drew from racialized depictions of Mexicans, and was bounded with racialized processes that paradoxically kept Mexicans geographically and socioeconomically segregated and marginalized.

Likewise, Sophie Spalding (1992), in an article published in the *Journal of Architectural Education*, noted contradictions in reformers' efforts in Los Angeles. Although it was a progressive public campaign for housing reform that razed the Flats to build Aliso Village in 1946, the construction disrupted the formation of positive community ties that had grown out of the Flats. In fact, the construction of Aliso Village institutionalized Mexican American poverty and marginality in Boyle Heights.

In sum, although the Chicago School's social disorganization perspective challenged racist views of immigrants, it ultimately reproduced paternalistic relations between whites and Latinos that reinforced Latino marginality. The social disorganization perspective undergirded the reformist push for fair housing by discursively associating race with substandard housing, congestion, disease, and delinquency. While Latino marginality and gang life remained entrenched in Boyle Heights—despite the social reforms of the Roosevelt era—other groups, such as the Molokans and Jews, moved out of the neighborhood. Residential segregation in post–World War II Los Angeles helped Southern and Eastern European immigrants advance ahead of blacks and Latinos, further entrenching marginality and gang formation. To understand the persistence of marginality in midcentury Los Angeles, it is vital to examine racial segregation.

Persisting Segregation during the Postwar Boom

In his landmark book *The Possessive Investment in Whiteness*, critical race scholar George Lipsitz (1998) noted that postwar Los Angeles's social policies purposefully facilitated the mobility of some groups at the expense of others. Instead of viewing changes in Los Angeles's demographic profile as an inevitable form of ethnic succession, as the Chicago School did, or as an unintended consequence of urban planning, as a planning perspective might, Lipsitz identified midcentury suburban housing development as a process that *intentionally* reinforced privilege. Los Angeles's postwar economic boom provided whites opportunities for social mobility by exacerbating racial inequality in two ways.

First, although postwar economic growth allowed many people to move into new, more affluent neighborhoods, the boom largely passed over Boyle Heights and the other major epicenter of Mexican settlement, East Los Angeles. Compared with other Los Angeles communities, they ranked in the bottom 10 percent in income and education (Moore 1991). Industrial plants established in Los Angeles during World War II were converted to industrial factories for production of rubber, steel, and automobiles; this provided new opportunities for Los Angeles residents. However, Mexicans and other minorities were largely excluded from prime jobs in the growing new economy (Moore 1991).

Second, although planned communities grew quickly to meet workers' needs for homes in residential suburbs such as Panorama City and North Hollywood, restrictive covenants explicitly stated that only persons of "Caucasian race" were allowed to buy new tract homes; Jews were included in this category, while Latinos, blacks, and Asians were excluded (Sanchez 2004, 638). The United States Supreme Court had ruled in 1948 that racially restrictive covenants were discriminatory and could not be enforced, but discriminatory practices continued against "non-Caucasians"; real estate agents, local property owners associations, and lending companies persisted in discriminating against non-whites until the 1970s (Sanchez 2004, 638). As a result, the housing market would not open for blacks and Latinos until decades after the war, much too late to for them to take part in the historic suburban housing boom.

In an ethnohistorical review of Boyle Heights' Cuatro Flats gang, sociologist James Diego Vigil noted that "in the late 1940s, largely due to their inability to move up the economic ladder as quickly as their Anglo counterparts in the boom years following World War II, gang membership provided a sense of personal pride in the face of social and economic powerlessness" (2007, 40). In turn, in the 1950s and 1960s, "gangs became so deeply rooted" in Boyle Heights due to "enduring social isolation and neglect of marginalized populations" (Vigil 2007, 43). Post-1970 deindustrialization and economic decline would subsequently limit blacks' and Latinos' prospects for mobility just as racially restrictive housing covenants finally lost their grip. As noted, the Chicano gangs that formed in Boyle Heights during the early twentieth century persisted decades later as among the oldest, largest, and most recognized in Los Angeles: along with White Fence, Primera (1st Street)

Flats, and Cuatro (4th Street) Flats, there were Big Hazard and Varrio Nuevo Estrada (Vigil 2007). Thus, Latinos on Los Angeles's Eastside became further marginalized and Latino gangs more institutionalized, despite progressive social reforms and advances made by other immigrant groups. Social reformers' racist/sexist depictions of immigrant poverty, social disorganization, and delinquency would be spun by the racial contests of the late twentieth century: the Civil Rights Movement, the backlash against it, and the War on Crime.

The Rearticulation of Race Relations: Civil Rights and the Rise of Colorblind Racism
The Chicano Civil Rights Movement

State-sponsored reform initiatives, which reproduced the paternalistic relationship between whites and Mexicans in Los Angeles's Eastside, receded by midcentury as civil rights activists began to contest the way state institutions and public policy upheld white privilege. The various battles that the African American Civil Rights Movement took on, such as school desegregation and voter registration in the South, rearticulated race from a concept of "ethnicity" to one of power and struggle (Omi and Winant 1994[1986]). Influenced by the black civil rights actions centered in the Jim Crow South, the southwest Chicano civil rights movement called attention to white/Mexican inequalities in education and labor. In 1968, in Boyle Heights and East Los Angeles, Chicano students walked out of class to protest educational inequality. Television news coverage captured students holding up "Chicano Power" signs, denouncing practices that oppressed and marginalized Latino students, and demanding a better education.

The Chicano civil rights movement spurred entrée-ism, which aimed to build "political organizations that could win elections, penetrate and influence state bureaucracies, and either exercise power in the Democratic Party or openly compete with it" (Omi and Winant 1994[1986], 110). Latinos had made large enough gains in public office that U.S. congressman Edward Roybal, who was first elected to represent Boyle Heights in the Los Angeles City Council in 1949, formed the National Association of Latino Elected and Appointed Officials (NALEO) in

1976. The large number of Latinos who entered public office in later decades, and contested racialized public policy, is attributable to the legacy of 1960s entrée-ism. In the 1980s, Gloria Molina, Los Angeles County's Eastside supervisor, made a stand against Latino poverty and gang violence by garnering support from a local Latino organizing group, the Mothers of East Los Angeles, to oppose the construction of a prison in the neighborhood (i.e., Sahagun 1989).

Far-left ethnic nationalism also emerged from the Chicano civil rights movement to combat racial oppression. Ethnic nationalists resisted "forcible imposition of the dominant white culture" and focused "on the recreation of the cultural framework by which their group recognized and understood itself" (Omi and Winant 1994[1986], 111). For Chicanos in Los Angeles, this meant embracing popular barrio culture, such as lowrider cars and graffiti art, but also rediscovering ancient traditions, such as Aztec imagery, language, and myths. Ethnic nationalism from the 1960s found expression in public murals in Los Angeles's Eastside, and this influenced the nature of poverty, gangs, and recovery from gang life. In an analysis of murals in Latino communities, Delgado and Barton found that murals "were painted on building walls that have been 'claimed' by the community as their own. . . . These spaces are transformed from their original purpose as part of a building structure to a message board for the internal and external community to see, read, and learn from" (1998, 347). Murals painted during the 1960s and 1970s on the walls of public housing complexes in Boyle Heights and East Los Angeles barrios wove together themes from the Chicano movement, such as protests and violence, with images evoking ethnic nationalist sentiment, such as the Aztec gods and the Virgen de Guadalupe. One long-standing mural in the Estrada Courts, home to one of Los Angeles's most established gangs, depicts Che Guevara's face and proclaims "we are not a minority." Another Estrada Courts mural depicts police beatings from riots following the 1970 Chicano Moratorium, the largest Latino antiwar protest.

White Racial Backlash

Civil rights gains provoked a backlash from whites resistant to social change and planted the seeds of 1980s restrictive crime policy (Omi and

Winant 1994[1986]). Nationally, conservative politicians and activists attacked forced integration and racial quotas. Former Alabama governor George Wallace, a prominent adversary of the Civil Rights Movement, gained support in traditionally democratic northern cities during the 1968 presidential campaign (Omi and Winant 1994[1986]). Based on the unexpected support for Wallace, political analyst Kevin Phillips advised Richard Nixon's campaign to turn to the right.

The "new right" drew from "coded language" that fostered anti-statism through political platforms supporting "family values" and "law and order," and lambasted the supposedly inferior "cultural values" of blacks and Latinos (Omi and Winant 1994[1986], 124). The backlash against the Civil Rights Movement led to the expansion of surveillance over racial and ethnic minorities. For example, the call for "law and order" emerged out of the reaction to race riots in northern cities and led to an increased police presence in segregated urban areas.

More broadly, the backlash against the Civil Rights Movement rearticulated white racial hegemony, from an explicit Jim Crow mode to a "colorblind" ideology that sought to roll back civil rights gains. A prime example is the first speech Ronald Reagan made as the Republican Party's presidential nominee in 1980, which he delivered near the Neshoba County Fair. A few miles away from the town associated with the 1964 murders of three civil rights workers, Reagan claimed that the government had distorted the Constitution's balance of powers by enacting the Voting Rights Act. By using the rhetoric of colorblind racism, Reagan tapped into white resistance against the Civil Rights Movement (Omi and Winant 1994[1986]). Later, as president, Reagan would advance crime control agendas that disproportionately targeted blacks and Latinos (Hagan 2010).

Neoliberalism and Mass Arrest Policing

In *The Culture of Control*, law and sociology scholar David Garland made the case that historical forces "transformed social and economic life in the second half of the twentieth century" in ways that not only wrought changes in crime control but revealed the limits of the nation state (2001, 75). The post–World War II decline of Keynesian economics "challenged the legitimacy and effectiveness of welfare institutions, and placed new limits on the powers of the nation-state," a condition that Garland described as "the coming of late modernity" (2001, 75). In turn, "the politics of post-welfarism" helped to produce "a new set of class and race relations and a dominant political block that defined itself in opposition to old style 'welfarism.'" America had concocted a new mix of state power, racist ideology, and crime policy to ensure another era of white privilege; neoliberalism was the crucial ingredient in this new recipe.

The Manhattan Institute, a neoliberal think tank founded in 1978, helped further efforts to rearticulate white racial hegemony. The institute published *Losing Ground*, Charles Murray's 1984 critique of Civil Rights Movement–influenced social reform. According to Loïc Wacquant,

> This book massages and misinterprets data to demonstrate that the rise in poverty in the United States after the 1960s was caused by the excessive generosity of policies intended to support the poor: such support, we are warned, rewards sloth and causes the moral degeneracy of the lower classes, and especially the "illegitimacy" that is alleged to breed all the ills of modern societies—among them "urban violence." (2009[1999], 12)

Murray's book, with its coded language, "would serve as the 'bible' for Reagan's crusade against the social-welfare state" (Wacquant 2009[1999], 12). Similar to the way Reagan lashed out against the Voting Rights Act, Murray's analysis tapped into white resistance against civil rights gains by framing Civil Rights Movement–influenced changes, such as the War on Poverty, as failed government intervention in redressing racial inequality.

Neoliberal ideology would provide the bedrock upon which to build the house of colorblind racism. Neoliberal discourse shifted the focus of criminal and penal policy away from spaces largely inhabited by affluent whites (financial regulation), to spaces disproportionately inhabited by blacks and Latinos (inner-city street crime). For example, the Anti-Drug Abuse Act of 1986 imposed a five-year sentence for possession of five hundred grams of powder cocaine, but only five grams of crack cocaine. The act criminalized an activity that poor, urban blacks and Latinos disproportionately engaged in on the street: selling crack. Despite the fact that per capita crime was dropping in the early 1980s, "tough on crime" platforms attacked the welfare state, as well as the gains of the Civil Rights Movement. Reagan and other politicians were able to accomplish this by skillfully avoiding the issue of *falling* crime rates, instead capitalizing on people's *rising fear* of crime, by creating the impression that crime was proliferating like never before and that street criminals were career felons who had to be incapacitated permanently (Hagan 2010).

As the War on Drugs was introduced, the federal government began a profound shift in making drug enforcement a federal priority. The resulting changes in criminal and penal policy led to a sharp increase in the U.S. prison population. After falling between 1960 and 1970, the U.S. incarceration rate began a steep, decades-long rise. Between 1970 and 1980, the U.S. incarceration rate rose from 161.4 to 220.4 per 100,000 adults. However, it soared to much higher levels following the Anti-Drug Abuse Act of 1986, reaching 458.2 in 1990 and 682.9 in 2000.[1] Marked racial differences are manifest in the rates of incarceration among different groups. While one in 106 adult white men were incarcerated in 2007, one in fifteen black men and one in thirty-six Latino men were incarcerated (PEW Center on the States 2008, 6). In fact, across the late twentieth century, the proportion of blacks arrested has increased while the share of total crime committed by blacks has decreased (Wacquant 2009[1999], 77).

Marc Mauer (2006[1999], 158), executive director of the Sentencing Project, a leading policy and advocacy organization, has proclaimed that "no policy has contributed more" to racially disparate sentencing than the War on Drugs. The War on Drugs increased imprisonment rates for blacks and Latinos in two major ways: through total arrests, and as a proportion of all arrests (Mauer 2006[1999]). Bringing together data from the Substance Abuse and Mental Health Services Administration, an annual household survey conducted by the Department of Health and Human Services to measure U.S. drug use, and arrest data provided by the FBI, Mauer (2006[1999]) demonstrated acute racial disparities in rates of drug use versus incarceration. In 2000, monthly drug use rates were similar across all groups (6.4 percent for blacks and Whites, 5.3 percent for Latinos). According to projections, however, one in six male Latinos born in 2001, and one in three black males, would

Figure 1.2. Incarceration Rate, per 100,000
Source: 1880–1970: Cahalan (1986); 1980–2008: Center for Economic and Policy Research analysis of Bureau of Justice Statistics data.

be incarcerated at some point—in contrast to only one in seventeen white males (Bonczar 2003, 1, cited in Mauer 2006[1999], 138).

The massive rise of incarceration rates following the War on Drugs and the vast racial disparities in incarceration have led law professor Michelle Alexander (2010, 11) to term the post–Civil Rights Movement era the "New Jim Crow." The redeployment of racist depictions of black and Latino communities as poor, socially disorganized, and crime ridden, has facilitated the racial state's transition from the Chicago School–inspired, racially paternalistic social reform approach, to the post–Civil Rights Movement colorblind racist approach of crime control.

The Field of Crime Control in Post-Civil Rights America

In the early 1990s, the Manhattan Institute continued to build on conservative ideas that emphasized mass arrest tactics targeting the urban—largely black and Latino—poor. The institute hosted a conference that led to a special issue in its journal, *City*, positing a relationship between urban disorder and crime that called for a heavy-handed policing approach to protect the interests of middle-class consumers of public space (Wacquant 2009[1999]). Rudolph Giuliani drew the idea for his "zero-tolerance" campaign from the conference, and used it to help him win the New York City mayoral race. This symbiosis of the Manhattan Institute's neoliberal perspective, mass arrest policing, and Giuliani's political success rekindled the fire lit by George Kelling and James Q. Wilson's 1982 *Atlantic Monthly* article that introduced the broken windows theory, which advocated mass ticketing and arrests of minor violations committed in urban spaces Wacquant (2009[1999]). After Giuliani took office in 1994, he appointed William Bratton as his police commissioner, and zero tolerance was implemented in New York. Inspired by these events, the Manhattan Institute funded Kelling and Catherine Coles to write *Fixing Broken Windows*. As crime was perceived to decline in New York under Giuliani and Bratton, the book could offer a seeming prima facie example of the application and success of the broken windows theory.

Kelling and Coles—like Bratton in his 1998 memoir, *Turnaround: How America's Top Cop Reversed the Crime Epidemic*—omitted significant evidence that clearly undermines their central assumptions. Scholars have pointed out that cities with softer "community-oriented" policing were posting similar decreases in crime, that crime had already dropped in New York before Giuliani and Bratton took office, and that complaints against the police soared in New York even as they dropped in cities that implemented community-oriented policing (Wacquant 2009[1999]).[2] However, the lack of evidence for the broken windows theory—which persists to this day—did not stop Bratton from becoming an internationally renowned expert on crime, exporting the neoliberal, broken windows, "zero-tolerance" approach to cities around the world. In 2002, he brought his suppressive policing approach to southern California, accepting the position of chief of the Los Angeles Police Department.

Bratton's approach reflected how post-1970s changes in crime institutions and practices were a "sharp reversal of policy and opinion and a remaking of the whole crime control field" (Garland 2001, 76). David

Garland has argued that contemporary crime control in the United States has led to the decline of the rehabilitative ideal and reinvented the prison as a mechanism to incapacitate supposed career criminals. Bratton's assertions about crime helped to further entrench the development of the contemporary field of crime control.

The current predicament for public officials is the fact that the "old myth of the sovereign state and its plenary power to punish" has not led to success in crime control, while "the political costs of . . . a withdrawal are liable to be disastrous" (Garland 2001, 110). Either the myth is reasserted, along with its failed policies, or instrumental action is abandoned, instead embracing the expression of "anger and outrage that crime provokes" (Garland 2001, 110). This predicament has undermined the development of coherent crime programs, and instead revealed the limits of the state in addressing crime. In return, public officials and citizens have reasserted the prominence of the state through excessive crime control targeting poor blacks (Simon 2009).

Criminologist David Kennedy (2011), in a highly personalized account of his attempts to help public officials and police officers institutionalize community-oriented policing and upend traditional (reactive) policing, maligned any analysis of racial conflict between inner-city communities and the police. Concerned not with drug use, but with the post-1980s rise of drug markets and the concentrated rise of homicide in segregated neighborhoods, he suggested that building on social programs such as Operation Ceasefire might be America's only hope of successfully addressing gang crime. However, as described earlier in this chapter, race has been central to twentieth-century American public policy efforts over the issues of poverty, marginality, and crime—preceding the rise of post-1980s drug markets by several decades. Following the end of the social reform era inspired by Roosevelt's New Deal and the Civil Rights Movement, conservative forces recast racial oppression by rearticulating notions of blacks and Latinos as poor, socially disorganized, and criminal, through post–civil rights movement, colorblind racist concerns over dependency, degeneracy, violence, and crime control. Dismissing twentieth-century America's highly racialized contests obviates the centrality of race in contemporary crime control projects.

The following section examines the City and County of Los Angeles, as well as the State of California, as paradigmatic cases of how neoliberal, colorblind discourse—machinated through both "tough on crime" approaches and innovative blends of proactive community policing—has helped to set the stage for much more aggressive racial domination in the contemporary United States.

The Latino Crime Threat: Los Angeles's War on Gangs as Colorblind Racism
Criminal Sentencing

Beginning in the 1980s, three laws were enacted in California aimed largely at black and Latino street gang members. These laws helped foster development of the Latino crime threat discourse by ensuring that Latinos would easily be targeted through the War on Drugs, the War on Crime, and the War on Terror.

- In 1982, district attorneys in California began to file "gang injunctions." These served as restraining orders preventing members from associating in certain public places, or appearing in public after certain hours (California Penal Code Section 166.a.4).
- In 1988, the California legislature created the "Gang Enhancement Law," which allowed misdemeanors to be tried as felonies, through the Street Terrorist Enforcement and Protection Act (California Penal Code Section 186.22). The Gang Enhancement Law increased sentences by up to four years, by judicial discretion, or five to ten years for serious and violent felonies.
- In 1994, the California "three-strikes" law" (California Penal Code Section 1170.12) was adopted in a referendum (Proposition 184). It required that persons with a violent first felony, a serious second felony, and any third felony face a mandatory life sentence.[3] (California Proposition 36, passed in 2012, revised the law, creating some exceptions for felons with a nonserious, nonviolent third felony.)

As the absolute number of incarcerated black and Latino inmates, especially gang members, grew in the post–Civil Rights Movement period, California became an extreme case of "law and order" racial reaction. Following post-1980s national trends in incarceration, the state became home to the largest prison construction project ever in human history (Gilmore 2007). In turn, mass incarceration has helped to construct men of color and gangs as threats to the state.

Operation Hammer (1988–1991)

The restrictive and punitive approach to crime, which focused on the outrage that crime provoked, pressed not only for tougher criminal sentencing but also much more aggressive policing strategies. In addition to increasingly punitive legislation on crime in California, law enforcement officials in Los Angeles began to adopt the "suppression" method—intense police surveillance and intimidation in communities with high crime rates (Klein 1995). The LAPD embraced this approach from 1988 to 1991, after Chief Daryl Gates declared a "War on Crime."

Law enforcement officials focused suppression efforts on black and Latino men, targeting gang members. Beginning in 1988, the LAPD began a series of sweeps intended to round up large numbers of gang members. Police officers raided residential neighborhoods in Los Angeles for the following two years in what was dubbed Operation Hammer, whose stated purpose was to reduce crime by "putting the pressure on" gang members, targeted due to rising gang violence in the region (see figure 1.3). The *Los Angeles Times* quoted Gates as having called gang members "rotten little cowards" at Operation Hammer's inception (Johnson 1989). Under Gates, Los Angeles policing fed into the discourse of the Latino crime threat through the implementation of approaches that implicitly or explicitly implicated street gang members as the most significant threat to public safety.

At the inception of Operation Hammer, gang membership and gang violence were growing in Los Angeles. The Community Youth Gang Services estimated that the number of gang members in the county had climbed from 30,000 in 1980 to 70,000 by 1988; the LAPD's figures for Los Angeles City alone stood at 15,000 in the mid-1980s, and 26,000 at Operation Hammer's inception (Himmel 1988). In addition, the number Los Angeles City gang murders had soared, from 205 in 1982 to 387 in 1987. In a 1989 television documentary, *Gangs, Cops & Drugs*, NBC News anchor Tom Brokaw referred to Los Angeles as the "gang capital" of the United States.

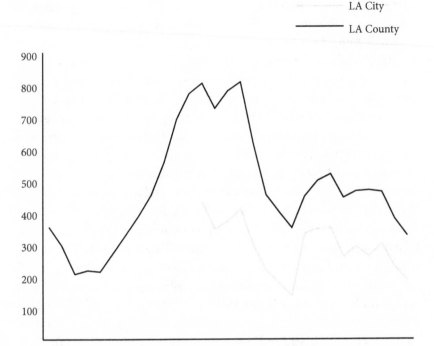

Figure 1.3. Gang-Related Murders in Los Angeles
Source: L.A. County Department of Public Health, Injury, and Violence Prevention
Program 2011.

On occasion, the *Los Angeles Times* simply ran short stories enu-
merating the size of large sweeps. In such instances, the paper briefly
reported the number of officers involved, the number of persons
arrested, and the number of those who were gang members. Sensa-
tionalistic headlines proclaimed, "700 Seized in Gang Sweep; 2 more
die in Shootings" (Welkos 1988); "237 Held in Sweep; Violence Continues" (Enriquez 1989); "Police Arrest 1,092 in Weekend Sweeps; Gang
Killings Continue" (Watson 1989); "618 arrested in S.F. Valley Gang
Sweeps . . . But violence plagues Southland as at least 15 people are
reported slain" (Enriquez 1990): and "'Hammer' Falls on 74 Possible
Gang Members" (Metro Digest 1990).

These raids exposed community members to a range of abusive behavior from police officers. For example, on August 1, 1988,

eighty-eight police officers swarmed two apartment buildings on 39th and Dalton, without any officer on hand executing a search warrant (Mitchell 2001). Officers smashed through residents' homes, destroyed furniture, walls, and family photos, and left their own graffiti: "LAPD Rules" (Mitchell 2001). One policeman recalled, "We were delivering a message that there was a price to pay for selling drugs and being a gang member. . . . I looked at it as something of a Normandy Beach, a D-day" (Mitchell 2001). An LAPD assistant chief would later compare the department's preparation for raids to that of going to war, and the treatment of the residents to that of dogs (Mitchell 2001). Officers left twenty-two persons injured, homeless, and under the care of the Red Cross; the city eventually paid $4 million in damages (Mitchell 2001).

As Operation Hammer waged on, community residents reacted in various ways. Some wanted more "hammers," "a whole toolbox" (Dawsey 1989), or claimed to be "all for police protection . . . it's pretty rowdy here" (Lee 1989). However, local faith leaders, as well as representatives of groups such as the black activist organization Us and the American Civil Liberties Union, accused the police of racial profiling. They argued that Operation Hammer harassed blacks and Latinos (i.e., Dawsey 1989; Katz 1990).

Op-ed pieces in the *Los Angeles Times* explicitly critiqued Operation Hammer as a failure. In one, Father Gregory Boyle defended the members of his parish, writing, "Gang members know all too well that mass roundups like 'Operation Hammer' and 'tougher' police presence in the housing projects only exacerbate the deep antagonism that already exists between law-enforcement officials and residents of the barrio" (Boyle 1990). He cited despondency as the main reason why gang members failed to respond to Operation Hammer's threat of tough policing and long jail sentences. Harking back to notions developed through the Chicago School of sociology, he claimed that gang violence was the result of the "failure of the educational system and the poor job market for minority youth," which had made it "almost impossible for gang members to imagine a future for themselves." Boyle pleaded for the city to address reform through reinvestment into jobs for young persons. *Los Angeles Times* readers responded by attacking the paper for its negative coverage of the sweeps, and positive coverage of reformers such as Boyle. High-ranking LAPD officers also attacked the *Times* for taking too "soft" a stance on crime (i.e., Vernon 1990; Gates 1991).

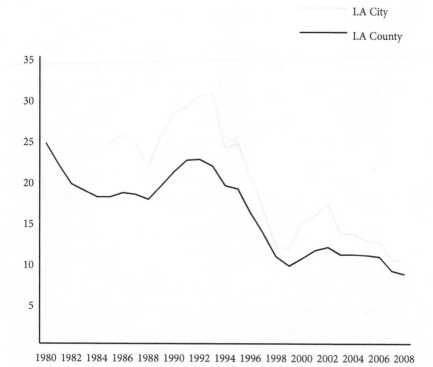

Figure 1.4. Murder Rate, per 100,000
Source: L.A. County Department of Public Health, Injury, and Violence Prevention Program 2011; L.A. County population figures from U.S. Census Bureau; L.A. City population figures from FBI Uniform Crime Reporting (UCR) statistics.

Following the implementation of Operation Hammer, the murder rate actually went up (see figure 1.4). The overall Los Angeles City and Los Angeles County murder rates, both in decline prior to the operation, rose from 21.6 (Los Angeles City) and 17.6 (Los Angeles County) per 100,000 residents in 1988, to peaks unsurpassed since, 30.3 (Los Angeles City) and 22.5 (Los Angeles County) per 10,000 in 1992, the year of the Los Angeles Riots. Gang scholar Malcolm Klein, one of the foremost experts in the field, noted in his landmark overview of policing and gangs that, nationwide, aggressive local law enforcement strategies have served only to foster an "us-and-them" climate that promotes gang cohesion, organization, and criminal activity (i.e., Klein 2006).

The "Internal War on Terrorism" (2002–2008)

The nation's War on Terror further exacerbated the Latino crime threat through the discursive framing of Latino gangs as threats to national security. Sworn in as chief of the Los Angeles Police Department one year after 9/11, William Bratton declared an "all-out assault" on gangs, called gang violence "homeland terrorism," and vowed to work with Mayor James Hahn to secure federal funds to fight the problem (Garvey and Winton 2002). Bratton also created a post to coordinate antigang efforts citywide—as the new "gang czar," he appointed Captain Michael Hillmann, a thirty-five-year veteran with experience as commander of the LAPD's antiterrorism division.

The LAPD strategically tried to distance itself from the racial history of 1980s and 1990s suppression policing. Captain Hillman's assistant chief, Jim McDonnell, said, "We don't want to come out like in the "80s with Operation Hammer. . . . We are planning a holistic, collaborative approach to the problem" (Garvey and Winton 2002). Nonetheless, experts feared Bratton's support for "community policing" was mere lip service, directed toward appeasing the activist Los Angeles citizenry organizing for expanded community engagement. Tony Muhammad, a Muslim community leader in South Los Angeles, highlighted the troubling facets of Bratton's framing of the gang problem. At one press conference, he declared, "We are with the police chief when he says: 'Get angry.' We are angry" (Garvey and Winton 2002). However, Muhammad was troubled by the racialized implications of such aggressive policing. He asked Bratton how he could "differentiate between a gangbanger and my brother" (Garvey and Winton 2002). Muhammad's fears were not unfounded. Over the previous two decades, the LAPD had documented between 38,000 and 64,000 gang members on their police files—most of them black and Latino (Los Angeles Police Department 2012).

Framing the gang problem through the War on Terror, Bratton consequently failed to work with local communities. Unsurprisingly, in his prior experience in New York, Bratton had also refused to address gang problems through community policing (Jones and Wiseman 2003).[4] Nationally, the effort to get police departments to implement community policing was an uphill battle; in the years after 9/11, during Bratton's tenure as LAPD chief, funds for federal community-policing initiatives, such as the Community Oriented Policing Services (COPS) grants, were withdrawn and redirected toward the Department of Homeland Security. In an effort to regain funding lost to the War on Terror Bratton and Hahn convened a workshop at an annual conference of mayors in Washington, D.C., in 2003, devoted to gang crime and domestic terrorism. However, Bratton's aims were either unclear or incompatible with community-oriented policing (Jones and Wiseman 2003). Homeland Security's main task was to expand the use of the military in domestic law enforcement, but Bratton did not explain how domestic terrorism funding could help fight gangs through community policing (Jones and Wiseman 2003).

Los Angeles County officials did eventually secure funding from the Department of Homeland Security. In February 2005, the county became the first entity in southern California to enroll in the Department of Homeland Security's 287(g) program, which provides funding for federal immigration officials to train local police officers how to screen, identify, and deport undocumented immigrants (Gorman 2009). Whereas Special Order 40 prevented police officers in the City of Los Angeles from participating with 287(g), the coordination between county jails and federal immigration agents created a means to screen for undocumented immigrants through the legal system.

Bratton's LAPD would adopt innovative approaches to community policing only after the election of Mayor Antonio Villaraigosa. But even after Villaraigosa's reforms, Bratton continued to flaunt research and evaluation on gang strategies. As mentioned earlier, academic researchers rejected the assertion that Bratton's tenure was associated with drops in crime rates. Rather, drops in crime were linked to overall national declines. Nonetheless, Bratton expressed his dismay in a 2004 *Time* article, "The Gang Buster," in which he vehemently proclaimed, "The penicillin for dealing with crime is cops. I thought I had already proved this. Criminologists who say it is the economics or the weather or some other thing are crazy" (McCarthy 2004).

Although he claimed to be in favor of community policing, Bratton actually favored measures that carved deep racial rifts between his police force and potential community partners. He advanced suppressive policing approaches that alienated leaders of minority communities, and his targeting and stigmatization of gang members along racial lines reinforced the ideas that undergirded the discourse of the Latino crime threat.

Recasting the Suppression Method (2003–2009)

Despite the central contradictions in Los Angeles's attempt to regulate crime—the simultaneous failure of the instrumental approach and the success of community activism against oppressive policing—local politics revealed the racial state's Teflon-like quality to absorb moderate demands, while largely insulating itself from more radical ones (Omi and Winant 1994[1986]). In 2005, the City of Los Angeles Ad Hoc Committee on Gang Violence and Youth Development funded the Advancement Project to conduct a study on the feasibility of a comprehensive plan for gang violence. Just as the funds were released, Villaraigosa's election as the first Latino mayor of Los Angeles also heralded a shift back to experimentation with community-oriented policing. In 2007, the Advancement Project released its findings in a report titled "A Call to Action: A Case for Comprehensive Solution to L.A.'s Gang Violence Epidemic." With community leaders and scholars, such as Father Greg and UCLA professor Jorja Leap, helping to coauthor the report, the Advancement Project framed gang violence in similar terms as Operation Ceasefire had done—an epidemiological approach focused on interrupting outbreaks of violence—and called for a "Marshall Plan" to end gang violence. Villaraigosa responded with the Gang Reduction and Youth Development (GRYD) plan. A publication released from the mayor's office, just before the first funds were released through GRYD, symbolized the progressive move toward community-oriented policing. Titled "Healing Our Neighborhoods: A Citywide Partnership to Combat Gang Crime," its front cover was adorned with a colorful mural by an acclaimed Homeboy Industries artist, Fabian Debora. The mural beautifully captured a dimension of compassion: a colorful tree bursting with a heart in its trunk, hugged on each side by two children with dark brown complexions.

GRYD effectively concentrated resources for fighting gang crime into twelve high-gang activity zones, cancelled the L.A. Bridges program, and built upon existing programs in each zone, largely following

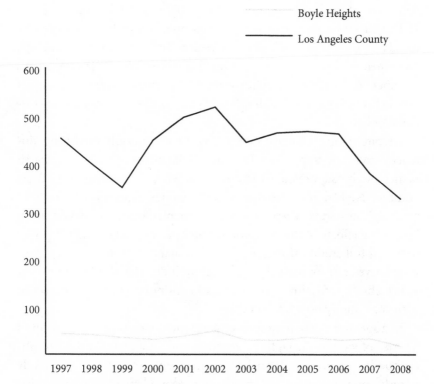

Figure 1.5. Total Murders, 1997–2008
Source: Los Angeles Police Department (LAPD), Citywide Gang Crime Summary.

the perceived success of Boyle Heights' gang reduction program. Ultimately, though, GRYD's major weaknesses lay in its focus on prevention and intervention strategies not yet proven to be effective. Prevention was addressed through funding for organizations that provided
social services for children aged ten to fifteen who scored "at-risk" on
the Youth Services Eligibility Tool (YSET). Yet only a small percentage
of at-risk youth were integrated into GRYD through this tool. In addition, intervention was heavily dependent upon an annual investment
of $200,000 through the Los Angeles Violence Intervention Acad-
emy (LAVITA), which was modeled after Operation Ceasefire. RAND
research on Ceasefire, however, suggested that in some instances, such
as its implementation in Pittsburgh, its outreach efforts facilitated cohesion among gang members and crime actually went up. No definitive

data existed on the feasibility of the programs carried out in Boyle Heights; murder rates may have inched up or down based on broader trends in Los Angeles County, as well as the nation (see figure 1.5). Nonetheless, despite the relative ineffectiveness of GRYD's programs, members of local communities were drawn into advisory committees for each GRYD zone, building upon the promise of community-oriented policing.

Despite progress toward developing community-oriented gang violence strategies, implementation of GRYD coexisted with the harsh tactics of the suppression method. Following the success of GRYD's Summer Night Lights program—murder rates dropped drastically in the neighborhoods where it was implemented—Bratton would again ignore the efforts of the city's community partners, claiming the police deserved full credit (Morrison 2010, National Public Radio 2012). Representatives of groups such as Homeboy Industries would lament the police chief's refusal to commend and continue to build relationships with community organizations.

In 2008 and 2009, hundreds of gang members were rounded up in a series of sweeps through the Avenues and Hawaiian Gardens neighborhoods, a revival of local law enforcement's efforts to aggressively punish gang infractions. Matthew, the respondent of mine who was picked up in the sweep mentioned at the beginning of this chapter, was to be tried for minor offenses four to five years old; he faced ten years in prison with a plea deal. At the same time that Los Angeles officials were attempting to shift to community-oriented strategies for curbing gang violence, the suppression method of policing gang members nonetheless perpetuated the discourse of the Latino crime threat. The Latino crime threat enabled public discussion of crime to materialize around the issues of race, immigration, and national security, and to more deeply entrench the neoliberal foundations of colorblind racism.

Conclusion

Los Angeles, in the latter half of the twentieth century, saw the rise of the Latino crime threat, a racialized image of the marginal, violent, urban Latino gang member. This image had its origins not only in racist assumptions that undergirded eugenics, but in the social structural representations of immigrant poverty that the Chicago School used to contest eugenics.

The Chicago School's assertions of the relationship between housing, disorganization, and crime shaped the way in which Los Angeles City officials engaged with Roosevelt's New Deal reforms. Reformers in Los Angeles attempted to make a case for housing reform by documenting poverty in ways that inadvertently exacerbated racist and sexist notions, inaccurately inscribing themes of absent mothers or male delinquency into depictions of Mexican households. Housing reform in Los Angeles rested on racial paternalism that elevated Americanism and social integration above existing social ties in Mexican neighborhoods. Los Angeles's contemporary Latino gangs have their roots in this racialized/gendered history of marginality, public policy, and reform.

The racist and sexist images of Mexican immigrant poverty, social disorganization, and delinquency that framed reformers' efforts during Roosevelt's administration were later recast through the post-1970s backlash against the Civil Rights Movement. Whites and conservatives sought to roll back civil rights gains by advancing notions of black and Latino dependency, degeneracy, and violence as threats to the state. Whites and conservatives used the coded language of "family values" and "law and order" platforms to support neoliberalism and roll back the same welfare state that had helped previous waves of immigrants, instead imposing mass incarceration and surveillance as forms of governance over black and Latino populations. Later, the rise of zero-tolerance policing strategies and the post-9/11 War on Terror further reshaped how the state engaged mass incarceration and surveillance to govern marginal, urban populations—by targeting urban gang members as "domestic terrorists." Thus, early-twenty-first-century debates over the state's role in public policy reformulated the same discussion of racial themes in the early twentieth century (i.e., immigration, poverty, social disorganization, and delinquency) by extending the reach of the racial state further into the branch of criminal law.

Contemporary immigration scholars have become especially concerned with the Latino experience of racialization and exclusion—in particular the tough-on-crime policing and stiff immigration controls in place today. The next chapter uses decennial census and American Community Survey (ACS) data to examine demographic trends in

Los Angeles' Latino-dominant, inner-city neighborhoods. It asks, are residents in these neighborhoods forming what William Julius Wilson (1987:8) once termed the "urban underclass," or are they moving up and out of the barrios? Segmented assimilation scholars have predicted Latino downward assimilation in a hostile context of reception, and have drawn extensively from the Mexican American experience in southern California to validate this idea. Similarly, critical sociologists have become concerned with the growth of neoliberalism, mass incarceration, and the surveillance state as processes that compound marginality, especially for blacks and Latinos. However, whether marginality will lead to cyclical and entrenched poverty remains to be investigated. As the following chapter reveals, although racialized dimensions of public policy in Los Angeles have helped to crystallize Latino disadvantage across the twentieth century, by no means do racialized policy and high rates of immigration and poverty create a context of cyclical poverty.

2

Into the Underclass or Out of the Barrio?

Immigrant Integration in Latino Los Angeles

[For] four days . . . I used too much coke. . . . I was laying
down on my couch, sweating. It was like if you have clothes
and you go inside of a shower, and then boom . . . my Jefita
was like, "Ey what's wrong with you? . . . Are you using
drugs?" I told her "You know what? You wanna hear the
truth? Yes, I'm using drugs. What do you care? What's it to
you?" And then, bro, she started crying. . . . She was crying, "*Mijo*, that's not the life I want for you! That's not what
I brought you here for! That's not what I want for you guys!"
Ramon, 24, Victory Outreach Bible study leader

amon is an undocumented immigrant, brought from Mexico
by a single mother when he was only twelve years old, and his
experience illustrates the risk that today's street gangs pose to immigrants (e.g., Portes and Rumbaut 2001). Although Ramon's mother
brought herself and her children to the U.S. to distance them from her
husband, and for better educational and occupational prospects, by age
fourteen, Ramon had joined a street gang and become involved with
gang violence. He had been shot at, nearly stabbed, and attacked with
baseball bats. He had carried guns to school, used drugs, ran "missions
with his homeboys," and even sold drugs with his uncle. By age twenty-
one, he was addicted to crystal methamphetamine and homeless. The
epigraph above captures Ramon describing, in an interview with me,
the moment at which his life changed: when his mother found out he
was doing drugs. Sometime afterward, she kicked him out of her house.
It was at that point that he found a flyer to the Victory Outreach–Eastside men's recovery home, moved in, and quit drugs.

Segmented assimilation scholars Alejandro Portes and Rubén Rumbaut (2001) have suggested that weak ties to coethnic communities and a hostile context of reception—such as the Latino crime threat described in the last chapter—help to foster formation of reactive ethnicity and to facilitate downward assimilation. Ramon's experience with Chicano gangs and drugs demonstrates these facets of segmented assimilation theory, as well as some other findings in immigration studies. First, in contrast to the earlier waves of European immigration, today immigration is more heavily influenced by women's agency and migratory networks. Gendered conflict emanating from Mexican patriarchal households can spur immigration, and women often prefer residence in the U.S. for the economic and educational opportunities it provides themselves and their children (Hondagneu-Sotelo 1994). Second, migration provides an opportunity for upward socioeconomic mobility, although acculturation into American street gangs and drugs can instead shape a trajectory of downward socioeconomic mobility (Zhou and Bankston 1998). Third, acculturation into street gangs and drugs is a product of, but is also exacerbated by, strained family ties. Ramon's experiences with gangs and reform not only illustrate but also challenge some of the dominant assumptions embedded in contemporary understandings of immigration.

The popularity of Samuel P. Huntington's *Who Are We* and Victor Davis Hanson's *Mexifornia* reveal that the context of reception for Latinos has become increasingly hostile, one in which assumptions are made that Latinos are prone to criminality or lack the capacity to socially integrate. These assumptions back the push for stricter immigration controls (Chavez 2008). In his review of twentieth-century crime policy, John Hagan (2010) suggested that such assumptions of immigrant criminality have a long history. An overemphasis on criminal ethnic succession has always colored the national imagination, as seen in books and films such as *The Gangs of New York*, the *Godfather* series, *Bugsy*, and *Scarface*. An overemphasis on criminal ethnic succession also characterizes more recent literature on Latino immigrants. For example, Tony Rafael's *The Mexican Mafia* ties urban street gangs with brutal, international drug cartels. Rafael's book promotes views of Mexican immigration and urban street gangs that fuel that immigration debate in ways that promote fear of immigrants, harsher sentencing, and restrictive immigration legislation—themes evoked, as shown in the preceding chapter, by many of the angry readers who commented on the *Los Angeles Times* coverage of the Avenues gang sweep.

Although illicit activities may very modestly endow some residents of immigrant enclaves, they tend to marginalize the whole community. Illicit activities "activate and exaggerate the general public's fears and anxieties, and they in turn relegate these ghettoized neighborhoods to the moral as well as physical periphery of the social and economic system" (Hagan 2010, 41). However, because of stricter crime policy, "America's ethnic vice industries are not the mobility ladders they might have once promised to be" (Hagan 2010, 40). As a result, as tiny as criminal ethnic succession may be, and despite the relatively low proportion of immigrants involved in crime, American immigration is entering a new epoch, one in which the romantic myth of assimilation and upward mobility has slowly faded and much more arduous obstacles—such as the restrictive crime policies covered in the last chapter—have obstructed American immigrant integration.

Whereas gang and delinquent youth in Frederic Thrasher's *The Gang* (1927) or William Foote Whyte's *Street Corner Society* (1943) eventually joined their peers in mainstream society by moving out of the immigrant neighborhood, marrying, and securing formal employment, contemporary scholarship paints a different picture of modern gangs and delinquent youth. Today scholars observe that the political economy of the urban neighborhood channels second-generation immigrant men into illicit activity as a cornerstone of adulthood (e.g., Bourgois 1995). Immigration scholars fear second-generation immigrants' potential to assimilate into a reactive ethnicity, which they see as rejecting the values of mainstream America. It is this trajectory which is thought to lead to cyclical and intergenerational poverty among post-1965 immigrants, most notably through gang membership and incarceration (Portes and Rumbaut 2006[1990]; Smith 2006; Zhou and Bankston 1998).

However, despite the salience of race, poverty, and crime in Ramon's adolescence and early adulthood, Ramon found a way to quit drugs, move out of the community where his gang was located, find a job, and mend his relationship with his mother. Despite the structural obstacles Ramon faced in experiencing upward assimilation, such as engagement with gangs and drugs, Ramon was able to buck a downward trajectory early in his adult life.

What can we make of Ramon's experience with gangs, drugs, and salvation? Do the experiences of today's marginal immigrant youth mirror those of a century ago, who largely aged out of countercultures and joined the mainstream? Is downward assimilation thriving among marginalized immigrant youth today? This chapter turns to census data to unpack some common and hidden assumptions about Latino marginality, before further examining gang recovery in Los Angeles in later chapters.

Segmented Assimilation in Inner-City Los Angeles

Segmented assimilation theory predicts downward assimilation among black and Latino immigrants, in low-income segregated neighborhoods with a hostile context of reception. Such a trajectory suggests cyclical, intergenerational poverty, such as that found in a lifestyle of drugs, gangs, and incarceration. To better contextualize this book's analysis of recovery from gang life, this chapter measures for evidence of downward assimilation in Los Angeles.

The following analyses draw from the U.S. Census Bureau's 5-percent Public Use Microdata Sample (PUMS) over the period 1900–2000, as well as the American Community Survey's 2005–2009 PUMS. The University of Minnesota's Integrated Public Use Microdata Series (IPUMS), which pools several PUMS files and offers measures of socioeconomic status, is also used.[1] These data measure for the defining structural features of downward assimilation: high rates of immigration and nonwhite demographics, as well as declining labor markets and high poverty rates. The analyses compare characteristics between inner-city Los Angeles, the area where virtually all of this study's respondents lived, Los Angeles County, the Los Angeles Metropolitan Area ("Los Angeles Metro," which includes both Los Angeles and Orange counties), and the United States. In addition to being the geographic context of this book, Los Angeles offers a paradigmatic case study for segmented assimilation theory. As mentioned in the introduction, segmented assimilation theory predicts a hostile context of reception for contemporary Latino immigration owing to settlement in neighborhoods characterized by racial segregation, bifurcating labor markets, high rates of poverty and gangs.

As previously mentioned, Victory Outreach and Homeboy Industries both originated on Gless Street, in Boyle Heights' former Pico-Aliso housing projects, in the City of Los Angeles. Victory Outreach and Homeboy Industries' rise in popularity, along with their geographic relocation, led to a growth in new memberships of recovering gang members. Their success caused a surge in membership that forced one (Homeboy Industries) to relocate to a much larger building in Chinatown, just outside the cusp of Boyle Heights, and the other (Victory Outreach) to continually expand to several urban areas inside and outside of Boyle Heights.[2] Nonetheless, a large number of members at both sites, and the majority of respondents in this book, hailed from four areas that could be characterized by high rates of immigration, segregation, poverty and gangs.

This book terms the four areas most respondents grew up in, and in many cases still lived in, *inner-city Los Angeles*. This consists of the areas where Latinos concentrate in the greatest numbers: East Los Angeles, Boyle Heights, Northeast Los Angeles, and South Los Angeles. East Los Angeles is the only one of these four areas to be considered "unincorporated"; it lies on the eastern fringe of the City of Los Angeles, but is not officially designated as a neighborhood or within its "Community Plan Areas." The other three areas are all designated Community Plan Areas by the city's Department of Planning. Boyle Heights is a Community Plan Area and neighborhood on its own. South Los Angeles and Northeast Los Angeles are each Community Plan Areas composed of several small neighborhoods. South Los Angeles consists of the following neighborhoods: Adams/Normandie, University Park, Exposition Park, Vermont Square, Vermont-Slauson, Harvard Park, and Chesterfield Square, as well as slivers of Vermont Knolls and Manchester Square. Northeast Los Angeles consists of the following neighborhoods: El Sereno, Lincoln Heights, Montecito Heights, Highland Park, Mt. Washington, Glassell Park, Eagle Rock, and Atwater Village.

A publicly available list from the City of Los Angeles Department of Planning details the census tracts in each of the three Community Plan Areas, and American Factfinder lists the census tracts in the unincorporated area of East Los Angeles. These lists of tracts correspond almost identically to the official boundaries of the four geographic areas most respondents were from. These tracts are drawn from in the following analyses of census and ACS data on "Age," "Poverty," and "Year of Entry into the U.S." In addition, the data also employ Public Use Microdata Areas (PUMAs) to present statistics on race and labor markets in inner-city Los Angeles, because PUMA geographies correspond well with the census tracts that comprise inner-city Los Angeles.

Most of the following analyses of census data on race and labor markets rest upon comparing Los Angeles and the U.S. across time, because geographically consistent data on inner-city Los Angeles is available only from 2000 to 2010. Characteristics associated with downward mobility are also measured, from the period of high European immigration to the current period of high Latino and Asian immigration, to get a sense of how the context of mobility in Los Angeles sets the backdrop for an analysis of gang recovery against the segmented assimilation paradigm.

Race

The post-1965 era has witnessed a decrease in whites' share of the American population. Nonetheless, this trend has become much more pronounced in Los Angeles, as large scale white flight from inner-city areas has tremendously increased blacks and Latinos' share of the population in urban neighborhoods. While Los Angeles's percentage of nonwhites among the native born was substantially higher than the national average in 1970 (26.8 percent versus 15.7 percent), it diverged dramatically by 2007 (62.9 percent versus 27.7 percent) (see figure 2.1). Inner-city Los Angeles, in particular, had a phenomenally high proportion of nonwhite residents (88.9 percent) in 2007.

In addition, the percentage of foreign born that are nonwhite has increased in the U.S. in the post-1965 era; again, Los Angeles Metro and inner-city Los Angeles serve as pronounced examples (see figure 2.2). Whereas the percentage of nonwhites among the foreign born increased in the U.S. from 26.5 percent in 1970 to 77.1 percent in 2007, it increased in Los Angeles from 48.6 percent in 1970 to 85.7 percent in 2007, and remained at an astonishing 97.6 percent from 2000 to 2007 in inner-city Los Angeles.

The tremendous rise in percentage of nonwhites, both among the native born and the foreign born, and especially in inner-city areas, has tremendous implications for the racialization of immigrants' children. Children of immigrants often search for an identity, and the racially homogenous landscape of urban immigrant neighborhoods may pull many second-generation immigrants away from the traditional practices of their parents' homeland, toward countercultural peer group associations in highly segregated neighborhoods. These changes in urban neighborhoods in Los Angeles should propel a shift in focus from straight-line conceptualizations of immigrant assimilation into the mainstream, to the segmented assimilation theory which posits varied pathways. For example, it is difficult to imagine how immigrant straight-line assimilation into the white mainstream would look in inner-city Los Angeles, which is overall over 90 percent nonwhite.

Labor Markets

Immigration today is situated in a context of economic decline, and this too has implications for immigrant integration. Whereas the first wave of European immigration was followed by rapid postwar economic growth, immigration in the post-1965 era has occurred during a long period of deindustrialization, declining wages, and increasingly unstable employment. The manufacturing industry and unionization have taken the hardest hits, depriving contemporary low-wage immigrants of a ladder used by previous immigrants to experience socioeconomic mobility (Lieberson 1980). Efforts to improve wages in niche Latino industries once dominated by unions, such as trucking, construction and janitorial services, have sometimes been successful in Los Angeles, but most Latino dominated industries remain characterized by low wages and no social mobility (Milkman 2006). The outsourcing of low-wage work to third-party firms specializing in providing unskilled labor has eroded the social mobility that once was once more possible with large enterprises (Milkman 2006).

Today, many more immigrants are concentrated in occupations that are at the lower end of the socioeconomic scale. Figure 2.3 illustrates this concept by drawing from a measure from the IPUMS, "ERSCOR50," which standardizes occupations based on their average earnings relative to average earnings in other occupations in the year 1950. An ERS-COR50 value of "55" suggests that an occupation had average earnings

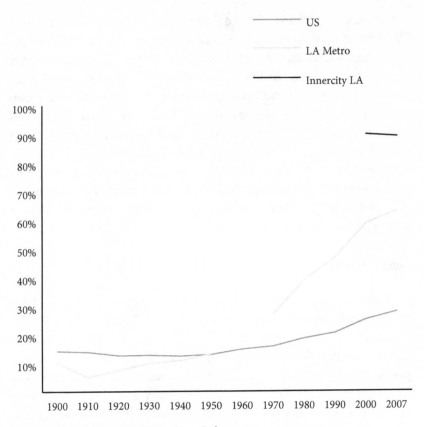

Figure 2.1. Percent Nonwhite, Native Born Only
Source: Census 1900–2000; American Community Survey 2005–2009.

that ranked higher than the average earnings of 55 percent of all occupations in 1950. However, in measuring Los Angeles workers' socioeconomic status (SES), there exist two caveats: (1) Los Angeles's labor market may not be characteristic of the nation as a whole, and (2) these changes may be tied to historic shifts. Thus, the average ERSCOR50 for Los Angeles workers is calculated (a) against the national average, and (b) across time. Figure 2.3 presents these calculations in terms of an *adjusted* ERSCOR50, one which aggregates data for the national labor market as a whole and presents the "percentage of workers above forty percent" of the ERSCOR50 socioeconomic scale. In other words, the adjusted ERSCOR50 presents the percentage of all workers with at least

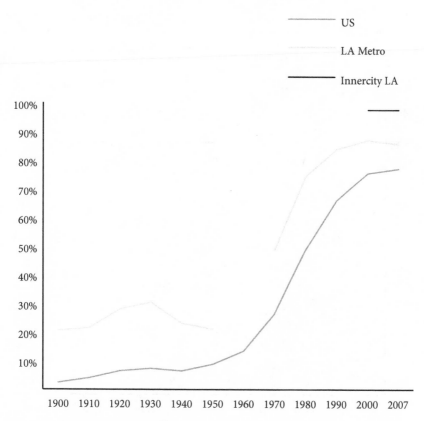

Figure 2.2. Percent Nonwhite, Foreign Born Only
Source: Census 1900–2000; American Community Survey 2005–2009.

a lower middle-class job. Equal distribution among high and low status occupations would result in an average of 60 percent; averages higher than 60 percent suggest a concentration in occupations with higher than average status, while averages lower than 60 percent suggest concentrations in occupations with lower than average status.

Figure 2.3 reveals what we would expect from segmented assimilation theory: occupations where the foreign born have concentrated have been more severely affected by economic downturns than other occupations. In 1950, U.S. workers—including those in Los Angeles—experienced a job market with relatively well-paying jobs. Roughly 69 percent of native-born workers were employed in occupations above

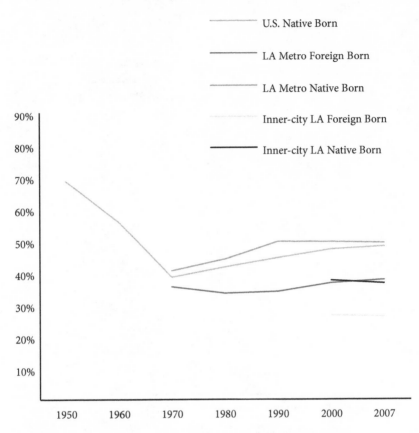

Figure 2.3. Percent of Workers above 40 Percent on ERSCOR50 SES Scale
Source: IPUMS-USA; Census 1950–2000; American Community Survey 2005–2009.

40 percent of the socioeconomic scale. For Los Angeles, this number was noticeably higher (79.2 percent). However, although the 1950 labor market provided relatively good jobs for most workers, the socioeconomic standing of all workers generally fell after the postwar period. By 1970, only 38.4 percent of native-born U.S. workers, and only 40.4 percent of native-born Los Angeles workers, worked in jobs that had average earnings above 40 percent of jobs in the labor market.

Across the late twentieth century, the disparity in socioeconomic standing between native- and foreign-born workers widened. In Los Angeles, in 1970, there was only a slim differential in the average of native-born workers above the 40 percent threshold on the ERSCOR50 socioeconomic scale (40.4 percent) versus foreign-born workers (35.4 percent). However, the most significant widening occurred between 1970 and 1980. In 1970, in Los Angeles, native-born workers held a 5.0 percent differential above that of the foreign born. By 1980 this differential widened to favor native-born workers by 11.6 percent (49.1 percent native versus 37.5 percent foreign born). Thus, foreign-born workers have concentrated in lower status jobs than the native born, and this inequality has grown even larger across time.

Inner-city Los Angeles provides an even more pronounced case of post-1965 developments in immigrant integration, than the nation or the Los Angeles Metro area. While broad trends in socioeconomic decline for Los Angeles and the nation virtually mirrored each other during several decades, the little recent data that exist for inner-city Los Angeles reveals that it was acutely affected. Inner-city Los Angeles ranked much lower than Los Angeles Metro in terms of average worker socioeconomic status. Only 36.4 percent of native-born inner-city Los Angeles workers had jobs that placed them above 40 percent of the socioeconomic scale, and additionally, and only 26.0 percent of the foreign born had such jobs (see figure 2.4).

Secondly, inner-city Los Angeles had a much higher poverty rate than Los Angeles or the U.S. (see figure 2.4). Although the 2007 poverty rate remained similar for the U.S. native-born population and Los Angeles native- and foreign-born populations—all between 13.0 and 16.8 percent—inner-city Los Angeles had a significantly higher rate of poverty. The inner-city Los Angeles foreign born had a poverty rate of 24.0 percent in 2007, while the inner-city Los Angeles native born had a poverty rate of 26.1 percent. The high rate of poverty in inner-city Los Angeles suggests that children of immigrants might be vulnerable to marginality during the experience of assimilation, and that this may lead to "downward assimilation." The second component of this equation, countercultures, is discussed in the next section.

Countercultures

Herbert Gans (1992), in an article that foreshadowed Portes and Zhou's (1993) segmented assimilation theory, posited that the changing racial make-up of urban neighborhoods, along with declines in blue-collar

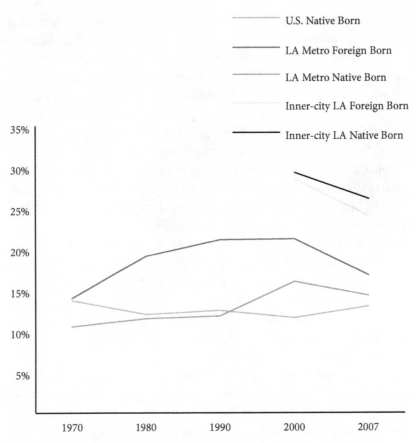

Figure 2.4. Poverty Rate, by Nativity and Place
Source: Census 1970–2000; American Community Survey 2005–2009.

middle-class employment, had created an environment that was cumulatively detrimental to the socioeconomic mobility of immigrants' children. Today, the children of immigrants are more likely to grow up in
neighborhoods where the impact of unemployment has been felt hardest by native-born blacks and Latinos, in an urban underclass that has
been tied to cyclical poverty—where lack of socioeconomic mobility
has negatively affected native-born black and Latinos' outlooks, and has
further cemented their marginalization from mainstream American life
(Wilson 1987; Anderson 1990).

Two trends suggest the growing importance of the relevance of countercultures in the study of second-generation immigrant integration:

rising incarceration rates and gang membership among second-generation blacks and Latinos. As described in chapter 1, the U.S. prison population has soared across the past few decades. From 1972 to 2007, the
prison population grew from 196,092 to 1,596,127 (Maguire 1995, 556;
Pew Center on the States 2008, 5). Including adults incarcerated in local
jails, this number rose to 2.3 million adults in 2008 (Pew Center on the
States 2008, 5). Including adults "on paper," which refers to probation
or parole, the number rose even higher in 2009 to 7.3 million, which
translates into one in thirty-one adults (Bureau of Justice Statistics
2010). These trends in incarceration have affected Latinos more so than
whites; while one in 106 adult white men were incarcerated in 2007, one
in thirty-six Latino men were incarcerated (Pew Center on the States
2008, 6). The first large scale study into the outcomes of immigrants'
children, the Children of Immigrants Longitudinal Survey (CILS),
reported that 20.2 percent of second-generation male Mexican Americans and 20.0 percent of second-generation male West Indians had
been incarcerated by age twenty-four (Portes and Rumbaut 2006[1990],
275).

Given its high number of gang members, Los Angeles presents
a good case study of segmented assimilation theory and the study of
downward assimilation and countercultures. Official Los Angeles Police
Department (2012) estimates put gang membership in the city at 60,561
in 1993, the first year such data was recorded, and 64,429 in the peak
year of 1997 (see figure 2.5).[3] Gang membership in Los Angeles City has
steadily declined since, to 38,974 in 2006, the last year such data was
recorded. The vast majority of documented gang members have been
black and Latino; never has the number of Asian, white, and "other"
gang members cumulatively topped 4,500. The National Drug Intelligence Center (2001) estimated 152,000 gang members in Los Angeles
County—the highest figure in the nation. In Boyle Heights, home to
some of the region's oldest gangs, about one in every three adolescent
boys is already documented as a gang member by the local police (Fremon 2004[1995]).

Whether they are the result or the cause of gang membership, gang
homicide statistics also indicate a fit with segmented assimilation theory. High rates of gang homicide suggest the development of oppositional countercultures. Figures drawn from the Los Angeles Police

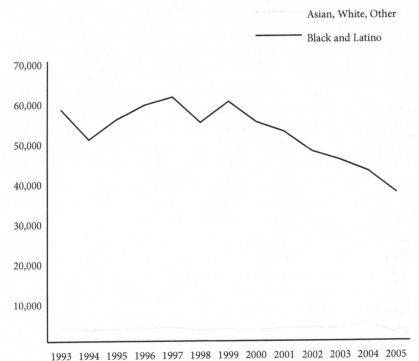

Figure 2.5. Gang Population in Los Angeles City
Source: Los Angeles Police Department (LAPD), Citywide Gang Crime Summary.

Department (2012) Citywide Gang Crime Summary, 1993–2008, placed Los Angeles first on the list of major American cities with the highest share of gang-related homicides (Howell et al. 2011). In 2009, gang homicides accounted for 50.3 percent of all Los Angeles homicides, while the next highest major city, Chicago, came in at a distant second with 32.9 percent (Howell et al. 2011). Los Angeles is an important case study for immigrant integration in urban America, precisely for its high rate of gang activity at a time when immigration scholars are noting the relevance of gang life in second-generation immigrant acculturation. Trends in race, poverty, and countercultures in Los Angeles—and especially inner-city Los Angeles—seem to support grim predictions of cyclical and intergenerational racism, poverty, and crime for immigrants and their children.

Revisiting Segmented Assimilation:
Mobility in Inner-City Los Angeles

The preceding figures cast a shadow on the prospects of intergenerational advancement among contemporary immigrants. The children of immigrants face a nation with growing inequalities in race and labor markets, and are raised in urban areas with a significant presence of countercultures. Are prospects for upward socioeconomic mobility doomed? The University of Southern California's Population Dynamics Research Group (PDRG), a group of scholars who apply demographic analysis to issues of international migration and integration, disagree. PDRG, led by renowned demographer Dowell Myers, has offered a counternarrative to segmented assimilation theory's pessimistic projections—one based on the classic American story of upward mobility and home ownership.

Research by PDRG scholars has suggested that, despite the inequalities which do exist, there is a "new maturity" of immigrants in Los Angeles (Myers et al. 2010, 12). In comparison to states where Latino immigrants have more recently begun to arrive, Latino immigrants in states where they are more long settled—such as California—have narrowed the gap in household income and homeownership compared to whites in the same states (Myers and Pitkin 2010, 25–27). As newer immigrants have arrived and struggled with a fickle labor market, immigrants who have made Los Angeles their home have begun closing in on significant benchmarks of income, education, and home ownership. However, despite the presence of settled migrants, cohorts of more recent migrants are more likely to move in and out of Los Angeles (Myers et al. 2012).

An Urban Institute research report funded by the Annie E. Casey Foundation also suggested that dynamic trends in socioeconomic mobility and home ownership may actually be obscuring urban upward mobility (Coulton, Theodos, and Turner 2009). When residents in low-income neighborhoods took part in a longitudinal study—an advantage that census data cannot provide—researchers found that the greatest gains and losses in poverty rates of many neighborhoods resulted not from the large-scale impact of economic cycles, but from the migration of residents from different socioeconomic backgrounds. Low-income neighborhoods often experienced growth among young persons who were experiencing poverty, but then they moved up and out of the neighborhood to better ones once they had experienced gains in income. Thus, poverty is best characterized as experienced at a period of the life-course rather than throughout it. Poverty rates in these urban neighborhoods did not reflect long-term cyclical poverty so much as a revolving door through which cohorts of persons impoverished as young adults moved in and out. Rather than characterizing these areas as stagnant urban ghettos, the Urban Institute conceptualized them as "launch pads" (Coulton, Theodos, and Turner 2009, 21).

Neighborhoods in inner-city Los Angeles, despite high rates of segregation, poverty, and gang membership, can also be conceptualized as launch pads. The latter half of this chapter examines tract-level data from Census 2000 (Summary Tape Files 1 and 3) and Census 2010 (Summary Tape File 1), as well as American Community Survey data from 2005–2009, to provide the most accurate data on age, poverty, and immigration in Los Angeles. This supplements earlier findings on race, labor markets, and poverty by examining demographic dynamism. The data suggests that age is a factor in settlement in inner-city Los Angeles, and that poverty may not be as entrenched across the life-course as much scholarly literature has suggested—dispelling a foundational assumption in the segmented assimilation paradigm.

Poverty across Age

Snapshot portraits of the racial demographics, poverty rate, and average socioeconomic status for Los Angeles seem to support the segmented assimilation hypothesis: contemporary immigrants are vulnerable to cyclical, urban poverty in a way that previous immigrants have not been. However, such assumptions rely upon snapshot data that fails to fully capture the dynamism of immigrant integration today. Table 2.1 shows that, despite the fact that Los Angeles and its inner city in particular are paradigmatic of segmented assimilation, between 2000 and 2007 there was a decrease in poverty in every age group except for newborns. In 2000, inner-city Los Angeles children aged four and under experienced a poverty rate of 37.9 percent.

Possibly, many children were born into their poverty as their parents were beginning their experiences in the labor market. But, by 2007, 35.1 percent of their relevant age group (ages six to eleven in 2007) were experiencing poverty—a loss of 2.7 percentage points. This suggests that though many children may be born into poverty, it is partially an outcome of their parents' youth and current socioeconomic situation. Such rates of poverty continue to decline across the life-course for residents of inner-city Los Angeles.

Every age group in inner-city Los Angeles experienced gradual improvements in their poverty rates, between 2000 and 2007. Although almost half of all inner-city Los Angeles children were born into poverty, a gradual trend out of poverty was simultaneously in effect (see figure 2.6). Most notably, the age group that was twenty-five to thirty-four in 2007 experienced an improvement of 10.6 percentage points in poverty, and the eighteen-to–twenty-four and forty-five–to–fifty-four age groups improved their poverty rates by 7.7 and 7.8 percentage points. Strikingly, inner-city Los Angeles's improvement in poverty

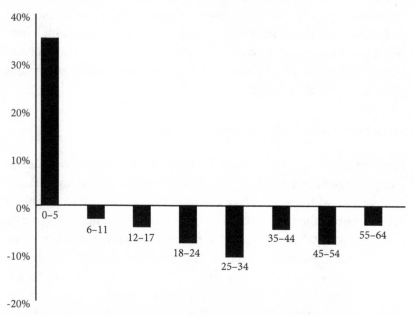

Figure 2.6. Change in Poverty Rate, 2000–2007, Inner-City Los Angeles
Source: Census 2000, Summary Tape File 3 (STF-3); American Community Survey 2005–2009.

Table 2.1. Change in Poverty Rate, 2000–2007, by Age Cohort

Age Cohort		Inner-City Los Angeles			Los Angeles County		
2000	2007	2000	2007	Net Change	2000	2007	Net Change
	0–5		34.9%	34.9%		23.2%	23.2%
0–4	6–11	37.9%	35.1%	–2.7%	25.5%	22.3%	–3.2%
5–11	12–17	36.7%	32.3%	–4.4%	25.1%	20.9%	–4.2%
12–17	18–24	34.8%	27.1%	–7.7%	22.9%	19.3%	–3.7%
18–24	25–34	31.6%	21.0%	–10.6%	23.6%	14.1%	–9.5%
25–34	35–44	26.5%	21.8%	–4.8%	17.7%	13.3%	–4.4%
35–44	45–54	25.5%	17.7%	–7.8%	15.1%	10.7%	–4.4%
45–54	55–64	20.6%	16.8%	–3.8%	11.6%	10.6%	–1.0%

Source: Census 2000, Summary Tape File 3 (STF-3); American Community Survey 2005–2009.

rate was much greater than the observed countywide change (see table 2.1). What makes this observation so much more remarkable is that it occurred across a span of only about seven years. Thus, the segmented assimilation perspective of downward assimilation in adolescence and early adulthood seems less plausible considering that, even in high poverty areas such as inner-city Los Angeles, there is a gradual, but significant, countertrend of movement out of poverty. Latino immigrants move up within the inner city.

Aging Out of Inner-City Los Angeles

Aside from declines in poverty rates, the turnover from various age groups suggests that inner-city Los Angeles is an outmigration "launch pad"—from which residents move up and out to better neighborhoods—rather than an isolated neighborhood of residents mired in cyclical poverty. Between 2000 and 2007, virtually every age group experienced a significant decline in population (see table 2.2). This trend was most pronounced for groups above the age of thirty: inner-city Los Angeles lost roughly 30 percent of population in each age group above thirty (see figure 2.7). The only cohort to experience a relatively small decline was the age group between twenty and twenty-nine, which lost 19,327 persons—or 15.7 percent—by 2010.

Table 2.2. Change in Age Cohorts, 2000–2010

Age Cohort		Inner-City Los Angeles			Los Angeles County		
2000 Age	2010 Age	2000 Pop	Change	% Diff.	2000 Pop	Change	% Diff.
0–9	10–19	136,811	−36,428	−26.6%	1,539,678	−107,203	−7.0%
10–19	20–29	123,202	−19,327	−15.7%	1,407,118	105,272	7.5%
20–29	30–39	129,020	−42,854	−33.2%	1,480,868	−49,104	−3.3%
30–39	40–49	112,300	−35,393	−31.5%	1,592,915	−171,482	−10.8%
40–49	50–59	88,258	−26,432	−29.9%	1,351,738	−128,613	−9.5%
50–59	60–69	58,140	−19,429	−33.4%	913,585	−138,062	−15.1%
60–69	70–79	39,030	−15,905	−40.8%	564,939	−126,875	−22.5%
70+	80+	28,571	−28,648	−65.6%	668,497	−364,149	−54.5%

Source: Census 2000 & 2010, Summary Tape File 1 (STF-1).

Migration to Los Angeles is partly responsible for why the loss in inner-city Los Angeles's 20–29 age group was relatively small compared to all the other age groups. Los Angeles as a whole gained 105,272 persons aged twenty to twenty-nine by 2010. This represented a 7.5 percent increase from that age group's 2000 population, and is hardly surprising considering Los Angeles is a major destination for young foreign-born and out-of-state migrants.

Thus, although small population losses were evident in inner-city Los Angeles between 2000 and 2007 for the ten-to-thirty age group, a significant percentage of inner-city Los Angeles's over-thirty population left in a span of seven years. As socioeconomic mobility occurs in adulthood, some leave inner-city Los Angeles for more affluent areas, or more affordable single family homes. The analysis now turns to the only census measurement of geographic mobility across time: "Year of Entry into the United States."

Immigrant Succession

Los Angeles County is trending toward high loss of immigrant population, as much immigration is being deflected toward new destination states in the Midwest and south (Light 2008). This was measured with three cohorts of international migrants: those who arrived before 1980

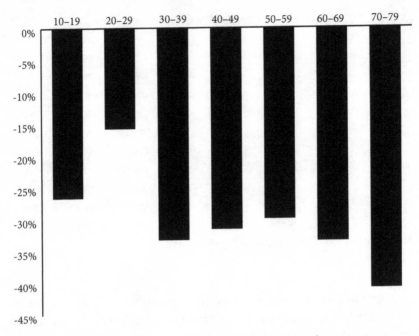

Figure 2.7. Change in Age Cohorts, 2000–2010, Inner-City Los Angeles
Source: Census 2000, Summary Tape File 1 (STF-1); Census 2010, Summary Tape File 1 (STF-1).

("pre-1980"), those who arrived between 1980 and 1989 ("1980–1989"), and those who arrived between 1990 and 1999 ("1990–1999"). Table 2.3 and figure 2.8 demonstrate how, between 2000 and 2007, the cohort of international migration which declined in greatest numbers from Los Angeles County was one of the most recent: the 1990–1999 immigrant cohort (a 22.4 percent decrease). Thus, new immigrants to Los Angeles left for new destinations while older residents settled long-term and became the "new maturity." Similarly, in inner-city Los Angeles, the same cohort out-migrated from inner-city Los Angeles at a rate of 27.1 percent.

The data suggest the dynamics of a "launch pad," or at least a revolving door for immigrants, when comparing all three "settled" immigration cohorts with the post-2000 immigration cohort. As older cohorts tended to move out, newer immigrant cohorts moved into Los Angeles County. Table 2.3 shows that, while all three settled immigration

Table 2.3. Immigrant Out-Migration, 2000–2007, by Decade of U.S. Entry

	Inner-City Los Angeles			Los Angeles County		
	2000	2007*	% Change	2000	2007*	% Change
Pre-1980	102,088	81,288	−20.4%	1,053,848	871,482	−17.3%
1980–1989	111,006	87,439	−21.2%	1,194,562	965,575	−19.2%
1990–1999	109,131	79,537	−27.1%	1,201,034	931,834	−22.4%
Post-2000		62,690			699,706	

Source: Census 2000, Summary Tape File 3 (STF-3); American Community Survey 2005–2009.

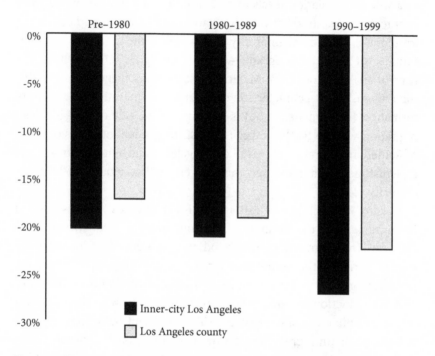

Figure 2.8. Turnover in Immigrant Population, 2000–2007, by Decade of U.S. Entry
Source: Census 2000, Summary Tape File 3 (STF-3); American Community Survey 2005–2009.

cohorts dropped from levels of over one million in 2000, to below one million in 2007, the same period saw an increase of 699,706 new immigrants in Los Angeles County. Figure 2.9 graphically illustrates that the number of new arrivals (699,706) to the county was only slightly larger than that of the decline in settled migrants (680,553). Focusing only on persistent poverty rates in the 2000s obscures the fact that, in Los Angeles, there is a continuous exodus of immigrant cohorts that have experienced socioeconomic gains, who are replaced by new immigrant cohorts.

Inner-city Los Angeles is even more of a launch pad than the county as a whole. Population levels in each immigrant cohort dropped from over to under 100,000 between 2000 and 2007. While 62,690 post-2000 immigrants settled in inner-city Los Angeles, the area lost a greater number of settled immigrants—73,961 (see figure 2.10). Belying the fears of an "invasion" from Mexico, these findings suggest that the ethnic replenishment characteristic of Mexican immigration and identity formation (i.e., Jiménez 2009) is receding. If the tide of new Mexican migration were to further recede against the gradual outflows of pools of settled immigrant cohorts, Los Angeles could enter into a post-replenishment phase and become an even shallower basin of Mexican ethnicity.

In sum, the high rate of exit among inner-city Los Angeles's settled immigrants, and the findings of age and poverty data—which indicated declining poverty in adulthood and high outmigration after age thirty—reinforce the notion that inner-city Los Angeles is a place for poor, young adults to form families in. A sizable number of adults experience a reduction in poverty, and others move out with their families to presumably more affluent areas. This movement out of poverty, and out of urban immigrant neighborhoods, counters the snapshot statistics of racial segregation, poverty, and countercultures upon which segmented assimilation's prediction of downward assimilation into the urban underclass has been based.

Conclusion

Los Angeles is a good fit for the study of segmented assimilation theory's concept of downward assimilation. It has a high percentage of

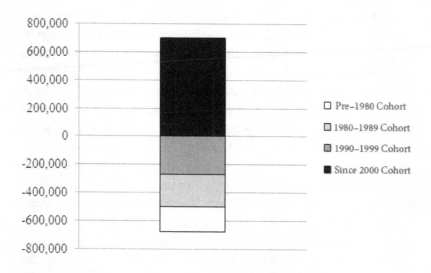

Figure 2.9. Turnover in Immigrant Population, 2000–2007, Los Angeles
Source: Census 2000, Summary Tape File 3 (STF-3); American Community Survey
2005–2009.

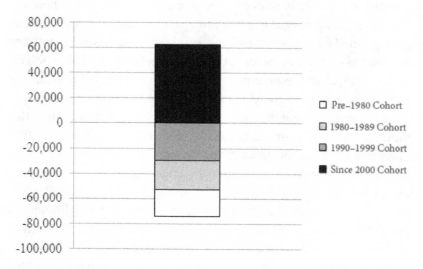

Figure 2.10. Turnover in Immigrant Population, 2000–2007, Inner-City Los Angeles
Source: Census 2000, Summary Tape File 3 (STF-3); American Community Survey
2005–2009.

immigrants and nonwhite residents, and a labor market with a large concentration of jobs with low socioeconomic status. It also contains high rates of poverty, a large gang population, and the highest rate of gang homicide among large U.S. cities. Census data across the twentieth century suggests that these trends are much more acute in Los Angeles County today than during the previous wave of European immigration. In particular, inner-city Los Angeles serves as an extreme case within Los Angeles County. Inner-city Los Angeles's population is disproportionately immigrant, nonwhite, and poor, and the area has a large number of gang members. These findings on race, poverty, and countercultures should lead to grim predictions of cyclical and intergenerational racism, poverty, and crime for immigrants and their offspring in Los Angeles—and especially in inner-city Los Angeles.

However, a snapshot analysis of immigration, poverty, and gangs fails to capture the mobility that many residents of inner-city Los Angeles seem to be experiencing: moving up and/or out of the barrio. There are several significant countertrends in inner-city Los Angeles that challenge the fundamental assumptions behind segmented assimilation's dour predictions. First, poverty rates decrease along every age of the continuum (except for children aged five and younger, who enter the world with no prior point of comparison), and poverty also decreases when examining age cohorts across time. Second, there is a large proportion of outmigration, hinting at socioeconomic mobility in adulthood. Third, economic progress among immigrants is masked by the simultaneous exodus of settled immigrants and the entrance of newer, younger immigrants. This movement of immigrants, in and out of inner-city Los Angeles, obscures upward socioeconomic mobility as newer, younger immigrants who take their place are more likely to be experiencing poverty. Fourth, population change among the immigrant stock in inner-city Los Angeles suggests a reversal in immigration: a stagnating or declining immigrant population. In inner-city Los Angeles, the immigrant cohort that arrived between 2000 and 2007 could not replenish the exit of immigrants from earlier cohorts. Thus, in the 1980s and 1990s, immigrants settled in inner-city Los Angeles's racially segregated neighborhoods, characterized by high rates of poverty and gang membership; the aftermath of this settlement, however, is typified not by entrenched, isolated poverty, but rather by modest socioeconomic mobility and outmigration.

Omar McRoberts (2003), in his book *Streets of Glory*, suggested that religious particularism among middle-class blacks who commuted to the inner-city Four Corners religious district every Sunday were not connected to the social life of the immediate physical neighborhood. The image evoked by the idea of middle-class congregants arriving from outside suburbs looks much different, however, if we try to reimagine those same congregants as recently migrated residents of the inner city. McRoberts's observations on religious particularism may hold true in locales populated by ethnic groups established in America for generations, such as Boston. But how feasible is the application of his findings on religious particularism to a neighborhood with a larger share of recent immigrant arrivals—many of whom are in the process of moving up and out?

The above analyses demonstrated that, as much as cyclical entrenched poverty may be a characteristic of inner cities and immigrant assimilation, so too is modest socioeconomic and geographic mobility. The next chapter investigates how Homeboy Industries and Victory Outreach attempted to facilitate socioeconomic mobility within Los Angeles's inner-city, by helping members cut ties with gang life, while also reintegrating them into their households and a broader faith or local community. Contrary to McRoberts's depiction of religious particularism in Four Corners, recovering Eastside gang members bore an intimate connection with both their ministry and the surrounding neighborhood. They experienced reintegration through helping mothers, partners, and children, as well as by reaching out to younger inner-city men. Although recovery from gang life and social reintegration are not rapid or linear, neighborhoods with high concentrations of gangs are still characterized by movement up and out. Thus, the neighborhood context of Latino immigrant integration, even in an era of "segmented assimilation," is not overwhelmingly entrenched in reactive ethnicity and cyclical poverty.

The next chapter takes a closer look at urban ministries to reveal how, within this context of subtle demographic changes, a segment of inner-city Los Angeles's population moves up and out: men use recovery to leave gang life, socially reintegrate into their households and the broader faith or local community, and contest the racist images that fuel the Latino crime threat.

3

Recovery from Gang Life

Two Models of Faith and Reintegration

You guys are doing a great job . . . never stop what you're doing. Reach the gang members . . . because you guys are doing a work for God.
Ramon, describing what a police officer told him

amon was able to leave gang life despite enduring obstacles that segmented assimilation theory predicts would yield downward assimilation: undocumented status, lack of middle class cultural capital, and lack of access to public resources. As mentioned in the previous chapter, Ramon had come to the U.S. as an undocumented immigrant, joined gangs in his early teens, and become a homeless drug addict by early adulthood. However, after entering the men's recovery home, Ramon became a drug counselor there and then, after years, a Victory Outreach church leader. At the time of his interview, he had been involved with Victory Outreach for three years and was a self-described "baby Christian." He lived in "reentry"; this consisted of a small room in the rear of the Victory Outreach church, shared with two other men, which he had moved into upon graduating from Victory Outreach's one-year men's recovery home program. He worked at a local aerosol factory where he earned just above minimum wage, led a Bible study, and had a self-sufficient lifestyle that kept him out of gangs and off of drugs.

During an interview at a local pizza restaurant, Ramon shared the story from which this chapter's epigraph is drawn. Not pausing to take his first bite for almost a half hour, he joyously recounted how he had attended an evangelizing "handball tournament" at the Maravilla projects, a stronghold of East Los Angeles gangs. At the tournament, a police officer who self-identified as a member of Cavalry Chapel (another Protestant church) came up to him and told him not to be discouraged by other police officers' racist harassment of Victory Outreach members. Ramon's reaction to me was, "He came with the good message . . . and it was a blessing to me because he was ministering to me, he was preaching to me, you know?" Victory Outreach's religious practices allowed for activities that distanced Ramon from the street and reintegrated him into the community.

Ramon's journey from gang membership to recovery is anomalous with the segmented assimilation theory, which has suggested that immigrant coethnic communities—in particular traditional religious practices—have a protective effect that shelters children of immigrants from the streets. The initial predictions of segmented assimilation theory—that there are three distinct paths of acculturation and mobility, and that they begin in adolescence and continue into adulthood—are belied by the data presented in the preceding chapter and by the fact that Ramon, and many other men whose stories are described in this book, broke from gang life in early adulthood.

One of the largest studies ever conducted on second-generation U.S. immigrants, the Immigration and Intergenerational Mobility in Metropolitan Los Angeles Study (IIMMLA), found that socioeconomic trajectories are not necessarily fixed. Findings from the IIMMLA study suggested that five factors can positively redirect immigrant socioeconomic trajectories: legal status, middle-class cultural capital brought from one's home country, family educational expectations, access to public resources and cultural memory. In an analysis of the study's findings, Zhou et al. stated, "Having experienced or being told of economic hardships in the homeland, traumatic escape from war, hunger, and political/religious persecution . . . many children of immigrants, regardless of national origin, can become self-motivated and resilient" (2008, 58).

Ramon's exit from gang life did not occur through Catholicism, the faith of his childhood, or through his parents' coethnic community. The

Catholic teachings with which his parents raised him never resonated with his personal life. Rather, he reformed from gang life through Pentecostal and majority-Chicano Victory Outreach. However, recovering gang members such as Ramon did experience recovery from gang life through cultural memory shaped by religious practice. While that Chicano cultural memory was not wholly situated in the Mexican coethnic immigrant community, or in the traditional religious practices of the Mexican American Catholic community, it still bore the features conceptualized by Zhou et al. (2008) as influential in resisting a trajectory of downward assimilation.

Social Reintegration

Most scholars agree that gang behavior and delinquency can be remedied through integration into family, religion, employment, and the military (e.g., Edin, Nelson, and Paranal 2004; Gans 1962; Hunt, Joe-Laidler, and MacKenzie 2005; Laub and Sampson 2003; Moloney et. al 2009; Roy and Dyson 2010; Whyte 1943). However, as described previously, the structural context of deindustrialization, outsourcing, and neoliberalism has made the path of gang exit much more elusive. The "maturing out" option, as sociologist Ruth Horowitz (1983) observed in her book *Honor and the American Dream*, was possible in the past, when a vibrant manufacturing economy provided relatively stable and good-paying jobs to men with low levels of education. Today's bifurcated job structure and hourglass economy offer few accessible job ladders to gang members or immigrant youth who have acculturated into gangs (Gans 1992; Hagedorn 1991; Kalleberg, 2011; Portes and Rumbaut 2001; Smith 2006). Nonetheless, at the turn of the twenty-first century, the issue of gang exit has been set against the surging relevance of religion and rehabilitation. Public policy changes allowing church ministries to compete for federal funds to provide social services have revitalized the American "religious marketplace."[1]

As mentioned in the introduction, in a policy report issued by the Urban Institute, Omar McRoberts (2002) suggested that it was problematic to assume that faith-based organizations necessarily facilitate community reintegration for ex-offenders. Sociologists of religion are quick to highlight that religious voluntarism—the choice of where to worship or attend church—may foster religious particularism, creating cohesive relationships within congregations but erecting social boundaries with outside groups (Ammerman 1997; McRoberts 2003; Warner 1993). Thus, religious particularism might reinforce social boundaries between church congregants and surrounding neighborhood residents, undermining the aim of prisoner reentry programs.

This volume contends that McRoberts's application of the religious particularism problematic to Latino ex-offender reentry does not extend to cases of gang recovery. As Ramon's experience with recovery in Victory Outreach suggests, social reintegration does not necessarily have to hinge upon the strength of a faith-based organization's ties to residents in the immediate physical neighborhood. Ramon's involvement with Pentecostalism, through the way it drew from Chicano cultural memory, reintegrated him with the church and the broader community while it helped him keep free from crystal meth addiction and out of gang life.

Homeboy Industries' and Victory Outreach's theological underpinnings—which also drew from the Book of Exodus and faith practices focused on the issue of marginality—played central roles in facilitating exit from gang life and social reintegration. Through symbolically rich religious practices, Chicano recovering gang members constructed a cultural memory of economic hardship, trauma from violence, and resilience that helped them to exit from gang life. The two urban ministries provided religious practices that fostered social reintegration and facilitated exit from gang life, irrespective of the organizations' social boundaries with the broader local community.

Theologies of Gang Recovery

Homeboy Industries and Victory Outreach both facilitated exit from gang life and social reintegration. As Robert Brenneman (2009, 164) noted in his study of Latin American Pentecostal and Jesuit approaches to gang recovery, "un-becoming a homie and joining the non-gang society represent two sides of the same coin." Homeboy Industries and Victory Outreach both offered communities into which recovering gang members could integrate, while leaving gang life behind. However, Homeboy Industries' and Victory Outreach's models of gang recovery differed vastly, due to fundamental differences in their theological underpinnings and religious practices.

Victory Outreach facilitated recovery from gang life through Protestant-centered religious theologies, while Homeboy Industries facilitated recovery through Catholic-centered theologies. Catholic theologian David Tracy (1981), in *The Analogical Imagination*, presented the idea that Protestant theology is rooted in a "dialectical imagination": God is radically absent from the world, and discloses Himself only on occasion (Tracy 1981, cited in Greeley 1990, 45; Greeley 2001). This characterization of Protestant theology advances an understanding of God as transcendent, as well as a vertical relationship that places God above the mundane world. In contrast, Tracy suggested that Catholic theology is rooted in an "analogical imagination": God is present in the world, and discloses Himself through creation (Tracy 1981, cited in Greeley 1990, 45; Greeley 2001). This characterization of Catholic theology advances an understanding of God as omnipresent, as well as a horizontal relationship that places God squarely within the mundane world.

Victory Outreach's theology of gang recovery emphasized understandings of God as transcendent; the ministry attempted to segregate recovering gang members from the broader community, encouraging them to climb the church's hierarchical structure—drawing them closer to God the further they distanced themselves from broader society. As mentioned in the introduction, Victory Outreach was organized with a top-down structure, and members were encouraged to climb the church hierarchy. In addition, Pastor Sonny Arguinzoni, Victory Outreach's founder, preached a vision to evangelize and start churches in urban areas worldwide; this "evangelism through discipleship" led to Victory Outreach's rapid growth in membership, which in turn provided new leadership opportunities.[2] This book refers to Victory Outreach's faith-based model of gang recovery, which offered integration through social distancing processes that paralleled the Pentecostal church's emphases on decentralizing hierarchies and rigid religious boundaries, as *segregated redemption*.

On the other hand, Homeboy Industries' theology of gang recovery emphasized understandings of God as omnipresent, but offered few opportunities for recovering gang members to climb the nonprofit's dense hierarchical structure. Homeboy Industries brought members closer to God by encouraging them to go outward and reintegrate into the broader community. As mentioned in the introduction, Homeboy Industries was also organized with a top-down structure, though one in which few members advanced to the very top. In addition, spiritual practices at Homeboy Industries reflected the religious ecumenism of modern Catholicism. The most popular spiritual practices at Homeboy Industries were yoga and meditation; in his memoir, *Tattoos on the Heart*, Boyle (2010) claimed that he found these spiritual practices to be highly compatible with Catholicism. This book refers to Homeboy Industries' faith-based model of gang recovery, which offered social integration through processes that paralleled the Catholic Church's emphases on centralized hierarchy and religious ecumenism, as *integrative redemption*.

In sum, Homeboy Industries and Victory Outreach provided two contrasting faith-based models of gang recovery. At Homeboy Industries, gang recovery took place through social integration that was shaped by Catholic theology: an understanding of God as omnipresent, an analogical imagination, and a theological emphasis on religious ecumenism, all of which emphasized recovery by way of reintegration into the mundane world. At Victory Outreach, gang recovery took place through social integration that was shaped by Protestant theology: an understanding of God as absent from the world, a dialectical imagination, and a theological emphasis on rigid religious boundaries, all of which emphasized recovery by way of segregation from the mundane world. These two models of gang recovery, integrative redemption and segregated redemption, created cohesive social groups, fostered cultural memory in distinctive ways, and resonated with the Chicano gang experience. The cultural memory fostered through these two gang recovery models paralleled the themes that Zhou et al. (2008) identified as key to facilitating socioeconomic trajectory shifts among adult children of immigrants: economic hardship, trauma from violence, persecution, and resilience.

Segregated Redemption

Victory Outreach's (2010b) mission statement called for evangelism, and claimed to instill within members "the desire to fulfill their potential in life with a sense of dignity, belonging, and destiny." The ministry's effervescent worship, amid a congregation of recovering gang members and drug addicts, inspired members with hope. The oft-used quote from Philippians 4:13, "I can do all things through Christ who strengthens me," best illustrated how Victory Outreach members experienced resilience through religion. To this end, worship sermons, small-group Bible studies, and evangelism at informal gatherings provided community and created a sense of belonging.

The church hosted weekly worship services on Fridays and Sundays at a storefront just off a major street in Los Angeles' Eastside. Sunday morning service usually drew the largest attendance, upward of one hundred adults. Worship service sermons were usually led by the pastor, and sometimes members from other Victory Outreach chapters visited to give guest sermons, though many members used call-and-response to shape the intensity of the speakers' messages. In addition, other leaders often "took the pulpit" to give announcements and lead prayers at the start of service. Several ministries, such as youth ministries and music practice, met throughout the week, though Tuesday Bible study groups were most intimate, congregating in members' homes, and serving homemade Mexican food after worship. Members of Victory Outreach affectionately called each other "brother" and "sister," terms popularly used in the wider Christian community.

Members of Victory Outreach engaged in what Maria Patricia Fernandez-Kelly defined as religiously based "oppositional" acculturation (2007, 4): marginalized second-generation immigrants regained their honor by ascribing to values deemed more moral than those in mainstream society. In line with criminologist Shadd Maruna's (2001) work on desisting career criminals, Victory Outreach members were "hypermoral." Not to be confused with the way in which immigration scholars often use the term "oppositional culture," oppositional religiosity suggests a moral "one-upmanship" that marginalized immigrants and men of color engage in so as to reclaim the honor they have lost by not fitting in with mainstream society's ideals (Fernandez-Kelly 2007, 4). Worship services that emphasized the "Holy Ghost" charisms—speaking in tongues, prophecy, and spiritual healing—defined Victory Outreach as on morally higher ground than dominant society.[3] Victory Outreach leaders spoke out against the materialism and pursuit

Figure 3.1. Victory Outreach members, just before church service (courtesy of Victory Outreach)

of wealth rampant in mainstream America. They asserted that events related to Christian worship and evangelism—especially events at their own church—were inspired by God, while other events were "worldly" and "evil." The space of the church was called the "sanctuary," and was deemed to protect members from "the world."

Victory Outreach's dichotomization of the church and the broader community offered a very sheltering environment, though it often imposed strict demands on members' schedules. Instead of allowing members to celebrate holidays outside of the church, which leaders claimed would leave them vulnerable to drug and alcohol use, the church arranged its own celebrations. Victory Outreach celebrated Halloween as a "harvest festival" at the local Boys & Girls Club, and hosted a Thanksgiving dinner and Christmas dinner at the church. In addition, Victory Outreach organized a collective viewing of the Super Bowl as a fundraiser at a member's house, and the region-wide ministry organized a Valentine's Day dinner for single men and women. Victory

Outreach's rejection of "worldly" concerns was not limited to holiday celebrations. Ministry leaders warned against employment in occupations with nonstandard hours, which were also seen as a threat to participation in church worship and events. Members were encouraged to quit any job that required work on Sundays, evenings, or overtime.

Victory Outreach leaders framed their strict demands of members' schedules through biblical scripture that portrayed the church as a necessary sanctuary. At one worship service, Pastor Raul said,

> Abraham didn't go to a place God sent him, out of fear of the famine. Maybe he was unemployed. He went to Egypt. But God didn't bring them out to send them back. Egypt was bondage, slavery. . . . There's some people like that . . . "I didn't come to church cuz I gotta work." . . . They go to places they're not supposed to be, and they're not at places they're supposed to be.

Through this parallel with Abraham, the pastor dichotomized church and the world, implying that one would find sanctuary in the church but bondage outside of it. Pastor Raul reasoned that Abraham might have returned to Egypt for the same reason that some members might leave church: fear of not having employment and income. The pastor strongly critiqued this behavior and urged members to demand a standard work schedule. He said, "Some of you are like this." He then spoke in a meek voice, unintelligibly, before yelling, "No! You have to learn to speak up!" The congregation cheered. The pastor then said,

> They used to ask me to have to work triple overtime, Tuesday, Friday, but I don't even work for regular time on Sunday. . . . They even say, "You know you don't have to stay," and some of you are just like, "okay," and you still stay! Why you working like a slave?! It's L.A., not Mexico or Chihuahua!

This display of Pentecostal protest masculinity sought to ground members' sense of cultural knowledge in Christianity. Pastor Raul drew upon biblical symbolism, Abraham's return to Egypt, to frame his concern with members missing church due to oppressive working conditions.

Despite the construction of rigid boundaries in opposition to dominant society, Victory Outreach members periodically left their sanctuary to proselytize in neighborhoods with drug addicts and gang members. They promoted the idea that every person needed to be saved and that the best way to encourage this was through personalized interactions. This was characteristic of the "voluntaristic absolutism" (Smith 1998, 210) and "personal influence strategies" (Smith 1998, 187) that lay at the heart of the American evangelical movement. Due to Victory Outreach's location in the U.S.-Mexico borderlands, such approaches are culturally pluralistic (León 1998; León 2004; Sanchez-Walsh 2003). During "street evangelism" at corner malls in low-income Latino communities, members performed Christian rap. At "feed my sheep" gatherings, members distributed *pozole* and refreshments in gang-ridden neighborhoods. Members also handed out blankets on Skid Row and baskets to needy families the weekend before Christmas. In their social interactions with non-Protestants, members passed out flyers, prayed for strangers, and said goodbye to everyone with the words "God bless." These outreach efforts combined elements of Mexican, American, and Mexican American culture, and members alternated between English, Spanish, and Mexican American slang, Caló. While members rapped with exaggerated mannerisms and wore the oversized clothes characteristic of inner-city style, they also listened to Christian worship music in their cars and made light-hearted Christian jokes about being "saved" or "rebuked" during social outings to restaurants.

Through these evangelizing efforts, Victory Outreach members created a self-enclosed community. For example, when Rick and the pastor's son rapped to customers at a Fourth of July fundraising fireworks stand in East Los Angeles, many members ate and socialized with their spouses, children, and other members. When Cecilia, a young, single female member of Victory Outreach, asked to go to Skid Row to practice evangelizing techniques she would use in missionary work abroad, Tony, an older member who always tried to attract her attention, offered to escort her. And when Ramon and Susana gave soup and prayed for a homeless, drug-addicted woman, Susana cheered her up by giving her several compliments, asking questions about her "cute" pet dog, and offering to take both in at the women's recovery home.

Victory Outreach members integrated into this tight community through the opportunities for advancement that opened up in the decentralized church structure. This experience was shared by Rick, a tall, fair-skinned twenty-seven-year-old recovered gang member from East Los Angeles. Rick was raised by his mother, a second-generation Mexican American, and his grandmother, from Mexico. After getting involved with street gangs and becoming a crystal meth addict, Rick's mother took him to the Victory Outreach men's recovery home, where he was forced to throw away his rap CDs. Rick recovered and became heavily involved with the church, performing Christian rap for Victory Outreach at street rallies and even running the men's home for a few months. Rick's ambition was to one day pastor a new chapter in Victory Outreach, a goal that seemed likely considering the church had grown to over six hundred chapters in forty years. This ambitious, but likely unlucrative, career path led to an argument between Rick and his mother, who wanted him to instead begin seeking a career in the conventional labor market. In an interview conducted with Rick as he ran errands in the church van for the upcoming Halloween celebration, he said,

> She doesn't really understand. . . . It's kind of addicting for me to help people now see the wonderful power of God. And she, she would rather me working, making money and doing other stuff. When I told her I wanted to be a pastor, the first thing she said was, "Well there's not too much money in that." God's not gonna let me starve and he's not gonna let me fall off. He's gonna take care of me, cuz my main goal in life is not like a lot of a percentage of America which is get all, money and that, you know. I don't, I don't, my drive is not that. That's not what I wake up to, all "Aw man." My drive, like I told you, is to see people get changed, to help people out.

As this quote illustrates, Rick felt that Victory Outreach sheltered him from participating in street life and filled his life with meaning through helping others. He hoped to one day become a pastor, have a family, and support that family. He juxtaposed these goals against the materialism and pursuit of wealth rampant in mainstream America. Victory Outreach's ascetic and evangelistic theological principles created a community, with rigid social boundaries, that quickly grew and provided Latino men with opportunities for advancement.

Integrative Redemption

In contrast to Victory Outreach's (2010) mission statement, which called for evangelism and advancement within the organization, Homeboy Industries' mission statement emphasized integration into society. Homeboy Industries' (2010) mission statement declared, "Jobs Not Jails: Homeboy Industries assists at-risk and formerly gang-involved youth to become positive and contributing members of society through job placement, training and education." Members were critical of the aggressive approach that the legal system had taken toward incarcerating low-income youth of color, and suggested that social problems—such as gang membership and drug addiction—could be better addressed through workforce development than incarceration. By advocating "Jobs Not Jails," Homeboy Industries members portrayed themselves as being unjustly persecuted by an increasingly punitive legal system.

In 2008, Homeboy Industries employed roughly five hundred gang members at any given time through the Homeboy Industries nonprofit, Homeboy Bakery, Homegirl Café, Homeboy Silkscreen, and Homeboy Landscaping. Legal services, tattoo removal, and self-help workshops were available to gang members in recovery. Members attended Criminal and Gang Members Anonymous and an array of group therapy classes such as Anger Management, Relapse Prevention, and Yoga. However, members referred to each other as "Homeboys" and "Homegirls," terms that revealed the porous boundaries between Homeboy Industries and the broader urban community. Homeboy Industries, unlike Victory Outreach, was influenced by spiritual ecumenism; gang recovery took place in a spiritually eclectic context. For example, fourteen years earlier, Mario was released from the courts to Father Greg's authority, then sent to live in a Christian men's recovery home. Despite the fact that Father Greg was Catholic, and that Pentecostals usually don't see Catholics as practitioners of the same faith, Mario told me that both he and Father Greg supported any form of spiritual development. When I asked him to explain this, Mario nonchalantly shrugged and said, "Whatever works."

Figure 3.2. Two Homeboys in the Homeboys Bakery (courtesy of Homeboy Industries)

Homeboy Industries' ecumenical leanings allowed therapeutic models of clinical rehabilitation to be used in gang recovery. Group therapy classes at Homeboy Industries often ended with the serenity prayer, a simple invocation that suggests no religious preference. The moderator would ask someone to "close us out with a prayer." As everyone formed a big circle, joined hands, bowed their heads, and closed their eyes, the volunteer prayer leader would say, "God, grant me the serenity to accept the things I can't change, the courage to change the things I can, and the wisdom to know the difference." Members would say "Amen," open their eyes, and adjourn the meeting with some light conversation on their way out the door. This type of social integration was spiritually more inclusive than the religiously particularistic tendencies observed with Pentecostal gang recovery.

However, members of Homeboy Industries, like those of Victory Outreach, did engage in a moral one-upmanship that positioned themselves over dominant institutions. I once attended a spiritual class in Homeboy Industries' Spreading Seeds program, in which Evo, the program's organizer, framed his class lessons through references to gang members' economic hardship, trauma, and persecution in the United States. He took us to a historic park across the street from the Homeboy Industries building to teach us meditation and breathing exercises. As we relaxed and sat cross-legged after finishing the exercises, he described how a circular plaque on the ground in front of us contained the history of different groups that had inhabited the space. Under the warm summer sun and with the sound of leaves rustling in the breeze, Evo told the story of how the indigenous Tongva, the Chinese, and blacks were all pushed into this same physical space, albeit at different times in history. Drawing a parallel between the past and present, between groups oppressed in the U.S. and urban gang members, he asked us if it wasn't merely a coincidence that Homeboy Industries, an organization helping recovering gang members, was now across the street. He then led us in more breathing exercises and talked about the concepts of yin and yang and positive/negative energy. Evo said that the U.S. government's penchant for imperialism, here, with the police in our streets, and abroad, through our continuing wars, was part of the negative energy. He encouraged members to not get "caught up in that," but to be part of the positive force, which could be experienced through spirituality. Evo both gave a sobering lesson on ethnic minority group oppression in the U.S. and demonstrated how to use spirituality to avoid aggressive police confrontations that could lead to further marginality and exclusion.

Homeboy Industries also drew upon Native American spiritual practices to facilitate gang recovery. At a daily morning meeting, where all members congregated before work, I once heard Father Greg tell a Native American parable as his "thought of the day." In the parable, a grandson told his grandfather that he felt he had two wolves inside of him: one full of anger and resentment, and the other full of love, kindness, and compassion. The grandson asked the grandfather, "Which one wins?" The grandfather responded, "The one that you feed, that one wins." As he told the parable, Father Greg related it to recovering gang members' experiences by talking about the feelings associated with relapsing into drug abuse or gang violence. He suggested that "feeding" those feelings would encourage one to act upon them. The use of Native American spirituality both facilitated the process of gang recovery and allowed members to reconstruct their foundation of cultural knowledge, from street gang life to Native American culture. Whereas Victory Outreach reconstructed members' cultural knowledge through Christian symbolism, Homeboy Industries did so, in part, through Native American culture.

A few members of Homeboy Industries attended a "sweat lodge," a traditional Native American faith ritual of cleansing, about once a month. One evening, I joined members of the Spreading Seeds class for such a sweat. Traveling about an hour north of Los Angeles, we arrived at an urban, Victorian-styled halfway house in the San Fernando Valley. We went directly to the backyard, which was largely grass covered, except for a patio area with a concrete floor and a few wooden benches. Three long-haired, soft-spoken, middle-aged Native American "elders" told us in a whisper that the ceremony was already beginning. We worked together to unfold a stack of blankets and place them over the tent's straw frame. The elders gave us instructions about the four directions painted on the wall, and how each person's path was different. We stood around the pit, feeling the sting and breathing the smoke of the hot burning rocks, while someone walked around and gave us leaves. We held them in the palms of our wet, sweaty hands. We were to move around the pit clockwise, individually throw leaves to the center, and pray, then go to the tent, kneel down, ask for permission to enter, and crawl in clockwise. The "umbilical cord" that connected the pit and the tent would be broken if we did not proceed behind the altar. Inside, we could barely see.

In the darkness of the tent, the elders explained that we could pray to whomever we wished; the sweat lodge was inclusive of all religions, including Christianity. We were told we would do four rounds, and if we needed to leave it would have to be between rounds. When the rocks were brought in the tent, I didn't think I could survive the heat. During the first round, I managed to sing along to the words, but I felt my face and lungs burning up and could not breathe. The elders said that we could put our faces on the ground to cool off, or put mud on them. I dug my feet and hands around the barren ground but found no mud. I felt as if I was about to faint from the heat, steam, and lack of air. I went outside after the first round ended, staggering and unable to walk properly. Drenched in sweat, I searched for water, trying to replenish myself.

Between the third and fourth round, Jaime, an undocumented 1.5-generation immigrant, and Evo came out together. Jaime whispered to him in the cold dark of the night that, inside the unbearable sweat, he had thought about what it must be like for people coming from Mexico to the United States, having to cross the desert in such a heat. Jaime's words touched me deeply. I was born to undocumented parents, given an English name, and told not to speak Spanish at school. My earliest memories are of my mother instructing me every morning, as she dressed me, about what would happen if she or my father did not come home that day. Jaime's words immediately drew forth those memories, and I thought of them as we returned into the sweat to pray for several more rounds.

Over the next year, I led a class at Homeboy Industries called College 101, designed with the aim to get Homeboys into college. I was delighted when my normally apathetic students would suddenly become interested in learning about "our history." This always referred to Spanish and English colonization of the Americas, or the treatment of Latinos in the United States before the Civil Rights Movement. I treated them as teachable moments to educate them on related sociological concepts, such as Marxism or feminism. This phenomenon was not unique to my class. In Find a Tree and Spreading Seeds, I saw instructors calm students' anger toward the cops and courts system by reminding them that in traditional Native American or African cultures, humility is a virtue and anger is frowned upon. Homeboy Industries' use of Native American and other non-Western cultures as repositories for symbolism was compatible with its facilitation of gang recovery through the Catholic creed of God's omnipresence. Homeboy Industries facilitated social integration into the broader community through porous boundaries and religious ecumenism.

Protesting Peacefully

Members of Victory Outreach and Homeboy Industries perceived a hostile context of reception for low-income Latinos in the United States. Latinos with a brown complexion told stories of being stereotyped and harassed by the police. This was true of Ramon, who had once been brought down physically in the Victory Outreach church parking lot and forced to confess that he used to be involved in street activity (see chapter 6). During that incident, Ramon was told by one of the police officers that members of his Latino-dominant ministry were "a bunch of gang members, "drug addicts," and "good-for-nothings." Conversely, Cecilia from Victory Outreach, an attractive, elegantly dressed Latina with Irish ancestry and a white phenotype, told me about an incident in which she was assumed not to have a criminal background because of her skin color. A police officer once came to her door asking if she knew a particular woman. Cecilia told him that she did, that she had met the woman while serving an eighteen-month sentence for drug trafficking. She said that the police officer jumped back, surprised. Cecilia coolly noted that, because police officers are so accustomed to harassing streetwise black and Latino men, they were always shocked to find out about her past. Racial boundaries are powerful factors shaping processes of racialization and assimilation among low-income Latinos.

Despite the power of racist images in shaping a hostile context of reception, Latino recovering gang members drew from spirituality to peacefully resist police hostility and experience social reintegration. Mario, a senior member and case manager at Homeboy Industries, claimed that his participation in gangs used to be a form of "violent protest"; it stemmed from resentment toward his mother for bringing him to the U.S. as a child, and manifested against the poverty and racism they faced. Upon further reflection, as a much older and wiser person, Mario now attributed his frustrations to processes of social inequality that spanned a much wider terrain than his Boyle Heights neighborhood. Similar to how John Hagedorn (1991) has taken a global perspective on gangs, the spread of neoliberalism, and urban marginality, Mario expressed that he now thinks that the problem of the rise of gangs is much broader and not limited to the United States. In an interview, Mario said,

> Some people commit suicide to protest. Like my brother, rest in peace, I think he protested saying, "I'm gonna take my own life. That's how much I don't agree with what's going on, and that's what I think is the ultimate way of protesting." I see in the Middle East people light themselves on fire to protest in something they don't like. You know [what] I'm saying? I think the world is a whole big ole' different gangs in big picture. And when you see gangsters in L.A. it's a small picture of what's really going on around the world. So it's like, we don't light ourselves on fire, but I tell you what, we'll sure put a gun to our heads and blow our brains

out. Just to tell you we don't agree with what's going on. And, maybe we should light ourselves up on fire and protest against discrimination, [discrimination] against races that are not born here but been here since babies, you know what I mean? Unfair treatment by the police because of stereotype, the color of your skin, or by the way you walk, or where you grew up at.

Mario's reference to discrimination against "races that are not born here but been here since babies" was about undocumented children that have grown up in the United States. Lacking the rights of their native-born counterparts, such as the ability to finance a college education or obtain formal employment, undocumented immigrant children shift from inclusion to exclusion from American society as they age. Sociologist Roberto G. Gonzales has called this process "learning to be illegal" and noted that it "makes for a turbulent transition and has profound implications for identity formation" (2011, 602). Mario's socialization into an inner-city neighborhood accelerated the already tumultuous process of maturation for an undocumented immigrant, as he came into contact with the legal system at a young age. Mario's embodiment made him vulnerable to racial profiling and the legal system, and compounded the frustrations he was already experiencing due to trauma, loss, a sense of having been uprooted, and social marginality.

Despite Mario's undocumented status and the systemic racism he perceived, he now opposed the destructive expressions he had engaged in through gang activity. In their place, he pursued less destructive forms of self-expression, or what he called "peaceful protest." He explained,

And now, I accept where I'm at. I'm not protesting in a violent way, but I think I still have that spirit of a protester. I still want things to change, but I don't do it violently, or I don't do it by hurting somebody, especially not the people that love me. But I speak with my youth . . . I talk to them in a way that how they can protest their life without hurting their loved ones. . . . I realized through pain that [violent] protesting is not gonna make it better. You know? . . . I look up to Martin Luther King. He was a protester, but in a peaceful kinda way. Ghandi, he protested against inhumanity, in a peaceful way.

Mario redirected his expressions of frustration to peacefully con-test dominant ideas rather than to self-destruct. As a case manager for Homeboy Industries, he talked with minors and told them not to engage in gang violence or riots. He was inspired by Father Greg's understand-ing of gang behavior as a form of discontent, as well as how he advocated progressive social change through social activism. As a result of his con-versations with Father Greg, Mario now sought peaceful ways of contest-ing his displeasure with discrimination and the hostile police presence in inner-city neighborhoods. Rather than trying to hurt his loved ones, he now embraced a faith-inspired, nonviolent approach to confronting systemic racism. Religious groups, in a context of anti-immigrant senti-ment, offer marginalized immigrants an alternative to the public sphere and facilitate settlement (Marquardt 2005). Through Homeboy Indus-tries, recovering gang members such as Mario experienced redemption and social reintegration into the broader local community.

Likewise, men at Victory Outreach also reformulated expressions of frustration from self-destructive gang activity to peaceful ways of con-testing dominant, racist images of Latinos. They challenged the popu-lar idea that gang members cannot change. This view was constructed through the ministry's representations of the legal system as an oppres-sive apparatus of the state, in contrast with Victory Outreach as a pur-poseful organization that could facilitate change in individual members' lives. At a Sunday morning sermon, Pastor Raul proclaimed, "People called us hopeless. . . . [They] think we can't change. . . . The State of California said, 'Give him 25 years.' Me!" He attributed his success in reforming from gang life and overcoming the challenges of the legal system to the church. He exhorted the congregation, "When you're in prayer, in the house of God, worry can't follow you, anxiety can't fol-low you." Concluding his story, he referred to the church as "sanctuary," "refuge," "security," and "reassurance." In response, members cheered, clapped, and roared, "Yes," "That's right," and "Amen." They validated the pastor's view that, although the state corrections system perceived inner-city gang members as unable to change, the church could redeem and socially reintegrate them, while simultaneously providing refuge.

Victory Outreach members took pride in professing to hold ideals that placed them on a morally higher ground than persons in main-stream society, despite their marginalized status as low-income ex–drug addicts and ex–gang members. In demonstration of this, they practiced peaceful protests through street evangelism rallies. Setting up microphones and large speakers at major intersections, they would give passionate testimonies and use Christian rap to spread their message to pedestrians. At one such event, two white police officers in a standard black-and-white patrol car stopped to make a left turn at the intersection, and a few members grinned, trying to hide their smiles. As the officers glanced at the church members, a woman from Victory Outreach chanted in their direction, "Je-sus, Je-sus, Je-sus!" The members who had previously hid their smiles joyfully joined in with the chants. Whereas people with backgrounds like those of the Victory Outreach members would generally be expected to have felt intimidated by the presence of police, the members delighted in contradicting the stereotypes of the urban poor. Through religious practices that emphasized redemption, but also rigid boundaries, they displayed themselves as standing on morally higher ground and reclaimed a sense of honor.

Conclusion

By virtue of American religious tolerance, gang members experience gang recovery in the context of a free "religious marketplace." Faith-based urban ministries and organizations compete for recovering gang members' membership, and offer models of gang recovery based on theologies and religious practices. Victory Outreach's decentralizing and ascetic model was influenced by Pentecostal theology, while Homeboy Industries' centralized hierarchy and spiritually inclusive model was loosely influenced by Catholic theology. Both approached gang recovery as a process of redemption and reintegration. Victory Outreach offered a model of segregated redemption, in which recovering gang members experienced recovery through activities meant to shelter them from the broader local community. Recovering gang members attended church activities, such as services and evangelism events, and abstained from drug and alcohol use or nonchurch activities. Homeboy Industries offered a model of integrative redemption, in which recovering gang members experienced recovery through activities meant to integrate them with the broader local community. Recovering gang members were encouraged to work and participate in spiritually inclusive prayers and meditations, although they left this setting and returned to their local neighborhoods when they were not working. In sum, recovery from gang life occurred through recovering gang members' integration into cohesive social groups, which offered rich cultural memory and resonated with the gang experience.

Though this study of gang recovery does not disprove the thesis of Omar McRoberts's *Streets of Glory*—that religious particularism is acute in inner-city ministries and may undermine faith-based efforts to help ex-offenders reintegrate into society—it certainly does suggest that the inverse is empirically possible. Recovery from gang life, and the other half of the coin, reintegration into broader society, can occur regardless of religious particularism. Furthermore, such recovery and reintegration need not be tied to traditional religious practice or a coethnic immigrant community. Segmented assimilation theory, in its effort to conceptualize the relationship between immigrant assimilation and socioeconomic mobility, has overlooked the central role that religion has played in facilitating immigrant integration (Warner 2007). Nonetheless, an element of Zhou et al.'s (2008) research on second-generation immigrants and upward socioeconomic mobility remains important in understanding immigrant integration: cultural memory.

The important role that cultural memory plays in facilitating recovery from gang life can be seen by highlighting the importance of theologies and religious practices in the construction of redemption. The recovering gang members described in this study had experienced racism, poverty, violence, drug addiction, and incarceration, and some were undocumented immigrants. These obstacles have all been understood to detrimentally affect immigrant integration. However, recovering gang members were able to begin carving out redemptive paths as these obstacles became understood through parables of the persecution of Christians, or through stories of minority groups oppressed by racism and colonization in the United States. These expressions of cultural memory, and the understanding of the paths that led out of gang life were shaped through Sunday morning church services, street evangelism, prayer, and meditations. These religious practices were reactive; in other words, they contrasted with the premigration religious practices of members' parents, grandparents, or other family members. Latino recovering gang members resisted trajectories of downward assimilation through religious practice in urban American ministries.

4

Reformed Barrio Masculinity

Eight Cases of Recovery from Gang Life

On a chilly November evening, Antonio, Homeboy Industries' drug counselor, held his first art show at the large Homeboy Industries building in Downtown Los Angeles. Two vintage 1960s era lowriders, one of them a Riviera airbrushed with Aztec images, sat on the concrete sidewalk outside of the Homeboys Bakery. Stocky, older Homeboys with thick *brochas*—mustaches—and sunglasses socialized and admired the cars. Closer to the entrance of the building, younger Homeboys and Homegirls exchanged elaborate handshakes, laughed and embraced. Inside the building, Antonio's large oil paintings lined the walls of the Homeboy Bakery, along with the colorful works of renowned Chicano artist Jose Ramirez, and a few small paintings by lesser-known Chicano artists with gang pasts. Homegirls Café waitresses served sangria and hors d'oeuvres to a large, diverse gathering of over a hundred visitors as they perused the fascinating, crowded scene.

I caught Antonio's eye as I walked in through the bakery, though I at first failed to say anything as I fought my way through small groups of people conversing. Antonio's appearance was curious: he was dressed in street garb, but the left half of his face was painted black and white, like a Día de los Muertos character while the right side was unpainted. He stretched an arm out to me through the crowd, shook my hand, and told me he was glad I had made it. After I made my way to the lobby, I waited with several others to watch a few Homeboys do poetry readings. The Homeboy poets did not disappoint. With thick East Los Angeles Chicano accents, stylish hats, and slightly oversized coats, they lamented their past gang activity and spoke passionately about leaving gang life behind. They amused the standing, captive audience by telling stories bursting with humor, sadness, and joy.

After the last poet spoke, Antonio took the microphone, and, spotting his mother in the crowd, warmly shouted, "Mom, thank you! *Sí, se puede!* I did this thanks to you. This, this is all for you." He followed with his personal testimony, a painful childhood memory. He spoke of not having had the patience for schoolwork, but of possessing a talent for drawing. Once, he was sent to the principal's office for vandalism, but Father Greg allowed him to paint the walls at Dolores Mission. Unfortunately, he became addicted to crystal meth. Nonetheless, his relationship with Father Greg helped keep him resilient, and he carried the hope of becoming employed at Homeboy Industries. Eventually, he succeeded in quitting drugs and gang life.

Concluding his testimony, Antonio told the audience, "If you wanna know why my face is painted this way, it's for Día de los Muertos. . . . It signifies the other life I've had that passed away." In contrast to his days on the street, Antonio's goal was now to "break the cycle of tragedy"— a subtle reference to his abusive father's heroin addiction—by being a nurturing husband and father to his wife and three children. Nervously taking one last deep breath, he lifted his hands and told everyone, "Thank you, enjoy the show." As the crowd cheered and clapped, and the background music became louder, Antonio disappeared into the crowd. When I spoke with him later, I told him that I was sure his mother was proud, and his eyes welled up with tears.

Antonio's experience with gang life was characteristic of Chicano gang masculinity. He was on a self-destructive, downwardly mobile path shaped by gangs and drugs. Likewise, Chicano gang membership in Los Angeles has been associated with a culture of *locura*, a hypermasculine "craziness or wildness," heavy drug and alcohol use, and "the appearance of a lack of impulse control" (Vigil 2007, 63), as well as street violence, crime, and neighborhood territoriality (Hunt 2003; Moore 1991; Moore, Vigil, and Garcia 1983; Vigil 2007). On the other hand, like many recovered gang members, Antonio engaged in a "redemption sequence" (Maruna 2001, 97); he dedicated himself to earning money through legal channels, working in a formal drug counseling job while doing some artwork on the side, and using his money to provide for his family. Furthermore, he sought to redeem himself for his prior actions, and to gain legitimacy for being reformed, by helping others as a drug counselor. Shadd Maruna (2001), in his research on career criminals who later avoided crime, found that redemption scripts facilitated social integration that helped maintain desistance from crime. The first major component of a redemption script was generativity—helping others who had once been in the same position (Maruna 2001, 99–100). As a Homeboy Industries drug counselor, Antonio used therapy to help gang members who were now in the position he was once in.

Chicano Gang Masculinity

Chicano gang masculinity has been articulated in the context of what Raewyn Connell has called the "gender order" (2009[2002], 54): institutional regimes that pattern gendered practices. Several expressions of masculinity are embedded within the gender order. "Hegemonic masculinity"—that which is implicitly normative—reaps the greatest reward in the gender order, while some men reinforce hegemonic masculinity through a "complicit masculinity" and share in the "patriarchal dividend" (Connell 1995, 77–79). However, other masculine expressions are positioned to receive less patriarchal privilege. Men whose masculinity is stigmatized, such as gay men, experience a "subordinate masculinity" (Connell 1995, 79). Men of "marginalized masculinity" also experience oppression through structural barriers to mainstream society, but they become preoccupied with the authentic expression of a competing form of masculinity (Connell 1995, 81).

Chicano gang masculinity has been a form of marginalized masculinity. In a context of industrial decline, racist images of low-income black and Latino men legitimated their marginalization and reinforced the dominance of white men (Connell 1995; Hondagneu-Sotelo and Messner 1994; Collins 1990; Espiritu 1997). The discussion in chapter 1 illustrated how twentieth-century public policy reinforced racial domination of Latinos in Los Angeles: first through the racial paternalism of Roosevelt-era "New Deal" social reform, and then through the color-blind racism of post–Civil Rights Movement neoliberalism. Laws that target gang members as domestic terrorists, have contributed to the Latino crime threat.

Although research on men and masculinities in the gender order has been advancing since the 1980s, the multiplicity of masculine expressions among Latinos was largely neglected until more recently (Mirandé 1997). In her study of Colombian evangelicalism and masculinity, anthropologist Elizabeth Brusco theorized that Latino masculinity was constructed in the context of a masculine duality. Brusco (1995, 85) argued that Latino "macho" masculinity was similar to the masculinity of the European-model patriarchy, in which men contributed economically and made decisions in the household. However, in a deindustrialized context, this ideal was out of reach for the vast majority of men who were unemployed. Conversely, Brusco argued that machista masculinity, machismo, was deeply immersed in a street-oriented culture of drinking. Latino machismo was characterized by unemployment, absence from the household, and substance abuse, as well as cold, distant relationships with partners and children, and romantic affairs outside of marriage.

The process of recovery among Chicanos was similarly framed by a macho/machismo distinction. The two portraits of Antonio's life, as represented by the way he painted his face and told his personal testimony, demonstrated the macho/machismo gendered duality. One side of Antonio's face represented the self-destructive gang member, and the other represented the affectionate family man. Pivotal to Antonio's reform was a shift in masculine orientation. He had begun to see himself as a father, husband, and son, instead of as a gang member. As a result, he left the streets and gang life behind in return for family life and the household. Antonio's involvement and exit from gangs reflected engagement with the macho/machismo dichotomy in a manner similar to that conceptualized by Brusco.

Figure 4.1. A Homeboy Industries member holding his son (courtesy of Homeboy Industries)

Reformed Barrio Masculinity

Gang recovery challenges the emasculating nature of racism and poverty by institutionalizing gendered arrangements that facilitate exit from street life and encourage social reintegration. Research on recovery has suggested that projects of spiritual restoration encourage reform of machista–influenced expressions of Latino masculinity, and align masculine expressions in recovery with dominant masculine expressions (León 1998; Brandes 2003; Brenneman 2009; Brusco 1995; Sanchez-Walsh 2003). Brusco, for example, found that men's socialization into evangelical codes of behavior fundamentally amounted to the "reformation of machismo." She reasoned that

> [a]scetic codes forbid much of the behavior associated with the machismo complex: men can no longer drink, smoke, or have women outside of their marriage. A man's social world becomes transformed also, from the male public world to a redefined private world were the family is the central focus. (Brusco 1995, 125)

Furthermore, she claimed that such a shift in gendered practices would reorient the flow of capital back toward the house, with the effect of stimulating consumption habits that influence the likelihood of upward mobility.

> Household consumption can include income-generating purchases, such as real estate (houses or land, urban and rural), live-stock, a car or truck, and of course education for children. It is important to note that such investment is distinct from individual entrepreneurship because it is strategically linked to consumption and it is household based. (Brusco 1995, 125)

Gang recovery was antiracist, as it sought to rearticulate notions of Chicano masculinity and to reposition recovered gang members within the broader gender order. Respondents hailed from poor families, lived in poor neighborhoods, had low educational attainment, and faced issues with their legal status. The marginality they experienced was compounded by drug addiction, the threat of violence, strained family ties, and a criminal record. However, similar to the Columbian example of evangelical conversion, recovery from gang life was shaped by masculine reformation and tied to upward socioeconomic mobility (see chapter 2 for a discussion of how mobility exists in a very modest form in Los Angeles's Latino-dominant neighborhoods). Recovering gang members sought to escape gang life by embracing the gendered image of the "breadwinner," the family man who was formally employed and provided for his family, despite having experienced a life mired in poverty, marginality, and crime. For example, Antonio's narrative of recovery involved leaving the self-destructive, downwardly mobile path of Chicano gang life by quitting drugs, earning a job at Homeboy Industries, and beginning a successful art career.

In a previous study that built upon Brusco's (1995) conceptual framework, I coined the term "reformed barrio masculinity" to describe Chicano recovering gang members' reorientation from the street to the household (Flores 2009, 1004). I found that recovering gang members sought to abstain from masculine gang expressions, such as gang violence, drug abuse, and extramarital affairs, and instead valued formal employment and the role of a providing, nurturing husband and father.

Table 4.1. Recovering Gang Members, by Organization

	Homeboy Industries	Victory Outreach
Leader	Antonio	Rick
	Mario	Ramon
Old Member	Sergio	Ivan
New Member	Gerardo	Santiago

This chapter more fully details the way in which gang recovery at Homeboy Industries and Victory Outreach was spurred by marginal, gendered oppression, as well as how it engaged the construction of reformed barrio masculinity. Two themes undergirded both successful and failed projects of reformed barrio masculinity. First, Chicano gang masculinity did not abruptly disappear after recovery. In gang recovery, there was continuity between the street style of the criminal gang member and the reformed gang member. As Antonio did, reformed gang members often retain some of the style of the barrio, expressed through such things as baggy clothes, lowrider cars, and airbrushed artwork. Second, Chicano gang recovery was constructed in opposition to Chicano gang life. As described above, while Chicano gang masculinity transgresses conventional expressions of manhood, reformed barrio masculinity is aligned with conventional expressions.

This chapter draws upon interview data, and some participant observation, to present eight cases of recovering gang members. Four cases were selected from Homeboy Industries, and four from Victory Outreach. Roughly half were older members, who had spent three or more years in one of the organizations, and half were newer members, who had spent less than a year (see table 4.1). These case studies are all based on different life stories, but they echo with similar themes. Many respondents experienced childhood poverty and social marginalization, and then adolescent gang violence and drug use. As recovering gang members, they expressed regret over their past gang activity. Above all, they wished to be redeemed for the pain that they had caused their own mothers, partners, and children. They desired to become employed, nurturing fathers and husbands, and furthermore, to pay it forward by being able to "give" to their "community," mentoring at-risk youth.

Giving Back to the Community: Leaders in Chicano Gang Recovery

Personal histories of leaders in gang recovery best illustrate the stark dualism between Chicano gang masculinity and reformed barrio masculinity; men left gang life as they engaged with recovery, and reoriented their masculine expressions from the street to recovery programs, the household, or the church. In this section, two cases from Homeboy Industries and two cases from Victory Outreach illustrate this gendered dichotomy—but also demonstrate how leadership responsibilities within recovery helped to amplify such shifts in masculine orientation. Whereas Homeboy Industries emphasized group therapy and job skills in order to reorient men from the streets to the household, Victory Outreach emphasized improving one's character through forms of spiritual growth, such as living in the men's recovery home, worshipping at church services, and spending time reading the Bible, to reorient men into the household.

Antonio, Homeboy Industries, old member

Antonio, a thirty-three-year-old Mexican American, was born in El Paso, Texas, to a family that had lived along the Mexican side of the El Paso/Juárez border for generations. At an early age, his family moved to Boyle Heights' Aliso Village housing projects, where his mother worked long hours to support three kids and a heroin-addicted father who was in and out of prison. During our interview, Antonio lamented that he had received little attention from his parents. Despite finding a father figure in Father Greg, who was then the local priest, Antonio became enmeshed in gang and drug life, writing graffiti on walls for his gang and using crystal methamphetamine. He worked odd jobs in construction to pay for his habit; for ten dollars, he once dangerously climbed a tall pole to paint a sign for a local store. Eventually his crystal meth addiction led him into a cycle of drug courts, running from the police, and incarceration. He frequently told the story of the night when he ran to a freeway center divider, where he contemplated suicide. Luckily, he pulled back and called his mother, and a few nights later he finally entered recovery.

Antonio first entered recovery through the Salvation Army, where he stayed for a few months. During that time he began regularly attending

Victory Outreach with a cousin who sang in the church. After finishing his time with the Salvation Army, Antonio continued to attend Victory Outreach with his family on Sundays and certain holidays, such as New Year's Eve. After a few months in recovery, Antonio got a job at Homeboy Industries. While working there, he took drug counseling certification classes and eventually became Homeboy Industries' drug counselor. As a drug counselor, Antonio used the language of clinical rehabilitation, such as referring to childhood trauma, addiction, and relapse, to talk about his experiences leaving gang life.

Antonio also experienced religion through artistic means. With a wiry frame and deep, dark, penetrating eyes, Antonio always spoke in a matter-of-fact way that masked the rich artistic talent he expressed through large oil paintings. His art often involved themes of regret and redemption, expressed through images of gang members, death, and children. Antonio also embodied an indigenous faith tradition, wearing a long ponytail, decorating his office wall with a Navajo dream catcher, and participating frequently in sweat lodges. In regards to the apparent contradiction between his practice of the Christian faith and indigenous faith, Antonio compared Pentecostal Holy Spirit manifestations with Native American vision quests. He said both were in his culture, and that he tried to "keep the balance."

In moderating his drug classes at Homeboys, Antonio drew upon notions of men as positive father figures. Sharing his testimony frequently, he told his class that he remained clean because, every day, he anticipated seeing his children as they waited for him to come home. He said that feeling was "not worth one hit of blast." Antonio said that he would like to have his kids see his work at a red carpet premiere one day, and that he had ambitions to be employed by the Dreamworks film company. To this end, he regularly organized art shows at Homeboy Industries. Antonio looked up to Dr. Ramirez, a professor at a leading art school who had "given back to his community," Father Greg, and Noah, a social worker at USC whom he did sweats with and called "uncle."

Mario, Homeboy Industries, old member

When I first met Mario, thirty-three, he described himself as a "family man" and said he wanted to be married to his girlfriend within the next five years. The sincerity of this self-description was confirmed the first time I visited him to conduct an interview. As we were well under way, Mario's girlfriend stopped by his apartment to fill out job applications and ask for his help. He generously agreed and asked me to finish the interview the following day. In our interview the following day, Mario told me that he and his girlfriend supported one another in their life goals.

Mario had been brought to the U.S. at age eleven against his will; he described this as an event that "shook his tree." Although Mario's mother came to the Unites States to flee an abusive relationship, it pained him to have been torn away from his father, without any closure. The adjustment to life in the U.S. was difficult for him; Mario's family settled in the Pico-Aliso area of Boyle Heights, and lived in poverty. He was the eldest son in his family, and several of his brothers, friends, and cousins followed in his footsteps. As Mario ran with a local gang, TMC, as a drug dealer at age thirteen, so did many of his relatives. Later, as I played chess at his house after leaving Homeboy Industries' Christmas party, he would reveal that he still had a strained relationship with his immediate family.

Mario first met Father Greg when he was fourteen years old, and was shocked by his efforts at outreach in such a gang-plagued neighborhood. Mario told me, "I mean you have a Catholic [priest] running around on a beach cruiser, at midnight, in the housing projects. I mean how do you picture a priest doing that?" However, Father Greg could not save all of Mario's childhood peers from gang life. One of his brothers committed suicide, another was doing a ten-year prison stretch, and another—as a minor—had been sentenced to life without the possibility of parole. After watching several of his peers get killed or get sent away to prison, Mario decided he wanted to change his life.

When Mario was eighteen, with a serious drinking problem and facing prison time, Father Greg intervened and sent him to a Pentecostal men's recovery home. There Mario quit drinking and learned to play chess with older ex-convicts who taught him about life over endless games. Mario maintained an unwavering allegiance to Father Greg as a "father figure" in whose footsteps he wished he could follow. He wanted to "give back to the community as much as Father Greg has given."

Mario started working with Homeboy Industries when it was still located in the old office in Boyle Heights. He had taken a course at the

California State University of Los Angeles, and got a certificate in gang intervention. His job title shifted from "gang intervention specialist" to "case manager" after Father Greg transitioned away from formally doing gang intervention work. As a Homeboy Industries case manager, Mario spoke with young people and encouraged them to think about peacefully solving their problems.

Mario said that he liked this job with Homeboy Industries because it gave him money, a job, and a sense of purpose in life; most of all, it was like a family. He said, "It feels like a community that is more than just nine to five. You build long term relationships there." Mario not only worked together with fellow staffers, but went out to dinner together after work with them, and they would help each other out in times of need, such as when moving in to a new apartment. Contrasting his experience at Homeboy Industries with the isolating experience he had at another church he had attended, Mario said,

> Even when I was involved really deeply in my Christianity . . . there was something missing, cuz all you see, the people at church on Sundays and Wednesdays . . . after mass you won't see 'em no more. You know what I mean? They live their own life. . . . You won't go out to their house. . . . I didn't like that. But Homeboys is not like that. Every day I see you and I'll call you during the day, tomorrow, in the evening, Saturday, "What you doin' Sunday?"

Mario had been with his girlfriend for a year at the time of our interview. He said, "We laugh all the time. We help each other out. We try to encourage each other to do good." In response to my question about where he saw himself in five years, he said, "Married, maybe have one kid already, and buy a house with her." However, Mario's life became extremely tumultuous over the following months. Just before his interview, and after fourteen years of sobriety, he had begun drinking again (which he attributed to his girlfriend's influence). Before the end of the year, Mario's relationship with his girlfriend became on-and-off.

Two months after I interviewed Mario, an old friend of his, Steve, was murdered. Steve had lost his job and his apartment, and Mario offered him his apartment to shower and rest. One night, Mario offered to let him sleep inside, but Steve refused the hospitality and instead chose to sleep in his car down the street. Old gang rivals recognized him that night as he slept in his car, and they shot him. At Homeboy Industries, a couple of mornings later, I ran into a teary-eyed Mario after the morning meeting prayer and he told me the news. I was concerned about Mario's drinking, which escalated severely. Father Greg demoted Mario from his Homeboy Industries position and sent him to drug and alcohol rehab for two months.

Upon returning from rehab, Mario moved to an apartment in Koreatown as an apartment manager, and he resumed work with Homeboy Industries. We played chess on Christmas Eve at his place in Koreatown. Mario and his girlfriend had broken up, and he had no plans to visit his family for Christmas.

Rick, Victory Outreach, leader

Rick, twenty-seven, was born to two Baptists, a second-generation Mexican American mother and a second-generation Italian American father. Rick's father left the family when he was seven years old, and he was raised by his Mexican grandmother and his mother. Rick grew up in the low-income Latino community of Paramount, where he joined a tagging crew in middle school. Later, after he got a scholarship to play baseball at a private high school, Rick's family moved to Montebello, a middle-class Mexican American community. He lettered in baseball, and was an all-star for four years straight. However, despite no longer being involved in street gang activity in high school, Rick started "experiencing and doing things other than living the Christian life." His teams won championships, and he lived a lifestyle of parties, "drugs and girls." In contrast to a childhood that was structured by discipline and customs, during his teenage years, Rick said, he had a feeling of freedom and did whatever he wanted to do.

After high school, Rick was recruited to enter the University of Southern California on a sports scholarship, but lacked the necessary grades. As a result, he joined the military. Even then, however, he would return home and party with drugs and women. After a short stint, he deserted and a warrant was issued in his name. For deserting the military and using drugs, Rick was kicked out of his mother's house.

After he was kicked out of his mother's house, Rick became home-less and hooked up with an old friend who was in a major gang on Los Angeles County's Eastside. Together with the friend, Rick became addicted to crystal methamphetamine and committed crimes with the gang to feed his habit. Eventually, he got pulled over by the police, ended up in jail, and was turned over to the military where he received an "other than honorable" discharge and was sent home. Rick's mother kicked him out of the house again, and he returned to the streets with his gang associate. He also met a woman who was a meth addict, and together they committed crimes that got themselves several stints of jail time.

At age twenty-two, after Rick went to court once again, a judge gave him another chance to get clean without significant jail time. His mother, though, gave him an ultimatum: enter recovery or get kicked out of the house again. She showed him a Victory Outreach flier, and Rick agreed to enter the men's recovery home. The next day, she dropped him off at a Victory Outreach men's recovery home, where they inspected his bag and threw out his rap CDs. Rick was disap-pointed to lose them, because he had just recently started performing live rap. However, he was glad to find out that the ministry encouraged Christian rap. He started writing Christian rap songs for entertainment, and later he had his gang tattoos removed at Homeboy Industries.

Rick moved up within the church hierarchy. When I met him, he was frequently on stage in the church band, singing, or playing the key-boards or guitar. He had a strong stage presence—he was tall and good looking, and wore flashy clothes such as leather jackets or dressy vests and suits. Eventually, although he relinquished the position after a few months, he became the men's home director. One staff member in the home told me he believed Rick was simply too young for such a respon-sibility. Nonetheless, Rick aspired to move up in the church hierarchy, because like many other Victory Outreach men, he looked up to the pastors and wanted to be just like them: to have a family and a home, and to pastor a church. Rick said,

There's a few pastors in the ministry that I would like to follow. There's a pastor in the city of Eagle Rock, my youth pastor. . . . He's about twenty-nine or thirty right now, and married, full-time ministry, he works in the church and he has a family . . .

Rick admired that the pastor from Eagle Rock had "favor" and knew public officials in the city. He also admired Pastor Raul from his own church, and he drew a parallel between their life experiences. He felt that his own mother was not supportive of his decisions to pursue a life in the ministry, but that Pastor Raul's success gave him hope. Rick said,

> [Pastor Raul's] family couldn't understand [why] he wanted to be in the ministry either. Kinda where my family is right now, but he stayed and stuck it out. And now he's a blessed man, with church, a family, a house . . .

Asked where he wanted to be in five years, Rick responded,

> Married like I said, living with my wife and just being a good man of God. Those are my goals. My goals are to finish school. I'm a little more than halfway done with our schooling to get the license to be a minister. And, after I become that, I just wait for the lord to send me out to another city. With my family and my wife and let's go.

In our interview, Rick told me his ideal mate would be a Christian woman that liked worship music and preaching, because he liked playing worship music and preaching. His ambition, to go to where ministry opportunities opened, required that he have a wife and children to follow him. He said, "That's why I gotta be careful with the woman that I marry, cuz she can either help fulfill my calling or take me out of it." Rick did not see himself as authoritarian. Rather, he hinted at elements of companionate marriage when he talked about his dreams, saying, "We're gonna go do our own city one day and we're gonna be pastors." At the same time, he made clear that there was a gendered hierarchy, "She's just gonna have to be ready and be willing to do whatever God wants us to do, and the woman's gotta follow the man."

Rick married Cecilia, a highly involved member of Victory Outreach, a year and a half later. The wedding was very humble, at the Victory Outreach storefront church. The day of the wedding, the church was adorned with simple paper decorations, and for dinner, members of the men's and women's recovery homes served chicken stew from large pots. At the following weekly Bible study group, Rick and Cecilia gave joint sermons at the following weekly Bible study, and said that they celebrated having each other in their lives.

Ramon, Victory Outreach, leader

Ramon, a twenty-four-year-old member of Victory Outreach, came to the U.S. with his mother at age seven. He described his mother's choice to migrate as an ambition for better socioeconomic opportunities. Ramon said Mexico was "real poor, man, that's why we moved over here, looking for a better future and everything." In addition, his father had been a drug dealer, and his mother "wanted to take us somewhere where our life was gonna be better." They settled in the low-income Paramount suburb, southeast of Downtown Los Angeles.

Ramon claimed that his mother was a good mother who valued education, and taught them how to be polite through traditional Mexican customs. He recalled being taught how to greet people when entering a house, as well as to use the Spanish phrases for "How are you," "Thank you," and "Good night." As she raised him, Ramon's mother told him to respect his teachers and his elders, and to be self-sufficient in cleaning the house and cooking for himself, as well as to take responsibility for chores when she wasn't around. In addition, he had a stepfather whom he described as "good." Ramon said that he "worked hard and did everything right." However, in thinking about his upbringing, Ramon said that he didn't value the lessons his parents tried to teach him.

When he was fourteen, Ramon started "hanging out with the wrong crowd" and joined a street gang in Paramount. His ideas of manhood began to be shaped by the street: romantic affairs, drug use, and violence. He said, "I was lost in a world that everybody desires to be a dope dealer, to die high, bro, women, money, cars, and all that stuff." Ramon began selling and using drugs, partying, and getting into fights with other gang members. He held down a job, but as he grew older he developed an addiction to cocaine that escalated.

Ramon held values that were at odds with his behavior, in what David Smilde (2008) has termed "akrasia"; he worried, for instance, what his parents would have thought if they found out he was using drugs. He said, "I'd always think about my mom. . . . You know, 'if my parents only knew what I do' . . . that would always cross through my consciousness." Ramon's guilt over his betrayal of his mother's support led him to feel uneasy and dissatisfied with his lifestyle. He reported,

> At the end . . . all my check was gone and all my money was gone, and my women were gone. And the homeboys and the drugs were gone, guess what, the reality would hit me. This is where you're at, man, bro. And inside of me it will be like "I don't want this no more . . . I could be doing something better."

Although he internalized his parents' values and ambition to succeed in the U.S., Ramon felt helpless in quitting his drug addiction in order to achieve that success. He reported,

> Every time I will get my check, every time I get paid, I would hit drugs again . . . but then when everything was gone . . . I feel . . . full of pain . . . wanting a better future man, wanting change, but really couldn't get myself the support to get that change. . . . I couldn't do it on my own. I tried too many times.

Ramon's mother kicked him out of the house when it became apparent that he was addicted to drugs. At age twenty-one, he spent the last day with his family on Christmas. After he was kicked out of the house and homeless, he called a few numbers for recovery homes. They were all full, except one—Victory Outreach. Although Victory Outreach is a Pentecostal church and Ramon was raised Catholic, he was willing to give it a chance.

Ramon described his first days at Victory Outreach as routine: waking up with several other men at about 5 or 6 a.m., praying for a few minutes, and then having breakfast—he added that the rice and beans back then were not very good. From there, they would go to a worksite, such as a carnival. The men would return at night for dinner, and then have a Bible study at about 9 or 10 p.m.

Although Ramon first entered Victory Outreach not wanting to stay longer than a few months, after eight months he began to lose the urge to leave the home. He thought, "I can't go back and do what I was doing before, getting loaded." Ramon subsequently became a counselor and enjoyed helping others with their addiction problems—a stark contrast considering that never before could he have imagined serving in the capacity of a counselor. He said that he recalled the day he suddenly began preaching inside the home. He was surprised to hear the words that he was using, and said that he felt it was the Holy Ghost speaking through him.

When asked how the Victory Outreach home helped him to quit a life of gangs and drugs, Ramon described the home as a "spiritual boot camp" that enforced rules, taught discipline, and made Christian "soldiers" of gang members and drug addicts. He said that the home forced drug addicts and gang members to work, and taught them that they had responsibilities, such as raising money for the van, for gas, for insurance, and so forth. In addition, working helped members learn how to obey authority. Ramon described the range of activities they did for pay such as working carnivals, unloading containers, washing cars, and cutting down and selling Christmas trees, as well as such "side jobs" as painting or tearing down houses, and disposing of scrap metal. In his view, working through the home taught men how to be disciplined, so that they could keep a job and be self-dependent. He said that the end result after living in the home would be for a man to "go out there and be willing to get a job and support his family, pay his rents, his bills, his car." In addition to work, the discipline of the home taught members "how to manage [their] finances."

Ramon, at twenty-four, was now proud to be a Bible study leader and youth leader in Victory Outreach. He still wore baggy clothes and slightly oversized plaid shirts. He still had a nearly shaven head and spoke with a heavy Chicano cadence. However, he no longer used drugs or saw his old friends. Ironically, he worked a factory job at a company that made spray-paint cans. As previously described, he lived in "reentry," a tiny room in back of the church that he shared with two other members, Chris and Kevin.

Ramon had one son, from a relationship he was in prior to entering recovery, whom he saw a few times a year. While he was in the Victory Outreach men's home, his girlfriend had gotten pregnant by another man and left for Las Vegas with him. When Ramon's ex-girlfriend and son periodically returned to town to visit, Victory Outreach members would accompany Ramon to see his child. This they did to ensure that he was accountable for where he claimed to be, and would not transgress into drugs and gang life. Ramon believed that it was for the best that his ex-girlfriend left him, because, in hindsight, he thought that their relationship was not God's will.

"Being a Man is Hard": Older Members in Gang Recovery

Recovering gang members without leadership positions within recovery often felt more ambivalent about their progress. As described above, older members generously expressed gratitude to their mothers, partners, and children. Men had ambitions to get married and have families, but they also tried to balance these ambitions by following in the footsteps of their organization's leaders and giving back to their communities. Some members were less immersed in the process of recovery, and found it much more difficult to "do" reformed barrio masculinity. Some, such as Sergio, felt the lure of gang life through persisting addictions, and this was enough to trigger episodic transgressions into gang life. Others, such as Ivan, experienced some doubts, but received a great degree of support from their partners, who were involved in recovery and pushed them to stay involved as well.

Sergio, Homeboy Industries, old member

Sergio, an extremely charismatic and bright twenty-five-year-old recovering gang member, had been with Homeboy Industries for fourteen years. Together with Antonio and Mario, Sergio was one of the few Homeboys who had known Father Greg since the early days of the Dolores Mission Church. However, unlike Antonio and Mario, he had persistent problems with substance abuse, and jumped around several jobs at Homeboy Industries following several firings.

At age twelve, Sergio came to the U.S. with his mother. Along the route, he remembered, coyotes (human traffickers) tried to force him and his mother across a river in which they could have drowned. They settled in the Pico-Aliso projects of Boyle Heights, where he had a difficult upbringing and experienced little of what he considered to be a "typical" adolescence. At twelve, he was already driving his mother's car; his mother regularly called, drunk, asking him to pick her up from other men's homes. However, Sergio was still labeled "gifted" in middle school, and said of himself, "I was pretty square and shit until I started hangin' out with the homies in the projects, and I started doin' other shit." He started ditching school as he joined a gang.

Sergio met Father Greg during the time he was in a gang. Once, when Sergio and his friends went to the priest's office, Father Greg asked Sergio, "How can I help you, my son?" From that point forth, Sergio said that he had been involved in some way with Homeboy Industries. At first, he worked for a few hours, cleaning, sweeping, and helping out; for this, he was sometimes paid about twenty dollars for a day's help. Sergio's mother was happy with the fact that Father Greg was involved in her son's life and trying to keep him out of trouble.

Sergio left school after he was sentenced to Juvenile Hall. He did six months during his first sentence, and fifteen months during his second. Reflecting on his teenage years, he felt that he felt he had let his family down. Sergio told me, "I'm not really proud of going to juvenile facilities, going to jail. . . . None of my family was gang members." He said that he felt he got lured in to a life of gangs and drug-selling because he was more concerned with fitting in with the culture on the street. However, he was afraid to leave gang life, afraid that he would be ridiculed and emasculated as a failed gang member. He explained, "I thought that I was supposed to go to the pen continuing with the way I lived, because if I didn't, I was gonna be a bitch, a phony, a fake if I didn't continue to do it."

Sergio's behavior finally changed when he realized he had fallen in with a crowd that had different values than his family. He said that at a pivotal moment he thought to himself, "My family ain't in no gang. I'm not a generation gang member. Just because I live where all the gangs are at don't mean I have to be into a gang." In contrast to his strained relationship with his mother, and his discontent with gang life, Sergio began building a relationship with Father Greg, whom he saw as a "father figure" because he was "there for him."

Father Greg once came to Sergio's assistance when he was seventeen years old, after he got into a fight and was kicked out of his brother's apartment. When Sergio called, Father Greg picked him up—despite the fact that he was on his way out to do mass in Juvenile Hall. According to Sergio, Father Greg taught him how to reflect on his behavior and refrain from violence. He said of Father Greg,

> When I do good, you get that fatherly thing, like, "Good job, my son, I'm proud of you." Like the shit a dad would tell his son. So I think that that, the fact that he's able to help—well, he helped me hold the mirror up to myself and see all my—where I'm wrong, where all the pain, where's all my anger at, all that type of stuff.

Their relationship influenced how Sergio thought of manhood, from being rooted in gang life to nurturing fatherhood. He said, "You know, dog, I can't do that anymore. I can't go back to my gangbanging ways. I can't do that shit. I've got a son. I have a son, man, I'm a single dad." Sergio felt that this commitment meant that there was no chance he would return to gang activity. He continued, "I think that if I would ever go gangbang now, I would probably lose respect for myself. . . . Before anything now, I'm a dad." Praising Father Greg for having changed his ideas about manhood and taught him how to be a nurturing parent, Sergio said, "If I wouldn't have had Father Greg as a father figure in my life, I don't think I would have been able to be a father figure for my son."

Participation at Homeboy Industries, where Sergio had been on-and-off from its inception, also helped shape his ideas about manhood. The day before our interview, he participated in a father's lunch at Homeboy Industries. The men at the fathers' lunch ate, then "did an eagle feather." Everybody passed around an eagle father, and gave advice about fatherhood. At the end of the event, Sergio felt inspired to hear testimonies from men who were separated from their children—but longed to see them. He said that he just wanted to go home and hold his son, Benito.

Around the time of his interview, Sergio had broken up with his ex-girlfriend, and was living with his two-year-old son. Although Sergio and his ex agreed to split custody of their son, she slowly stopped visiting him, until finally Sergio had lost contact with her and not seen her in several months. Tensions grew when Sergio's ex-girlfriend found out that he had a new girlfriend—a waitress from Homegirls' Café. Just before Sergio lost contact with her, Sergio's ex bashed his car's back windshield. Sergio willingly received her when she reappeared in his life, but after visiting she ran out with Benito in an attempt to kidnap him. Sergio managed to pry him away before she could throw him in a running car. In a subsequent incident, Sergio called me—instead of the police—when she became violent outside his house and tried to break in. Sergio was fearful of being apprehended by immigration officials and deported. The last time I heard Sergio mention his ex was when he found out that she had opened a fraudulent case file with the Department of Social Services, getting food stamps through her son though she never visited him.

Despite the hope and ambition he had to be a good father, Sergio did not feel that "being a man" was an easy accomplishment to maintain. His own grasp on the role still felt very tenuous. "Being a man is hard, dog," he said. "It's a daily thing. It's not something that you work on for six months and then you're a man and you're never gonna fuck up as a man."

Sergio faced the obstacles of strained relationships with his family and ex, as well as drug use. He was unable to quit smoking marijuana daily, and then, "while hangin' with the homies," he was introduced to crystal meth, which he was trying to quit when I knew him. Distancing himself from old friends, Sergio asked if I would be willing to invite him along to things that I did and to teach him customs for interacting with "educated people." Sergio told me that he felt he could be fine if he simply surrounded himself with Father Greg, his therapist, his drug sponsor, and me. Sergio said he wanted to go to school, get a degree, work with youth, and have health insurance—a lifestyle he described as "normal."

Reminiscent of Sharon Hays's (2004) work on poor, single mothers, Sergio said he felt like he had to choose between working and being a good father. When I pushed him to think about returning to school in order to improve his career opportunities, he turned the idea down. Gesturing toward his son, he said, "He's everything to me . . . I've got to put him first. Because a lot of things that I want to do, I'm secondary. This is the number one, and I feel bad sometimes." Sergio's problems with his legal status led him to feel that his time was better spent being together with his son than working toward a degree that couldn't offer him better employment. He confessed that he "hated saying that," because he felt that such a statement implied being content with "being mediocre," but said that at the same time he really did want to put aside his selfish desires to be a good single father.

Sergio said that his idea of "being a man" meant being a father first and foremost, as well as creating positive change in the world. But, because he was limited in his ability to get an education and land a good job, he knew that the likelihood of improving his economic situation or creating social change would be unrealistic. Instead, his notion of manhood pivoted on providing those opportunities to his son. He said that he was willing to place his son's needs before his own, and that he wanted his son to succeed and create positive change in the world. Closing our interview, Sergio said, "To me, being a man, dog, is like, trying to . . . understand what life is giving you . . . to do something significant. If I don't do nothing significant that contributes to this world in a positive way, then I want my son to do that."

Ivan, Victory Outreach, old member

Ivan, forty-six, had biological parents who were Native American and white, but looked like he was of Mexican descent. Ivan was adopted at birth by his biological mother's half-sister (who was of Mexican origin), was given a Spanish name and surname, and was raised in a Mexican American community. Ivan's parents sent him to Catholic school so that the neighborhood would not have an influence over him.

However, Ivan started his own gang, smoked marijuana, and got expelled from school by the seventh grade. A year later, he joined what he called "a real gang," a Chicano gang in a barrio south of Los Angeles. He was introduced to PCP and began selling drugs. During our interview, described himself as having grown up a "ghetto kid," becoming a "playboy" on the streets and living his life dangerously.

At the age of twenty-one, Ivan was shot in the chest with a .38-caliber gun. As I interviewed him, he recalled calling out to God and wanting to change his life. Still, he persisted with his lifestyle. Two years later, he saw a Victory Outreach play called *Ese Homie*, to which he related; however, he remained seated during the following altar call because he felt that answering it was an expression of "weakness" for those who "were trying to get out of gang life."

Five years after attending the Victory Outreach play, Ivan stood in a courtroom, facing a five-year sentence in the state penitentiary. However, Victory Outreach members came into the courtroom and asked if he would be willing to "go into a program." Reflecting on this experience, he reasoned that the Victory Outreach members must have planned to meet someone at the courtroom but that the intended person hadn't shown up. Instead he crossed paths with Victory Outreach members by "divine appointment." He subsequently entered the home, and recalled this as the moment when his faith was born. However, after his first graduation from the Victory Outreach men's home, Ivan retreated into gang life and ended up back in prison. After his release, he immediately returned to the Victory Outreach men's home, and he never retreated again into gang life.

Ivan remained committed to the church, through which he eventually met his wife, Lucia, a tall Latina. He claimed that he met her "the proper way." Ivan avoided making eye contact with any women at church, because to do so would break Victory Outreach's social norms. One day, however, a sister approached him and told him that, if he wanted to, he could talk to Lucia after church service. He said that he did, and that they had a good conversation. They subsequently started dating, though with a chaperone present at all times. During his interview, Ivan defended the practice of dating with chaperones. Ivan reasoned that "the flesh is weak" and suggested that unsupervised dates could have led to transgression into gang and drug life. After two years of dating, Sister Lucia and Ivan married.

Embodying a Chicano *veterano*, or veteran of gang life, Ivan wore plaid shirts with nice dress slacks, and sported a thick *brocha* that reached down to his jawline. With his stocky build and standard expressionless demeanor, he looked intimidating. When he took the pulpit at Victory Outreach, however, his demeanor entirely transformed. At weekly Bible study gatherings in his backyard, Ivan drew on powerful Christian symbolism to talk about reforming from gang, drug, and prison life. Once, Ivan enacted walking off to prison with his hands behind his back, and described the experience as "following the devil into a pit of hell." Ivan would exclaim that he had been changed through belief in Jesus, and urged members to similarly follow the "covenant" of their local church leadership.

Despite being committed to the church, and embodying the cha-
risma of a great Victory Outreach leader, Ivan was unable to fulfill his
dream to become a pastor and lead his own church. Stable employment
was a requirement for becoming a pastor. However, he paid his apartment with a Section 8 voucher, and the church wouldn't allow someone
on Section 8 to become a pastor. He lamented that he could only find
employment through sporadic, informal construction projects. In private conversations with me, he occasionally mentioned that he sometimes felt like "throwing in the towel," but that he persisted because he
had faith in God. In front of congregation members, he demonstrated
this resilience by telling members that, as he cleaned toilets, he was
filled with the joy of "the Holy Spirit."

Ivan said his pastor and wife were the main reasons he was still in the
church. He looked up to his pastor, and wanted to follow in his footsteps. However it was his wife who most urged him to remain committed. His wife "pushed," "rebuked," "encouraged," and loved him, and
he felt he would not be where he was without her. The deep commitment that Brother Ivan and Sister Lucia shared with Victory Outreach
became a kinlike bond, one which Ivan described as not only "ministry" but also "family." Soon enough their kin network would expand
through Victory Outreach. Sister Lucia had a daughter from a previous marriage, Cecilia, who was twenty-four years old. Ivan considered
Cecilia his own daughter, and she began attending services a couple
of years before fieldwork for this book began. As fieldwork ended, she
married Rick (as described earlier), and they later had a child.

"I Felt Like I Let Them Down": Newer
Members in Gang Recovery

Newer recovering gang members were, at times, still engaged in
destructive gang activities that were at odds with their broader ambitions to exit gang life. While recovering gang members forged relationships with mothers, partners, and children, and became involved in
their local communities, they also resisted gang life. However, this often
did not occur in a strictly linear fashion. Rather, patterns of gang activity and recovery crisscrossed in various ways. As the preceding vignettes
suggest, the seeds of recovery sometimes grew into and significantly

overlapped with gang life, while at other times no element of gang life (hanging out with gang members, drugs, violence or romantic affairs) appeared after entering recovery.

The following case studies illustrate a third theme: how substance abuse may undermine a deeper immersion into gang recovery. Newer recovering gang members, such as Gerardo and Santiago, struggled to develop a secure sense of masculine identity outside of the gang and alternated between expressions of Chicano gang masculinity and recovered gang masculinity. Neither Gerardo nor Santiago had been members of their organizations for very long when they alternated between gang activity and gang recovery. Both had struggled with strained relationships, unemployment, and self-destructive behavior. These are two cases of men who sought recovery from gang life, but simultaneously engaged facets of Chicano gang masculinity that prevented reorientation away from street life.

Gerardo

Gerardo, a twenty-one-year-old member of Homeboy Industries, came to the U.S. with his mother and younger brother, Victor, when they were two and one years old, respectively. Gerardo also had a fourteen-year-old sister, whom his mother was trying to prevent from becoming involved with the street.

Gerardo's mother worked two jobs, one at night, when she was a single parent caring for him and Victor. Although early in their lives, both Gerardo and Victor were honor students, no one was left at the house to care for Gerardo and Victor. As a result, Gerardo and Victor went out at night unsupervised and ended up associating with other males in the neighborhood. In their early teens, they joined the Playboys, a street gang based in South Los Angeles.

Despite his family's struggles, as an adult, Gerardo held no resentment toward his parents. In fact, when asked who he admired and tried to be like, he said his mother. Much of the respect he had for his mother had been earned through his family's struggles and through the troubles he and his brother had with the law. Gerardo said, "My mom, she's done a lot. She's done a lot for me, for our family. It was like she never gave up on me."

Although Gerardo's biological father tried to come back into his life and be a positive influence, Gerardo had no interest in building a relationship with him. He said, "I never had that dad figure. . . . My dad wanted to come over when I was like thirteen, fourteen. I was already gangbanging you know? It was already too late for that." Gerardo did his first stint in Juvenile Hall soon after, when he was fourteen years old. He served six months in Eastlake, then remained out for eight months before serving another three for violating probation. From that point, he went back and forth between Juvenile Hall and placement several times.

By the time he was eighteen, Gerardo had no interest in immediately returning to the streets, and he volunteered to stay in placement for six months in order to finish receiving a high school diploma. After receiving his diploma, he enrolled in summer school for Los Angeles Trade-Tech and started studying to be an electrician. However, Gerardo eventually went back to the streets. He tried to rob someone, got arrested for armed robbery, and went to prison for two and a half years. After his sentence, he was subsequently deported to Mexico.

Gerardo's mother, Yvette, is now married to a man who plays guitar at the local church. Yvette became more involved with helping out at the church, and dragged Gerardo to a support group at the church. Yvette was hoping that he would become more involved in church, and less involved with the street, but he did not think highly of the experience. He liked only one person in the group, whom he described as "a thug" who "didn't have a dad figure in [his] life" but nonetheless was "trying to do with his son the things that he didn't do with his dad." Because he had a toddler and an infant with his wife, Gerardo was able to relate to this person.

I asked Gerardo where he saw himself in five years, and he responded that he wanted to move up and out of the neighborhood. He didn't like the idea of his son growing up in a gang-infested area or of following in his footsteps. Gerardo said,

> I want to see myself in five years doing good, but with a better job. Like hopefully enrolled in school, doing more studying, something like that. In five years out of my neighborhood where I'm stayin' at now. I want to move. Why? Because of my kids. They're growing up and I don't want 'em to grow up around the same environment I grew up in.

Asked what options he saw available, however, Gerardo commented that he couldn't imagine any because of his legal situation. Construction was one of the only options available, but ideally, he would have preferred to go into the social service field. He said,

> Something about being in social work. My cousin wants to be a psychiatrist, so she's going to school for that. I was thinking about that, [because] I don't want to do construction. . . . If I was born here legally, if I was legit here in the U.S., I would go for that dream. . . . [But] I never heard about somebody that was a counselor that's here illegally.

Gerardo also faced personal obstacles in achieving his ambitions of moving up and out. he mentioned that he kept retreating into attitudes and behaviors that he described as his "old ways," and a "gangster mentality" of "not giving a fuck, doing whatever the fuck you want to do." When I probed, all he said was, "That gangbangin' thing is still in me. It's still livin' in me."

Gerardo felt he was unable to fulfill the demands of manhood either at home or on the street. On the one hand, he was not the patriarch of his family that he expected to be. At times, Yvette checked up on him and would tell his wife, "Don't let him go out." At other times, she would take sides with his wife in an argument. As fights recurred with his wife and mother, Gerardo said he felt an even stronger push to spend time with his gang friends. In addition, he claimed that avoiding the gang would emasculate him, make him look like a "weenie" or "a bitch," and that this would leave him open to harassment and beatings.

Gerardo's solution was to try to hang out with his gang associates in nonviolent ways. He smoked marijuana and drank with friends daily, behaviors that to him seemed benign and not necessary to desist from. He tried to justify hanging around the gang by saying, "I won't put my family in danger, and I won't take my family somewhere where I know that I can't take 'em and they're gonna be in danger, but . . . I still kick it. I still drink with the homies."

Gerardo's strategy toward limited gang involvement was strongly undergirded by notions of manhood. When asked if he still tagged on walls or shot at rivals, he replied, "No, I don't go doing that. That's what little kids do. I'm done with all that. . . . [I meant that] still be in my hood, that I drink. That's what I mean by 'fucking around.'"

Gerardo did see the value in what his mother and wife preached. He told me that he didn't want to be like older gangsters because, they were in their thirties, and

> They ain't got shit now. I try and do something better for myself. "Excuse me, I'm trying to get a job," you know? To have something going for me . . . I'm tryin' to be out of here in five years. I'm not gonna be around my neighborhood.

However, Gerardo's justification for hanging out with gang friends rested upon his assumptions that he felt he was much more mature and in control of self-destructive behaviors now. He said,

> I think about things twice. Say if I want to go fuck around, just for example, if I want to go tagging or go shoot somebody or go fuck around, I think about it twice, because my mom and my wife.

At first, I believed Gerardo was capable of navigating the social terrain between street and domestic life. However, I began to doubt the viability of his attempts to remain only peripherally engaged in the street without placing himself or his family in harm's way. Months after our interview, an accident occurred that tempted him to become active with his gang.

While Gerardo was in a grocery store, an enemy gang member spotted him and followed him out onto the street. As he raced away on his bike, the gang member chased after on foot, shooting hollow-tip bullets, which explode on impact. Gerardo was shot in his leg, but managed to get away. When I visited him, he was wheelchair-bound with his leg in a full cast—but he was lucky. Had the bullet hit his bone or any major arteries, he could have lost his leg. Had he been hit in a vital organ, he could have died.

As I inquired about the incident, it became apparent that Gerardo was contemplating taking revenge for having been shot. When I visited him at home, he was happy to see me and have me sign his cast. Worried about his well-being, and that of anyone else that might fall

victim to another shooting if a radical intervention was not successfully attempted, I asked if he would allow me to take him to a Victory
Outreach Bible study. I explained that there would be no chance of him
running into enemies, and he agreed. The next week I drove him to a
small Bible study at a member's home in East Los Angeles.

The day of the Bible study, I walked into the apartment with Gerardo
as he hobbled on crutches. There, members took the time to meet him,
get to know him, and let him know that they too had experienced gang
violence. They told him that it was possible to leave gang life, and that
they had done so through their faith. During the Bible study, he sat quietly, listening to Brother Ivan's lesson on repenting and forgiveness, as
Ivan used call-and-response to engage the church members. The gathering, as usual, seemed more to me like an opportunity for the Bible
study leader to play the part of pastor and deliver a mini-sermon than a
true democratic discussion.

As the sermon ended, Brother Ivan asked if anyone wanted to be
prayed for. Gerardo, to my surprise, quietly volunteered when all fell
silent. As Brother Ivan turned to him and got on one knee, he asked
Gerardo if he was willing to accept Jesus, and Gerardo said yes. Three
members gathered around Brother Ivan as he laid hands on Gerardo,
and they prayed passionately, in stream-of-thought prayers. Brother
Ivan then succeeded in getting Gerardo to repeat the "Sinner's Prayer"
after him. When they finished, the congregants invited Gerardo to their
church, but he seemed hesitant. However, when we got back into my
car, he seemed to be in a state of serene peace, and asked if I thought
that God could forgive all of someone's sins.

Months later I had lunch with Gerardo, and found out that he was still
struggling with the same issues. He was still trying to distance himself
from the gang without being called "a bitch" and risking a beating. He was
still trying to build a good relationship with his three-year-old son's teacher
and counselor. He was still trying to get rehired at Homeboy Industries.
He was still using some drugs and hanging out with his old gang.

Santiago, Victory Outreach, new member

When I looked at Santiago, I felt like I was almost looking at a reflection of myself. Despite the tear drop tattoo beside his eye, he was about

five-foot-nine, had a thin frame, and hailed from west-central Mexico. Santiago's parents were from Tepic, Nayarit, and they had brought him to the U.S. when he was three years old. They settled in South Los Angeles, where his father became pastor of a church. Santiago's father was the first to receive permanent residence, and then he arranged for the whole family to receive legal residence. However, his father eventually abandoned his family and divorced his mother, and he grew up exposed to the influences of the street.

Santiago was a successful boxer. He was undefeated, with several knockouts. However, he was also running with South Los Angeles's 38th Street gang, one of the region's oldest and most notorious gangs, implicated in the Zoot Suit Riots of 1942. Before his arrival at Victory Outreach, he had been in and out of jail for drug or weapons possession most of his life.

At age twenty-four, Santiago went walking down an Eastside street, looking for a rival gang member he wanted to kill, when a Victory Outreach–Eastside member greeted him outside the church and asked him if he had "God in his heart." Santiago didn't want to talk to them because he was carrying a gun. But Victory Outreach members offered him food. He was hungry and high on drugs, so he walked inside.

Santiago recounted his first impression of Victory Outreach to me: the men were "sissies" because they were "all gang members and now they're turning their back on their neighborhood. What kind of gang members are these guys?" As a result, he said, he was ambivalent about attending Victory Outreach. In addition, while he was looking for a positive change in his life, he thought that he could not improve his life through Victory Outreach. He recalled thinking, "These guys can't teach me nothing. These guys are the same as me."

However, one thought did weigh heavily as Santiago deliberated attending Victory Outreach: he felt shunned by other churches that would "judge" his tattoos or his appearance, and would not accept him with open arms. So he gradually accepted Victory Outreach members' invitations to attend worship services and fellowship events. He soon became more closely involved with the organization, helping out, cleaning, and setting up food.

For the first two years, Santiago's involvement in Victory Outreach was back and forth between the church and the gang. In our interview, he said he felt guilty being involved with gang activity—but that he didn't change because he was not truly "seeking God." He told me he wanted to attend services and feel the presence of God, but at the same time, he did not want to let the church or his faith reform his behavior.

Soon after he began to attend Victory Outreach, Santiago found out that he had developed a blood clot and was forced to retire. He managed to find good work thereafter with the Edison electric company, for $25 an hour. He was employed there for a year and a half before his personal life began to unravel.

Santiago continued to use drugs and drink, which eventually led to the loss of his job. In turn, his wife left him and wanted to take his daughter away completely. He lost the desire to live. At age twenty-six, he attempted to overdose on "three eightballs" of crack cocaine and two bottles of tequila. When the overdose failed, he pulled out his 9mm handgun and tried to shoot himself. The gun jammed. After a desperate search for alternatives, he climbed up a two-hundred-foot-high bridge and jumped. The fall from the bridge shattered many of his bones and cracked his head open, but, amazingly, he survived.

Santiago was taken to an emergency room, where he was in surgery for eleven hours and in a coma for two weeks. The accounts of the surgery sounded horrific to me. Doctors had to cut open his wrists and knee to vacuum out bone fragment. They gave him a knee implant, replaced his jaw with metal, and planted screws in his head. He spent about seven months in the hospital before he was allowed to leave.

Despite the amazing recovery, Santiago was too embarrassed to head back to Victory Outreach. "I felt embarrassed going to Victory Outreach, because I felt like I let them down." Instead, along with his wife, he began attending a Christian training center in a nearby suburb, which he described as a "Christian boot camp." The couple returned to Victory Outreach after he graduated from the other church's men's home.

After his return, he joined Victory Outreach's men's home, where he was at the time of his interview. This time, he said he was making great strides to leave street life behind. Unlike the first time he attended Victory Outreach, he claimed that this time he was searching for God. And, this time, he claimed that they were successfully instilling discipline in his life. Quoting to me from the Book of Matthew, he said that he was finally learning about having a "heart of wisdom" at Victory Outreach. Also, for the first time, he called his mother on Mother's Day.

Santiago said he was motivated by the prospect of becoming more involved in the church, and by preaching to persons through the prison ministry. he explained, "I'm tired of going back to the same environment. I'm tired of being that nobody. Now I could become a somebody and help somebody." After a few months of sobriety, and encouraged by the changes they finally saw happening in his life, Victory Outreach leaders were enthusiastic about sharing his testimony with others.

When I asked if Victory Outreach was ever a part of his life, Santiago said that they were more than just a part. He considered Victory Outreach members "family" and felt that the kin relationship he shared with them was founded upon their ability to teach him how to be a "better man, and a better person." In particular, he saw Brother Alex as a father figure, and his wife Sister Josefina, as a mother figure. Through having household-type responsibilities at Victory Outreach, and through living in the men's home, they reformulated his notions of manhood from being rooted in the street to being rooted in the household and church. Santiago said of Brother Alex and Sister Josefina,

> They helped me be the man of the house, not the drug addict of the house. They helped me to be the father for my daughter, the husband for my wife, and to be that son for my mom that she always wanted to have. Instead of being the black sheep, I was being an example for my little brothers.

After his long spiritual journey through Victory Outreach, Santiago said he had finally achieved what was expected of all members, to accept "God's will." Asked where he saw himself in the next five years, he said he wanted to be "with my wife, my house, my daughter. . . . Bein' in a ministry, having my own church, having my own men's home, [or] having my own youth home . . . I see myself teaching and going to school." However, in reflecting upon his response, he voiced the concern that it might not be the best situation to be reunited with his family and said that he was open to accepting an alternative if it was God's will.

Conclusion

The cases of eight leaders and members of Homeboy Industries and Victory Outreach presented above illustrate the description of behaviors that were common across all of my interviews with recovering gang members. As they distanced themselves from gang life, they attempted to build companionate relationships with their partners and better relationships with their mothers and children. In addition, recovering gang members admired and looked up to their leaders, and hoped to follow in their footsteps by giving back to their communities.

Men who had been in recovery for at least three years were more likely to mention companionate aspects of relationships with their partners or spouses when asked where they saw themselves in five years. This trend toward companionate relationships is one of the legacies of feminism, even in mainstream institutions such as the evangelical church (Stacey 1990). However, these companionate, romantic relationships were not necessarily egalitarian. Men at Victory Outreach more often expressed wanting to be "where the Lord takes me," and men at Homeboy Industries expressed wanting to "give back to the community" in ways that downplayed women's ambitions and elevated men's status in the public sphere.

Respondents reported admiring and trying to be like persons who endorsed or espoused positive expressions of masculinity. This included family members (usually one's mother), leaders from their organization, or historical figures. Men often admired persons they knew who gave to or provided for family members—and usually these were women. But men also admired how their organization's leaders gave to the community. Men who had been in recovery for at least three years often mentioned admiring men who were leaders in their organization because of their community work. Several recovering gang members at Homeboy Industries mentioned that they admired Father Greg for demonstrating unconditional love and helping inner-city residents, and these men in particular talked about giving back to the community. Much the same held true for recovering gang members at Victory Outreach, who often talked about Pastor Raul and about wanting to become a pastor at a new church. Significantly, when asked these two questions, not one respondent made reference to any member of his gang, or any aspect of gang life—even though some were often still tangled in gang life through violence or substance abuse.

How does the construction of manhood in recovery mirror broader trends observed among American men in religion and society? We can draw lessons from two examples of social and economic change in the U.S., which have at times shifted the balance of power between men and women or challenged the structure of patriarchy. As Michael Kimmel noted in *Manhood in America*, during the Victorian Era, industrialization, modernization, and the gendered division of labor helped to expand American women's influence from homes to schools, churches, and civic groups. Men reacted to what they perceived as the feminization of traditionally masculine social spheres by retreating in order to retain privilege. They reconstituted hegemonic masculinity through fraternities, homosocial men's groups, and displays of "muscular Christianity" (Kimmel 1996; Messner 1997). A second example can be drawn from the 1960s, when the feminist movement helped to increase women's labor force participation, and deindustrialization eroded men's grasp on manufacturing employment. Judith Stacey (1990) noted that as evangelical women became influenced by the feminist movement and began to demand egalitarian relationships, the evangelical church adapted by absorbing some changes and insulating itself from many others; for instance, while the church successfully negotiated the character of marriage from corporate to romantic, it affirmed patriarchy through the idea of marriage as a male-headed institution.

Similar to women's gendered negotiations in sub-Saharan Africa or the Middle East, U.S. women's negotiation of a "patriarchal bargain" rests upon access to the means of production (Kandiyoti 1987; Stacey 1990). However, the patriarchal bargain found among recovering Chicano gang members had a different point of departure. Whereas men in Kandiyoti's patriarchal bargain had more access to production than women did, a case could be made that many Chicano recovering gang members have less access to formal employment than their partners. As observed above, many Chicano gang members have limited education, little job experience, criminal records, and substance abuse problems.

Chicano men in gang recovery used civic and religious engagement to claim a sense of privilege in the public sphere after shedding gang masculinity. For example, through Pentecostal recovery from gang life,

Rick adopted masculine expressions with institutionalized privileges. As a ministry leader, he hoped to one day become pastor of a church and expected to marry a Christian woman who would allow him to act as head of the household. He talked about meeting a Christian woman who would help him "fulfill his calling." "Giving back to the community" was, on the one hand, a way to exit gangs and reintegrate into the community. On the other hand, it seemed to be a strategic sacrifice. Evangelical groups have often reformulated masculinity in ways that construct men as subservient to God, yet allow them the opportunity to retain the title of head of the household (Stacey 1990; Messner 1997; Heath 2003). Recovering gang members were willing to take up an offer to reform their masculine expressions, so long as it conferred privileges in the domestic and/or public sphere.

Michael Messner, citing the example of the Promise Keepers movement, has suggested that some faith-based men's movements organize for a "new patriarchal bargain" (1997, 34). Men shed what Messner terms the "costs of masculinity" in the new bargain, trading self-destructive behavior for household responsibilities (1997, 19). Many men, according to him, fear the dominant idea that "[r]eal men deal with their own hurt and doubts through destructive and self-destructive practices, such as drinking too much alcohol, taking other drugs, and/or multiple sexual conquests of women" (Messner 1997, 34). Unwilling to pay such high costs of masculinity, men in faith-based movements may reformulate masculinity insofar as it allows them to become household patriarchs (Messner 1997; Heath 2003). In Messner's words, "What a relief it is for many of these men to learn that a real man is simply one who faithfully keeps his promises to be a responsible husband, father, and family breadwinner" (1997, 34).

Similar to white men's faith-based movements, men in gang recovery often expressed weariness over the costs of gang masculinity: drug addiction, violence, incarceration, financial instability, and strained family relationships. Recovering gang members shared an overwhelming sense of self-loathing for having participated in gang activity; they lamented having had poor relationships with their mothers, partners, and children, and wanted to mend these relationships. They desired the self-respect and privilege that they perceived came with reintegration into the household and the public sphere. Recovering gang members sought to trade in the costs of gang masculinity for the privileges associated with conventional expressions of masculinity. In a localized adaptation of the patriarchal bargain, Chicano men used gang recovery to shed the costs of machista-oriented gang life for the privileges of macho, patriarchal domesticity.

The next chapter focuses more closely on the construction of reformed barrio masculinity, examining the articulation of conventional masculine expressions and the rearticulation of Chicano gang masculinity within the site of gang recovery. As Maruna (2001) has argued, the reformation of criminal behavior is not accomplished on one's own but through negotiations in social interaction. Likewise, reformed barrio masculinity is not accomplished through one's own accord, but through interactions within the space of gang recovery.

5

Masculinity and the Podium

Discourse in Gang Recovery

"I want you to walk away knowing what empathy is today," announced Alfredo, a bearded, late-twenties ex–gang member, in a soft voice. Homeboy Industries' Anger Management class had just begun. A few Homeboys and Homegirls trickled in late, joining about a dozen others who sat behind tables arranged in a large square. This chaos was generally reflective of classes at Homeboy Industries. Alfredo, the moderator of Anger Management, stood at the end of the circle with a hand on some manila folders. Previously joking and flirting, the class participants fell silent once he started to talk. "Empathy means to put yourself in someone else's place," he explained.

Alfredo set the two ground rules of the class: everything had to be kept confidential, and everyone's opinion needed to be respected. One final Homeboy walked in, interrupting him. Alfredo chastised the Homeboy for being late, but continued with the ground rules, confessing that he was not above the frustrations of group therapy. He then made a comment that suggested that the style of public talk in recovery had reshaped his ideas of manhood. He confessed, "Me . . . I've been called names, I wanted to walk out. . . . Sometimes it takes a better man to walk away." Alfredo urged the class participants to submit to his authority as a leader in the organization. Inviting them to follow a similar path of recovery, he said, "This is a starting point, Homeboy Industries."

Alfredo started with "check-ins," asking Homeboys about their weekend. He stood over the one nearest to him, who was slouching in his seat. The Homeboy said in a hasty voice, "My mom's been tripping lately." Alfredo paused for a moment and then honed in, asking in his soft voice, "Okay, why do you think that is, dawg?" The Homeboy shrugged and simply replied, "I dunno." Alfredo, tapping his folders on the table and kindly urging the Homeboy to think about his problem, asked, "Empathy, big dawg, what does it mean?" The Homeboy answered, "To put myself in someone else's place." He continued to talk, but about a sickness in his family, how his mother took on the burden, and how he believed that's why she was upset lately more than usual. Alfredo listened attentively, without making any remarks; then, once the long story had ended, he slowly, calmly worked his way down the room.

Ruben, a recovered gang member in his mid-twenties and the survivor of a gunshot wound to the head, sat in his motorized wheelchair wearing a Los Angeles Dodgers hat to hide his scar and thick, clear glasses. Short of breath and speaking in terse sentences, he revealed that his uncle had passed away. Ruben said he thought it was wrong that his uncle's wife had left her kids behind in the U.S. to go to the funeral. Alfredo mediated the somber tone of Ruben's check-in, kindly asking questions such as, "Where are the kids staying?" Nonetheless, Ruben's tone became increasingly negative, until he finally questioned why he was even participating in group therapy. "I got hit in the head with a .357 and lived. I dunno why I'm still here," he said, tearing up. Alfredo then performed a courageous gesture. Guided by the "tragic optimism" of ex–offenders' redemption scripts (Maruna 2001, 11), he placed a hand on Ruben and, for the whole group to hear, assured him, "Naw, you're here for a reason, dawg. When you share your story, dawg, you're fulfilling it, dawg." According to Maruna, career criminals who have maintained desistance from crime often frame their past as a necessary precursor to a later path of redemption—one that has led them to help others. Alfredo's tender interaction with Ruben demonstrated such tragic optimism.

Following his bittersweet exchange with Ruben, Alfredo shared an emotional story of his own: this week was the three-year anniversary of his brother's death. Although his' brother had not been a gang member, in a paranoid delusion a drugged gang member fatally shot him. Alfredo regretted his previous gang activity, lamenting, "Karma came back and bit me in the ass. I never thought it would happen to my brother." But his story had a different spin than the usual tragic tale of an innocent life lost to gang violence. He said that he had seen his brother's murderer cry and confess on the witness stand, declaring that he didn't care how many years he got in prison—he just wanted Alfredo's family to forgive him. In a trembling voice, Alfredo said that he wanted to live without resentment; he wanted to write the murderer a letter and tell him that he forgave him.

Alfredo framed experiences through tragic optimism to create group communication dynamics distinct from those on the street, though they drew from street interaction modes. For the rest of the Anger Management class, he led readings on facial expressions and body language, and members clearly related to the examples Alfredo illustrated his lecture with. When he discussed how gang members' exaggerated, threatening stares (i.e., "mad-dogging") could lead to violence, members chimed in. When he dryly noted that one text's suggestion that the reader listen to opera music wouldn't work for him, members laughed along with him. Alfredo's ability to relate to the class participants' lives allowed him to take effortless command of the class. The use of tragic optimism to put a positive spin on negative events created an inclusive environment that not only welcomed gang members, but also invited the discursive possibility of reform.

Reform from gang life is not an individual effort, but is rather negotiated through social interaction. In his study of career criminals who maintained desistance, Maruna argued that reform was negotiated through "looking-glass rehabilitation" (2001, 158); in order to experience reform, ex-offenders needed to know they were seen as reformed. However, Maruna also found that employment was precarious for persons with records, and that, as a result, ex-offenders often used volunteering or therapy to carry out generativity (see chapter 4). Similar to how marijuana users learn to experience a high, ex-offenders with more experience desisting from crime helped newly desisting ex-offenders by relating to their frustrations and interpreting experiences in ways that helped to maintain desistance. Alfredo's use of tragic optimism, in helping Ruben cope with his burden and in sharing his own testimony, framed some of the struggles of recovery from gang life—trauma and emotional pain—in ways that upheld nurturing as opposed to violent expressions of manhood. Gang recovery provided the space that allowed for acts of generativity that maintained desistance from street gangs and validated members as being reformed.

Dwight Conquergood has convincingly made the argument that, deeply rooted in intracommunal communication, gangs are "preeminently a communication phenomenon" (1994, 52). The importance of generativity to the space of gang recovery, as demonstrated by Alfredo's use of tragic optimism in reinterpreting traumatic events in members' lives, suggests that gang recovery is also a communication phenomenon. Gang communication, as deviance, is "an adaptive response . . . against dominant spaces and structures of exclusion and oppression," ideologically challenging bourgeois individualism (Conquergood 1994, 52). Similarly, as described in chapter 3, gang recovery also allows members to experience reform—and to be seen as reformed—while using communication to collectively foreground issues of racism, poverty, and inequality.

The previous chapter examined how reformed barrio masculinity was central to exit from gang life; this chapter probes deeper into how this gendered redemption sequence operates as a discursive process. Gang recovery programs, through the spaces they provide for public talk, centrally negotiate masculinity and facilitate reform. Public talk in gang recovery reformulates Chicano gang masculinity into warm, nurturing expressions, by affirming it as well as by negotiating it. Leaders such as Alfredo used the word "dawg," and other Chicano slang, to gain members' respect and to take command of the class. In addition, leaders in gang recovery used talk to negotiate Chicano masculine expressions. In the Anger Management class, Alfredo drew from the model of group therapy and used "check-ins" to facilitate interactions with recovering gang members. He inquired about recovering gang members' personal lives and encouraged them to talk about family and to feel "empathy" for family members. This discourse enabled him to shift the focal point of Chicano gang manhood from the streets to the household and family. Thus, although Alfredo's use of the word "dawg" helped to affirm Chicano masculinity as characterized by street style, it also negotiated the meaning of Chicano masculinity to encompass nurturing and household-oriented behavior. These negotiated meanings helped to distance men from the street and reintegrate them into the household.

Shame and Reintegration

Under the rubrics of "recovery," "restoration," and "rehabilitation," social programs have emerged as a significant force in facilitating exit from gang life. In religious settings, such as Pentecostal churches (Brenneman 2011; León 1998; Sanchez-Walsh 2003; Smilde 2007), recovery is often promoted through spiritual restoration. In secular settings, recovery often operates under a broad umbrella of state-sponsored recovery programs, such as clinical rehabilitation, twelve-step programs, and recovery homes (Bourgois 2009; Carr 2010; Fairbanks 2009; Haney 2010). However, not much is known about how programs for gang exit work, and even less is known about how these programs engage masculine expressions deeply embedded in men's personas. As suggested in the preceding chapter, Chicano gang members are structurally blocked from resources necessary to display conventional markers of manhood, such as stable work, which has historically induced maturation from gang life. These structural obstacles stymie the reformulation of Chicano masculinity and the path of gang exit.

Despite the structural obstacles created by racism and poverty, recent research has suggested that persons with long rap sheets can desist from crime through positive processes of shaming and social reintegration (Braithwaite 1989; Brenneman 2011; Hagan and McCarthy 1997; Rios 2011). Braithwaite (1989) theorized that contexts which allow "rituals of reacceptance and reabsorption" following disapproval produce reintegration and reduce deviant behavior (Hagan and McCarthy 1997, 181). On the other hand, in contexts where no rituals for reacceptance followed deviant behavior, stigmatization is relentless, reintegration does not occur, and deviant behavior is more likely to continue (Braithwaite 1989; Hagan and McCarthy 1997). Most central to this perspective is how actors from mainstream institutions engage in and produce permanent stigmatization and alienation of gang members, and how community-level groups that reach out to gang members may allow them to learn, make amends, and become socially reintegrated (Brenneman 2011; Hagan and McCarthy 1997; Rios 2011). This conceptual framework of reintegrative and disintegrative shaming has been adopted to frame the Chicano or Latin American experience with gangs, masculinity, and recovery from gang life (Brenneman 2011; Rios 2011).

Bob Brenneman (2011), in a study of Pentecostal- and Jesuit-based programs, found that gang recovery hinged on reintegrative shaming. Pentecostal groups allowed men to publicly cry, challenging the dominant status of hypermasculinity, and built bonds between shamed recovering gang members and sympathetic church members. This type of shaming distanced recovering gang members from their gangs and allowed them opportunities to build trust in other contexts. Brenneman's research suggested that Pentecostal programs institutionalized processes of shaming much more than Jesuit programs, which placed less emphasis on religiosity. In addition, Victor Rios (2011) has proposed that reintegrative shaming can be effective in reforming gang members' hypermasculine delinquent behavior. Finding that mainstream institutions (i.e., education, corrections, jail) facilitated disintegrative shaming through a school-to-prison pipeline, he suggested that community-level organizations had the potential to facilitate reintegrative shaming.[1]

Shaming Masculine Gang Behavior through "the Podium"

Both Homeboy Industries and Victory Outreach conceptualized the problem of gang activity in the same way, as a pathological masculinity grounded in addictive and destructive behavior. Leaders used public talk to encourage verbal testimonies that involved transgression, guilt, and for those who had begun to experience recovery, salvation. Such talk articulated conventional expressions of manhood, such as working, providing for a family, and being affectionate, and rearticulated the ideals of Chicano masculinity, distancing it from violent, self-destructive gang masculinity. Both programs constructed reformed barrio masculinity by distancing themselves from gang masculinity and aligning themselves with hegemonic masculinity. The accessible manner of such performances allowed any member to learn how to craft an appropriate testimony and to perform it as such evidence of reform.

In one of the few ethnographies of men in recovery, a study of an Alcoholics Anonymous group in Mexico City, anthropologist Stanley Brandes (2003) found that public talk shaped recovery through reformulation of masculinity as well as latent religiosity. Much of the therapeutic work in the group centered on talk performed through use of the "podium," a platform for public speaking. Through the podium, men redefined manhood from being rooted in drinking culture to domesticity. Such public talk negotiated traditional notions of masculinity. Men communicated that they wanted egalitarian relationships with their significant others, elevating their spouse's status by referring to them as "partners" instead of wives and relinquishing absolute authority at home. Furthermore, through the podium, men renounced alcohol use, shared their private struggles, and created "a space in which the expression of regret is interpreted as strength rather than weakness" (Brandes 2003, 163).

Similarly, gang recovery also offered a podium: spaces for public talk where sharing regrets over gang life or concerns related to family could be reinterpreted as strength. Interactions such as Alfredo's "check-ins" or his testimony as class moderator elevated warm and nurturing behavior over violence, aggression, and toughness. However, the podium can also be used to affirm traditional masculinity through stories laden with uncontrollable sexual activity, violent defense of honor, or cursing (Brandes 2003). Homeboy Industries and Victory Outreach members affirmed some traditional notions of Chicano masculinity through the podium at the same time that they used it to affirm nurturing behavior.

Though the topics brought up at the podium were very similar, Homeboy Industries and Victory Outreach employed radically different forms of verbal communication to create the space of the podium. As previously described, social interactions at Victory Outreach were overtly spiritual and effervescent, while those at Homeboy Industries were much more secular in nature. At Homeboy Industries, the podium was created through sermons, class lectures, moderated group therapy discussions, and testimonies. Men in Homeboy Industries attended

Criminal and Gang Members Anonymous, group therapy classes like Anger Management and Relapse Prevention, and spirituality classes such as Yoga and Spreading Seeds. At Victory Outreach, leaders used sermons at church services, informal Bible studies, or evangelism on street corners. Discussion leaders at each organization nurtured men who gave testimonies, and each encouraged displays of nurturing behavior. Nonetheless, they both reflected the mix of spiritual and secular concerns observed in the AA movement. Both sites exercised many of the prescriptions and proscriptions of verbal communication in AA: putting the recovery group ahead of self-interests, admitting powerlessness, practicing humility and kindness, frequently attending meetings, telling one's story, and not allowing "cross-talk" during testimony (Hoffmann 2006, 675). It was in this space of public talk and the podium that Homeboy Industries and Victory Outreach did the critical work of gang recovery.

Men of God: Victory Outreach's "Restoration" Model

Victory Outreach drew upon the Pentecostal church's "spiritual restoration" model of recovery, emphasizing redemption through the ecstatic, collective worship of being "set free." The tradition has roots in late-nineteenth-century America among Christians who sought to replace what they saw as an overreliance on Scripture with a more experiential expression of faith—baptism in the Holy Spirit. Pentecostal worship services involve public testimonials that relate past sins and the experience of redemption to biblical parables. Congregations often adopt the "call-and-response" mode: pastors call out to their flocks in the pews, who respond with enthusiastic shouts and exclamations. By 2000 there were 250 million Pentecostal adherents worldwide, with rapidly growing numbers in the global South, many of them attracted both to charismatic forms of worship and the array of Pentecostal social ministries (Miller and Yamamori 2007). Pentecostalism has made big inroads with Latinos, both in Latin America and in the United States, often taking root in the poorest urban neighborhoods (Sanchez-Walsh 2003). Storefront Pentecostal churches serving "socially and culturally homophilous" congregations of marginalized Latino immigrants have been successful in converting formerly Catholic Latinos, fueled by the promise of spiritual redemption and the amelioration of economic marginality (Stohlman 2007, 62). In the U.S. and abroad, Pentecostal churches have facilitated gang exit (León 1998; Sanchez-Walsh 2003; Vásquez, Marquardt and Gómez 2003; Vigil 1982; Wolseth 2010).

A typical Victory Outreach–Eastside Sunday service opened with forty-five minutes of "praise worship," in which members clapped and danced to church music. The sound blared out onto the major street where the chapter was located. Recovering gang members from the men's home wore orange "Security Guard" vests, and warmly greeted church members as they walked in well-dressed and with Bibles—but especially those recovering gang members who could easily exchange familiar, elaborate handshakes and hugs. The music oscillated between upbeat catchy "praise choruses" and slower, melodic hymns, as congregation members sang and swayed. Many in the pews lifted their arms and mumbled improvised, stream-of-thought prayers. Aside from singing, dancing, and clapping, members of Victory Outreach also sometimes spoke in tongues. Church leaders drew upon the energy of this collective effervescence in their sermons, which often focused on the tragedies of gang life, drug addiction, and alcoholism. Leaders and staff members frequently asserted that attendance at services was key to the Christian project of recovery, which they referred to as "spiritual restoration."

Victory Outreach practices employed forms of communication that were oratory rather than conversational, using sermons, testimonies, and Bible study classes. They shamed recovering gang members by casting marginalized, drug-addicted, drug-selling men as inferior and subordinate to church-going, family-oriented breadwinners. Most Victory Outreach members spent a lot of time sitting in the pews as the pastor spoke, but the ritualistic communicative form was much like the "call-and-response" verbal repertoire found in many black churches. After a statement from the pastor, the Chicano attendees in the pews regularly shouted out affirmative and enthusiastic exclamations such as "Amen"; "Woo!"; "C'mon now, bring it!"; "That's right, tell it Pastor!"; "Hallelujah"; and "Praise the Lord." They clapped, cheered, stood up immediately, lifted one hand for several seconds, or "raised the roof"—motioning with two palms pulsing upward as if to push the ceiling. In addition, certain remarks explicitly asserted the hierarchical and oratory nature

Figure 5.1. A testimony at a Victory Outreach fellowship event (courtesy of Victory Outreach)

of sermons and testimonies, and compelled members of the congregation to respond with heightened enthusiasm. If Pastor Raul thought that the congregation was not being sufficiently participatory or loud, he would shout, "Can I hear an 'Amen'?" Tapping the microphone, he would rhetorically ask, "Is this thing on?" Gang masculinity was cast as subordinate through such communication, as gang members in the congregation had no institutional means by which to resist the call-and-response interactions mocking gang life, or the pastor's performances of recovered gang masculinity as a dominant masculinity.

Victory Outreach leaders larded sermons and testimonies with religious parables and symbolism. After the musical introduction, Pastor Raul, or another speaker with a gang background, would deliver a sermon from the podium or request congregation members to testify how they had been "set free" from violence and addiction. The main speaker was always male and well-dressed in a suit and tie, and always presented himself as a family-oriented "man of God." These leaders portrayed gang members in gendered ways (hypersexualized and violent gang members vs. nurturing mothers or fathers), and described them as being "in the stronghold of the devil." They scorned the images and behaviors associated with gang masculinity, and often satirically and dramatically performed Chicano gang masculinity, drawing examples from Chicano culture and slang, such as calling guns, drugs, and barrio characters, "*chuco*," "*feo*," "*lenio*," and "*quete*." While these parodies of Chicano gang life were jabs at older members' histories, they were also criticisms of newer members. As older members casually laughed, younger members sat attentive and quiet, reluctant to voice dissent in the public space of recovery.

Pastor Raul, as well as the half-dozen Bible study leaders, embodied the masculine transformation of recovery. They were former gang members, with testimonies of several prison stints or lengthy rap sheets, who shamed their previous gang behavior and resistance to reform. They spoke of the problems of drug addiction, violence, and family separation, and urged members to "submit to the Lord," rather than to be "prideful." They insisted that God wants to "see you broken" (i.e., crying), "touch your heart," "heal you," and ultimately "build you up" as a leader in the church's patriarchal hierarchy.

In one sermon, Pastor Raul drew from Scripture, an experience with a pit bull (a dog that is popular among Chicano gangs and barrios), and a contemporary Christian book (Kenneth and Jeffrey Gangel's *Fathering Like the Father: Becoming the Dad God Wants You to Be*) to verbally convey the masculine transformations of recovery in desirable terms. He began by citing Matthew 7:24 and proclaimed, "Those who believe in God are like the wise man who built his house on a rock. Those who don't believe are like the foolish man who built his house on sand." The congregation nodded and murmured in affirmation. He then bellowed that there had just been a three-day storm, with accidents followed by blaring sirens and howling from his pit bull. He declared that there were also other storms we would weather in life: affliction, problems, pain, loss, and abandonment. He urged the congregation to "stand, survive, and thrive in the storm with God," because, "in the Scripture, the house is symbolic for life. There are things like layoffs, death, and sickness in the family." He called on congregants to go to church services, Bible study, and VETI classes. He spoke directly to the men, exhorting them to "invest in a Christian book . . . learn how to be a good Christian husband or parent." In this sermon, as in others, Pastor Raul wove examples from barrio life and biblical scripture to advocate a notion of manhood as strong, yet nurturing.

Lessons taught through Victory Outreach sermons almost always related to family, work, and interpersonal behavior, but no topic received as much attention as the ideal of responsible fatherhood. Many Chicano gang members have fathered children while still in their teens, and Pastor Raul regularly lambasted the "epidemic of missing fathers" in America. In one sermon, he drew from a quote from the diary of one of the sons of President John Quincy Adams to preach that men should become significant figures in their children's lives. Pastor Raul pointed out that, in his diary, Charles Francis Adams—who served as the chief American diplomat to Great Britain—wrote, "Went fishing with my son today—a day wasted." He proclaimed, however, that Henry Brooks Adams wrote in his diary, "Went fishing with my father—the most wonderful day of my life." As the pastor preached about fathers' responsibility to provide guidance and comfort, members from the congregation responded affirmatively with, "C'mon now," and several men clapped especially loud. The pastor then showed a video clip through the projector, introducing it with the assertion that this is "how a father should be." As the lights came down, a clip rolled of the 1992 Olympics in Barcelona, in which Derek Redmond ripped his hamstring during the 400-meter semifinal. Christian hard rock blasted through the church speakers as the church members saw Redmond's father come to his side and help carry him, crying, to the finish line. As the clip finished, the pastor again addressed the congregation. Weeping, the pastor said that although he and his wife had experienced struggles with raising a family, they were able to lean on God "as a father." The pastor announced an altar call, the sound system played a soft song, and congregants gathered at the foot of the stage to worship, embracing each other. The quote from Henry Brooks Adams's diary, the clip of Derek Redmond, and Pastor Raul's testimony provided both visual and verbal celebrations in which men learned how to associate masculinity with nurturance, healing, and strength. It was common at church services to see tattooed, overweight men with shaved heads and gang clothing touching, embracing, or whispering affectionate words in each other's ears.

Although verbal communication often cast gang members as inferior and subordinate to church-going, family-oriented male breadwinners, the rituals of verbal communication allowed for recovering gang members' social reintegration. Pastor Raul's sermons and testimonies, such as in the examples above, were often followed by an altar call. During one sermon, he walked up and down the aisle, and made parallels between himself and the congregation. He said that he understood how some members were still "dealing with issues on the inside," such as depression, traumatic childhoods, not being able to wake up the morning to go to work, and anger. But he reproached them, saying, "It's not normal to want to kill someone cuz you're mad!" At that moment, the male congregant next to me burst into tears. He clumsily put his hand in his T-shirt sleeve, and awkwardly pulled it up to wipe them away. After the end of the sermon, the band played music and the pastor invited church members up for an "altar call," during which they could accept Jesus and be forgiven for their sins. More than one hundred people crowded the altar; speaking in stream-of-thought prayers, church leaders rested their hands upon them and prayed for them. Despite the overt shaming of gang behavior, and the presence of active gang members in the church, the pastor's sermon and altar call offered redemption, inclusiveness, and a sense of belonging among gang members at different stages of recovery.

The spectacle of Pastor Raul's sermon, his fiery proclamation that he could relate to "issues on the inside" that were "not normal," and the collective effervescence of the altar call reflected the second major component of a redemption script that Maruna found among reformed career criminals: the articulation of their "real me" in opposition to their past crimes (2001, 88). To demonstrate that they no longer engaged in the same behavior, members of Victory Outreach—from the pastor down to newer members—collectively joined together to renounce their past transgressions during the altar call.

Although church leaders asserted that for recovery from gangs to occur one had to accept Jesus and "surrender," they did not expect all vestiges of Chicano gang life to be erased. Recovering gang members verbally declared abstention from substance abuse, violence, and extramarital affairs, but they still spoke with the accent and language of Chicano gang members. Rather, Pastor Raul urged members to redirect their gang behavior, to become soldiers for Jesus and "fight for Christ," building on the aggressiveness of gang masculinity by evoking the image of a masculine Christian warrior. However, in contrast to real violence, the "spiritual violence" practiced by Victory Outreach men was to be characterized by compassion and a determination to help drug addicts and gang members. Recovering gang members at Victory Outreach fervently sought out these evangelical missions.

Recovering gang members carried out the third component of Maruna's redemption script, the "compensatory model" (2001, 148): they did not blame themselves for their past crimes, but did want to be responsible for helping others. Victory Outreach members tried to guide new church members who still seemed "lost," held Bible studies in areas with high gang activity, and conducted evangelism on busy street corners. During street evangelism, some performed the "cool pose" of urban male rappers while proclaiming the "good news" of the Gospel, trying to get persons off the street and into the church. Street evangelism validated that recovering gang members' were experiencing recovery, rather than "backsliding" into gang life. Encounters with old acquaintances during street evangelism helped confirm Victory Outreach members' status as recovered gang members: men with gang histories who no longer engaged in gang behavior but sought to help others.

Family Men: Homeboy Industries' "Rehabilitation" Model

Homeboy Industries' approach to gang recovery was based upon the Jesuit social justice mission, encapsulated in their slogan "Jobs Not Jails." Homeboy Industries sought to reintegrate violent and drug addicted gang members into broader society through a variety of job training, services, employment, and twelve-step support groups. In addition, Homeboy Industries drew from the model of therapeutic rehabilitation, providing an array of classes to gang members.

At Homeboy Industries, the most spiritual event would take place at the daily morning meeting, at which Father Greg had institutionalized a ritual he once started; at the end of every morning meeting, even when Father Greg was out of town, one person was selected to tell a spiritually reflective story in front of the hundreds of members about to start a day of work. These stories, many of which dealt with substance abuse or death, were often heartbreaking, thoughtful, and inspirational. Aside from the morning meeting, there was no other moment in the day when all members of Homeboy Industries collectively shared the same space. Those in need of the most personalized help sought out Homeboy Industries' group therapy classes.

A typical Homeboy Industries' group therapy class opened with the moderator stating the ground rules of communication ("respect" and "confidentiality"), before doing "check-ins" to probe into class participants' personal lives. Homeboys and Homegirls would trickle in a few minutes late to class and join about a dozen others sitting at tables arranged in a large circle formation. Classes, lasting about sixty to ninety minutes, were held in rooms of Homeboy Industries' sparkling new twenty-three-thousand-square-foot building. Some members attended classes voluntarily, while others participated as a condition of probation or court conviction.

Homeboy Industries classes had names such as Substance Abuse (including levels I, II, and III), Anger Management, Building Relationships, Speech Class, Parenting, Baby and Me, Circle of Youth, and Spreading Seeds. Several support groups were available through classes, such as Alcoholics Anonymous (AA), Narcotics Anonymous (NA), and Criminals and Gang Members Anonymous (CGA). These groups are mutual aid societies that provide spiritual support to participants who strive for abstention. AA, founded in the 1930s, is the grandfather of several twelve-step programs that are today international. NA and CGA are modeled after it.

Rooted in nondenominational Protestant Christianity (Rudy and Greil, 1989), AA also closely parallels Mexican Catholicism's cultural focus on rituals, trajectories of transgression, guilt, confession, and salvation (Brandes 2002). Foucauldian critics of the twelve-step model of recovery have argued that personal testimonies which force subjects to accept fault, blame, and individual accountability thereby impose governmentality and panoptic surveillance (e.g., Bourgois 2009; Fairbanks 2009; Haney 2010). In *Scripting Addiction*, E. Summerson Carr (2010) argued that AA and other twelve-step programs could be seen as a process of "rehabilitating the drug user's relationship with language." Participants had to learn to follow a recovery narrative, which featured a

Figure 5.2. A Homeboy gives the spiritually reflective "thought of the day" at Homeboy Industries' daily morning meeting (courtesy of Homeboy Industries)

linear plot line that stretched from a dirty past, to hitting bottom, and then pointed to a clean future.

Homeboy Industries' model of recovery was overtly shaped by the AA and twelve-step group model, centering verbal communication upon group therapy talk and testimonies. After "check-ins," the class moderator gave a short lecture, and called on class participants to answer discussion questions or to talk about their own addiction. The moderator was almost always an ex–gang member or a man with extensive experience in street life. He would use terms popularized by a therapeutic culture to uphold the image of the "family man" oriented toward work and the home. Leaders and some participants portrayed gang life in gendered ways, contrasting violent gang masculinity and femininity with nurturing fatherhood and motherhood. They used the therapeutic vocabulary of AA, referencing "cravings," "relapse," "the cycle of violence," "secondary emotions," "codependency," "denial," and "accountability."

At Homeboy Industry classes, recovering gang members reassessed and appraised Chicano gang masculinity through talk in the semipublic group setting. As seen in this chapter's opening vignette, Alfredo admonished the aggressive behavior of some class participants as well as his old behavior. By portraying gang behavior as defensive and immature, and characterizing acceptance of criticism as a marker of manhood, he thus reformulated notions of Chicano masculinity. Likewise, Jeremy, the CGA moderator and an ex–gang member, once ridiculed the aggressive nature of gang masculinity. Disparaging the behavior of previous participants, Jeremy told the men in the room not to bring gang rivalry problems into group therapy because "a real man won't go doing something like that." Gang recovery leaders taught newer members that manhood was associated with the acceptance of criticism, not aggression. In these settings, as with Victory Outreach, newer members sat intensely quiet, reluctant to break discursive rules in the public space of recovery.

Against the scorned image of gang masculinity, Homeboy Industries leaders positioned themselves on a higher ground; they constructed masculinity in recovery as normative—and superior to gang masculinity. The leaders referred to themselves as "family men" who were oriented toward family and work rather than street life. In CGA, Jeremy spent a great deal of time shaming gang masculinity and contrasting gang life with fatherhood and domestic responsibilities. Jeremy urged gang members to shift from the street to the home often by enthusiastically describing the joys of fatherhood. One day, after recapping a weekend of fishing and off-roading with his son, Jeremy warned, "You can't do that stuff if you're locked up." Moderators encouraged participants to reform their behavior for the benefit of enjoying time with their family and children.

Moderators encouraged reflection, compassion, and nurturance among those members who were more reserved and spent less time with their family. At one CGA meeting, Joseph, an older Homeboy in his late forties, shared a moving testimony encouraging the men to show affection to their mothers. With close to thirty people crowded into a room, some lined up against the wall, Joseph addressed us, repeatedly using the word "*carnalito*" (an affectionate way of saying "little brother" in Spanish). He told members of the class to avoid making the mistakes he had made failing to build relationships earlier in his life. He talked about how he tried to be a mentor to adolescents in his neighborhood, giving advice in "a respectful tone of voice" even to boys who were not from his gang and trying to talk to young mothers he always saw crying.

Joseph suddenly had trouble speaking loudly. Taking several deep breaths, he revealed that his mother was about to pass away. He said he was trying to emotionally support her. He asked us not to wait until it was too late, to say the things to our mothers that we would want to say. Tearing up, he said he didn't want the kids he mentored in the neighborhood to see him hurt, as he was showing us, but that "it's hard." Joseph repeated himself, as he said, "Hug your mother and tell her that you love her." A silent moment passed as he wiped his tears, looked up for a second, looked back down, and finished wiping. After he gave one last quick, silent glance, Jeremy solemnly said, "Thank you, Joseph." Everyone in the room clapped. By demonstrating the practices of verbally coaching and nurturing others, Homeboy Industries moderators taught communication skills and nurturing behavior to their class participants. These interactions helped to create "strength" rather than "weakness," as men learned how to use speech to reinterpret vulnerability, forgiveness, and regret as strength.

Through CGA, Jeremy also taught members how to hold on to certain aspects of gang embodiment that protect one's self-esteem and prevent transgressions into gang activity, while desisting from aspects of gang embodiment that could lead to transgressions into gang life. Having spent the majority of his adolescent and adult life incarcerated, he often talked about what a joy it was to be spending time with his wife and kids, and to not be on the streets anymore. He also claimed that they could be more "down for their neighborhood" if they were doing well in life with good jobs and able, for instance, to provide for someone who needed to get bailed out of jail. Moderators harshly criticized the destructive facets of Chicano gang masculinity, in light of their apparent contradictions.

In an instance of moderators' upholding of the "family man" image, Antonio, Homeboy Industries' drug counselor, once chastised participants in his Substance Abuse class, telling them that the money they spent on drugs could instead be used to buy their children shoes. He then shared his personal testimony. He told the participants that he used to rely on income gained from employment at Homeboy Industries to support his family, while he went to school at night to take classes for his drug counseling certification, and that it was the thought of his wife and children waiting for him to arrive home that prevented him from relapsing. Antonio and other moderators encouraged class participants to reform for the well-being of their family members, and several times moderators even pointed to me and said that I was a "real man"—not like gang members in the class or on the street—because I was in college and able to take care of my mother. In turn, in the same way that ex-offenders in Maruna's study disassociated themselves from crime by stating that their past behavior was not reflective of their "real me" (2001, 88), men in Homeboy Industries disassociated themselves from gangs by claiming that, during their gang days, they were misled about what it meant to be a "real man."

Recovery was a process in which one learned how to be a "real man." Candace West and Sarah Fenstermaker (1987), in a landmark article titled "Doing Gender," argued that gender is so deeply ingrained in social interaction that it is impossible to escape; efforts to merely pass only serve to reinforce assumptions of gender as natural. Similarly, men in gang recovery were always aware that by default they would be seen by many as nothing more than gang members: hypermasculine and prone to criminality. Gang recovery was an effort to overcome this "controlling image" (Collins 1990, 72). Gang recovery leaders often actively celebrated conventional and nurturing displays of manhood (e.g., working and providing for a family) that contested controlling images of Latino gang members. Members sought to perform reformed barrio masculinity convincingly enough to pass as reformed.

The threat of failing at the performance of reformed barrio masculinity loomed large. Matthew, whose arrest during one of the LAPD's gang sweeps was mentioned in chapter 1, was publicly chastised by his arresting officer though there was no evidence that he had been recently involved in any gang activity. As described, Los Angeles Times readers judged Avenues gang members through the racist/sexist discourse of the Latino crime threat. They framed Latinos and gang members as a social cancer that needed to be treated by castrating them, turning our military resources onto them, deporting them, and militarizing the U.S.-Mexico border (see chapter 1).

Heavily investing in gendered performances aligned with conventional expressions of manhood, Homeboy Industries leaders contested the racist discourse of the Latino crime threat. At one CGA class, Jeremy dramatized how to contest racial profiling when being unnecessarily searched by a police officer. Standing up, clutching his phone to his ear, and looking over his shoulder with an irritated expression, Jeremy loudly remarked that the cop was wasting his time searching his car. However, this type of resistance was different than that expressed through Chicano gang masculinity; it was intended to challenge stereotypes. Jeremy said that when asked for identification, he would pull out both his state and college ID cards, and ask, "Which one do you want?" These dramatizations demonstrated to class participants how to resist emasculation while also contesting racial stereotypes and state surveillance. Similarly, as described in chapter 3, Mario discussed how he redirected his frustrations with racism and inequality from acts of gang violence to peaceful resistance. Declaring that this radical shift was influenced by Father Greg's use of Catholic social teachings, Mario commented that, if he were to ever study to be a Catholic priest, he would want to be a Jesuit, because, like Father Greg, they favor social justice and activism. Mario and Jeremy, like the desisting career criminals described by Maruna (2001, 148), highlighted problems external to themselves—racism and poverty—when talking about their past crimes, but felt the responsibility to be part of a solution, what Maruna called the compensatory model. As they talked about injustice and recovery from gang life, and as they mentored men still active in gang life, Homeboy Industries moderators contested racial stereotypes while maintaining desistance from gang life.

Faith and religion helped shape communication in gang recovery. Just as Alfredo acted the role of secular priest, hearing recovering gang members' confessions of pain, regret, and existential crisis, Victory Outreach leaders commanded members to "surrender" to God. These verbal interactions encouraged what Hoffmann identified as AA prescriptions: a belief in God (or a higher power) and acceptance of "things beyond your control" (2006, 675). One-on-one interactions between moderators and members, in class, allowed watchful class participants to benefit, demonstrating yet another cornerstone of AA-style therapy: "put[ting] the group of AA ahead of self-interests" (Hoffmann 2006, 675).

However, in contrast to Hoffman's findings that both direct and indirect criticism are rare in AA, at times both Homeboy Industries moderators and Victory Outreach pastors and speakers criticized members as part of their heated, passionate orations. Homeboy Industries members overtly shamed gang activity, indirectly attacking class participants who were still known to be active in gangs. Jeremy once forcefully pointed his finger at a few young gang members sitting near me and said, "You think it's fun, and you think it's fun, and you think it's fun. But it ain't fun. It is not fun! As a juvenile I got life in YA [Youth Authority], but today I would've gotten life in the pen." Jeremy continued by talking about the harsh realities of prison life, and told the young men that they were naïve because "real men" were "family men." Jeremy had used Chicano culture and slang to construct an image of gang life, but then mocked Chicano gang masculinity for being destructive. This was clearly an attack on the young men, meant to shame them and to position their expressions of gang masculinity as subordinate and inferior.

Homeboy Industries class moderators shamed and ridiculed masculine gang behavior: activities such as substance abuse, selling drugs, and violence. Jeremy would ask men in class if they preferred to be lined up "dick to ass" with prison inmates (relying on not-so-subtle homophobia) rather than live a straight life outside of jail and have romantic relationships with women. Jeremy sarcastically ridiculed many of the major tenets of gang life, such as the extreme preoccupation with violence, but used some tenets, such as loyalty, to rearticulate Chicano masculinity. As with Victory Outreach, moderators were not doing away with all facets of Chicano masculinity, but only those elements associated with street life.

Conclusion

Chicano men distanced themselves from gang life and the streets by interacting in spaces of gang recovery and by earning legitimacy as reformed gang members. This was facilitated through two related processes: the practice of new discursive rules and the negotiation of Chicano gang masculinity.

At both Homeboy Industries and Victory Outreach, the process of gang recovery centered upon gang members learning new discursive rules of interaction in order to participate in the public space of recovery. At Victory Outreach, the pastors and leaders relied on sermons styled after Pentecostal oratory, as well as call-and-response interactions from congregation members. They used these orations to discuss how gang behavior led to transgressions, pain and regret, and ultimately redemption. They framed their experiences through religious symbolism and parables, melding Scripture with lived gang experience and Chicano slang and references to barrio life. At Homeboy Industries, the twelve-step model structured group therapy sessions. As they led class discussions, moderators drew from members' testimonies and troubles as well as their own. These group therapy discussions hinged on shame, regret, and redemption.

It has been suggested that rituals that allow for reintegration can help facilitate desistance from crime or gangs (e.g., Braithwaite 1989; Brenneman 2011; Hagan and McCarthy 1997; Rios 2011). The research described in this book suggests that ritualized verbal communication facilitates desistance from gang life, and that it does so through gendered negotiations. The negotiation of Chicano gang masculinity is woven into verbal rituals in two major ways.

First, recovering gang members learn nurturing behavior that negotiates notions of Chicano manhood. During testimonies, sermons, or group therapy, leaders acted as secular priests or spiritual leaders, encouraging members to accept a higher power, accept things beyond one's control, and put the recovery group ahead of one's interests. The men not only verbally renounced substance abuse and gang violence, they also publicly expressed regret and empathy for the plight and suffering of others. In doing so, they reformulated regret as a sign of strength rather than weakness, and learned how to perform dominant expressions of masculinity that facilitated their reintegration into the church, home, and workplace.

Second, the discursive practice of talking about transgression, regret, and redemption portrays gang masculinity in negative terms, while the image of the male breadwinner, rooted in hegemonic masculinity, is constructed as dominant in relation to marginalized expressions of masculinity. In recovery, Chicano family-oriented breadwinner masculinity was repeatedly described and encouraged, and practices and behaviors of Chicano gang masculinity, such as the use of gang monikers, territoriality, substance abuse and addiction, and violence were ridiculed and shamed. Because aggressive posturing allowed leaders to elevate recovered gang members' masculine expressions above those of newer members, such performances casted reformed barrio masculinity as a dominant masculine expression. However, although these expressions were made accessible to recovering gang members, neither program sought to erase all vestiges of their past identities. Instead, organization leaders integrated Chicano culture, nicknames, and slang with normative conceptions of masculinity. Thus, through verbal communication in gang recovery, men learned to distance themselves from gang behavior and to align themselves with dominant masculine expressions: working, and providing for and nurturing one's family.

Recovering gang members experience themselves as "reformed" only through their interactions with others. Gang recovery provides spaces for public talk where such interactions can occur, and where recovering gang members can experience reform through redemption scripts. They seek opportunities to help others who now experienced drugs and gangs. They articulate a renewed sense of self divorced from previous behaviors. They hold themselves responsible for helping others—even if it means making a difference in just one person's life.

Gang recovery's communal orientation to communication forcefully rejects one of the major problems posed by late modernity. During the late modern period, large populations have been uprooted, displaced, and marginalized, as the neoliberal discourse of "overpopulation" and "superfluous" human beings has gained traction—fueling fears of immigrants, poverty, and crime (Bauman 2004).Gang recovery resists these discursive trends, creating spaces in which some of the most marginalized persons are humanized and recentered. The communal nature of discourse in gang recovery challenges the premise that there may be superfluous, "wasted" lives, instead asserting that even the lives of the most marginalized are profoundly significant.

6

From Shaved to Saved

Embodied Gang Recovery

One day I was harassed by a cop, man. They pull me over I
think because of the way I look. Me and two brothers from
the home. They pull guns at us, bro. They brought me down
like I was a gang member . . . and I wasn't dressed as a gang
member no more. And you know what, man? In front of the
church, in the parking lot of our church.

Ramon

amon's recollection illustrates the hostile relationship between
the police and poor men of color. As Ramon and another Victory Outreach member arrived at the church for an event, two police
officers stopped and frisked them. According to Ramon's account, during the search, he and his fellow Victory Outreach member remained
polite and quiet, speaking only to answer questions. While Ramon
obeyed the police officer's commands and attempted to demonstrate
that he was not involved in gang life or criminal activity, the police
officer rebuffed him and accused Victory Outreach of harboring Mafia
activity. As Ramon recounted this story to me, during our interview at
a local pizzeria, it seemed as if the police officer's reproach certainly did
not fit with Ramon's present lived reality as a Christian convert, recovered gang member, and law-abiding resident.

Ramon's experience with the police is not unusual. Black and Latino
men often perceive themselves to be targets of police harassment and
fear it (Rios 2011). However, Ramon's experience with the police and

racial profiling illuminates two dimensions of gang recovery. First, although he was no longer an active gang member, Ramon still embodied gang life. Second, although the police mistook him as an active gang member because of the way he looked, when Ramon recounted this story to me he did not think that he did look like a gang member.

Ramon's definition of what a gang member looks like was probably different from most people's. Despite his use of somewhat form-fitting clothes, I could tell that he was from the barrio. He typically wore plaid or two-toned striped polo shirts with slightly baggy jeans and had his hair cut extremely short. He spoke with a Chicano accent and used his hands when he talked in a style similar to that of many men from the barrio. The type of masculine expressions that recovering gang members, such as Ramon, try to distance themselves from is *masculine gang embodiment*. They make adjustments to masculine gang embodiment, such as Ramon's use of form-fitting khakis in place of baggy jeans, through *reformed gang embodiment*.

Many recovering gang members still gave off subtle signs that they had a gang background. Despite distancing themselves from gang life, men at both gang recovery sites still bore some elements of masculine gang embodiment, such as shaved heads, barrio-style tattoos, and particular ways of walking or gesturing. Many recovering gang members were not aware that they still displayed these signs of gang life, but they were apparent to me (and others).

Reformulation of embodied masculine meanings is pivotal to the process of gang recovery. Bob Brenneman (2011), like Stanley Brandes, found that men's negotiation of the meaning of crying helped facilitate recovery. As men shaped embodied meanings, they constructed new ideas of manhood that centered around recovery and domestic life rather than the streets. Embodied faith practices in gang recovery undergirded the reformulation of masculinity. As Luis León observed in ecstatic Pentecostal worship, "[T]he experience of the body is central to worship and to the construction of a social body that coheres with other male bodies; men's bodies are ritually, emotionally, spiritually, and physically connected to one another" (2004, 238).

Recovering gang members' largest obstacle in resisting gang behavior involved reshaping their bodies to feel and respond in a manner in line with reformed barrio masculinity. Cravings for drugs or aggressive behavior were examples of embodied gang life that sometimes led to gang behavior, such as drug use, drug selling, or gang violence. The permanent, physical markings of gang life that can lead to gang behavior are *hard embodiment*. Within hard embodiment is a spectrum of expressions that are on the one end relatively constant, such as the urge for drugs, and on the other end surface situationally, such as the aggressive vocal tones that arise during hostile interactions.

The previous chapter portrayed how recovering gang members used the podium to affirm, negotiate, and contest Chicano gang masculinity. This chapter extends the analysis of reformulated Chicano gang masculinity to the body and bodily practices, to help fill a theoretical gap in the masculinities and crime literature. Recovery offers embodied practices that facilitate the construction of reformed barrio masculinity. In turn, as recovering gang members attempt to leave gang life, they learn how to embody reformed barrio masculinity in such a way that prevents transgressions into gang behavior.

Both Homeboy Industries and Victory Outreach made use of embodied practices that reformulated Chicano gang masculinity and facilitated gang recovery. Leaders in gang recovery urged members to grow their hair out, remove gang tattoos, and dress with form fitting khakis. These malleable, physical markings of gang life are *soft embodiment*. Theologies of gang recovery facilitated practices that reshaped and redirected soft embodiment, but also redirected hard embodiment. Whereas Homeboy Industries' model of gang recovery drew upon therapy and meditation to reshape embodied gang masculinity, Victory Outreach's model of gang recovery drew upon worship and evangelism to redirect embodied gang masculinity.

Gang Embodiment

Racial minority status and years of growing up in a context of poverty and violence shaped the way respondents carried their bodies. However, instead of shielding themselves from violence, Chicano gang members' compensatory masculine displays further deepen their risk of being victimized by gangs and the police. Several men carried themselves in ways that displayed embodied fear and invited violent confrontations.

In addition, some respondents were from immigrant backgrounds; immigrant settlement in low-income neighborhoods exposes black and Latino second-generation immigrants to violence from other blacks and Latinos, and the police (Waters 1999; Smith 2006). While in recovery, some respondents would often look around anxiously and, at times, inappropriately stare at strangers. Despite the fact that the setting of recovery posed no threats to subjects' well-being, they still responded with mannerisms that embodied fear; they had been habituated in a context of violence and fear, and this surfaced in their interactions even after threats were no longer present.

Embodied fear surfaced one day as I sat in on a class at Homeboy Industries' continuation school. One homeboy, Eucario, turned and asked if I could help him with his work. I replied "no" and told him he needed permission from the teacher. Eucario, skeptical that the teacher would allow me to tutor him, joked, "He's afraid you're gonna take his job." As another homeboy across the class burst into laughter, Eucario walked over to give him a fist bump. Immediately after, though, Eucario became serious. In one fluid motion, he quickly walked past the homeboy and looked out the window behind the teacher, as if he were on a high level of alert and watching for danger. The act of looking out the window struck me as absurd. We were on the second floor, and the only notable object in sight was a Los Angeles Metro Gold Line platform with no train visible. Eucario's behavior, fitting for a street corner but not for a safe classroom, demonstrated how bodies become embedded with particular masculine expressions as a form of self-protection from violence (Messerschmidt 2004). The fist bump seemed to trigger a fear that was largely subconscious. Such masculine displays fall within the realm of what Julie Bettie (2003) conceptualized as gendered performativity.

Luis Rodríguez captured the gendering and embodied effects of racialization in his autobiographical memoir of East Los Angeles Chicano gang life. He wrote, "I began high school a *loco*, with a heavy Pendleton shirt, sagging khaki pants, ironed to perfection, and shoes shined and heated like at boot camp" (2005[1993], 83). His embodiment of Chicano gang masculinity was met with disdain and hostility from schools and the police, and this led him to further embrace masculine gang embodiment and become even further involved in gang life. Rodríguez wrote:

> If you came from the Hills, you were labeled from the start. I'd walk into the counselor's office for whatever reason and looks of disdain greeted me—one was meant for a criminal, alien, to be feared. It was harder to defy this expectation than just accept it and fall into the trappings. It was a jacket I could try to take off, but they kept putting it back on. . . . So why not be proud? Why not be an outlaw? (2005[1993], 84)

His experience, of dressing as a gang member because it was "harder to defy this expectation than just accept it and fall into the trappings," illustrates the gendering effects of racism on adolescents: those who fail to meet gender ideals and experience discrimination strengthen their association with same-sex peer groups to receive validation (Ferguson 2000; Lopez 2003; Bettie 2003).[1] Likewise, recovering gang members had negative experiences at home, in school, or on the streets, which led them to cultivate masculine gang embodiment and engage in gang behavior.

Gang life was often embedded in recovering gang members' bodies and continued to surface as they engaged in gang behavior. Two members from Homeboy Industries, Marcelo and Sergio, experienced the markings of masculine gang embodiment after engaging in gang behavior. One evening after work, Jaime and Marcelo were drinking when they decided to head to the apartment of Sergio, Jaime's uncle. Marcelo, however, made the mistake of flashing gang signs in front of Sergio's apartment—a behavior that is highly disrespectful when done in a neighborhood not belonging to that gang. Sergio, as Jaime told the story, was in a foul mood after having gotten into a fight with his ex-girlfriend. As a result, Sergio aggressively approached Marcelo and confronted him about his disrespectful behavior. Marcelo, drunk, did not back down and fought with Sergio. They battled on the street, giving each other black eyes, until the police intervened and restrained them. Ultimately, they were released and not charged with any crimes. However, the next day at Homeboy Industries, their black eyes got attention from senior staff members, who scolded them.

As I stood with Jaime and a clearly bruised Marcelo in a corner of the Homeboy Industries building, Jaime recounted to me the previous night's street brawl. Laughing, Jaime said, "I just went to go get some 40s, and I come back, and the cops are there and this guy is like this." Jaime walked down the Homeboy Industries hallway, imitating a staggering Marcelo with two hands behind his back, as if arrested, and stumbling forward with his head bouncing in an intoxicated manner. Antonio happened to walk by and saw Jaime's performance. From across the hallway, after Jaime finished telling his story, Antonio made a seemingly casual joke about the Homeboys' lax attitude toward work. But he took advantage of the interaction to walk closer and confront Marcelo. Invading Marcelo's personal space and peering at him intently, Antonio asked in a scolding voice, "What happened to your eye?" Marcelo smirked, shrugged, and softly told Antonio that he was simply tired. Antonio briskly walked away with a sour expression on his face. Jaime and Marcelo nervously remained quiet. It was clear that Antonio had accurately interpreted Jaime's drunk walk and Marcelo's swollen eye, and was upset that they had engaged in violence.

The embodiment of gang life easily led to discrimination. Wilfredo's experience, long after exiting gang life, demonstrated how gang embodiment could lead to hostile interactions with the police. Wilfredo, a short, stocky, late-twenties Latino with white skin and light brown hair, had been in a notorious northeast Los Angeles gang, but no longer engaged in gang activity. He worked as an employment counselor at Homeboy Industries, after earning a master's degree in social work from the University of Southern California. Smiling and dressed in business casual attire, with form-fitting khakis, a colorful shirt, and a checkered sweater, Wilfredo recounted to me a night a few years back when he had woken up in a police car. Wilfredo's mother asked him to pick up his brother from a drinking session with buddies at a house in a nearby neighborhood. When he arrived, his brother did not want to leave. Wilfredo grabbed him and put him in his car, just as an LAPD officer watched. As the officer arrived on the scene he opened the door of Wilfredo's car and pulled him out hard enough to knock him unconscious. The policeman then took off Wilfredo's shirt and found a gang tattoo from his teenage years. Although Wilfredo was no longer an active gang member, under California's gang enhancement law, some misdemeanors could be prosecuted as felonies if gang tattoos were present. In addition, he was apprehended in an area from which his gang was banned, violating California's gang injunction law. He did not serve any time in jail, although two previous felonies on his record would almost certainly have led to a mandatory life sentence. Wilfredo's body had been shaped by gang life, which had consequences for his interactions with law enforcement and his criminal record long after he had left gang life behind.

Gang violence left some men with permanent disabilities, such as limps, paralysis, or missing limbs. These handicaps also led to discrimination, like that experienced by Jose, a blind member of Homeboy Industries. Jose wore large black shades to cover his eyes and was forced to hold his head up with a hand to keep it from falling to the side—he had lost the ability to keep it up straight after being shot in the head and neck. With his scalp shaved, the black shades made it appear that Jose was still an active gang member. To his frustration, the police continued to break into his house and search for signs of gang activity.

Disabled recovering gang members sometimes grew frustrated with being unable to reformulate Chicano gang masculinity into a dominant expression of masculinity. Ruben, as described earlier, suffered such extensive nerve damage after a gunshot wound to the head that he was confined to a power chair. Ruben, when giving his testimony, always recounted how a nurse once told him he would never walk again. I once witnessed the impact of this statement on his emotional state in a "Building Relationships for Men" class at Homeboy Industries. A group of three men and two moderators sat around a small table in a tiny, candle-lit group therapy room. Esperanza, the middle-aged Chicana moderator from a nongang background, tried to tie the men's day-to-day struggles to lessons on forgiveness and redemption. She told the men that it was easier to live without resentment and that to forgive others for misdeeds, they had to endure pain with God. Esperanza asked the group about the struggles they suffered through. "How often do you think about it?" Ruben remarked of his paralysis, "Many times a day." He was upset about not being able to do leisurely activities, such as go camping on retreats with the other Homeboys, or work at a proper job. In his weak voice, Ruben mourned, "I used to be able to make money. What they make you do here at Homeboy Industries is not like a real job. Homeboy Industries is not shit." With a solemn expression, and shedding a few tears, Ruben recalled that he was earning $800 a week making food deliveries to restaurants before his accident. He commented that there were not many sixteen-year-olds who could legally make what he had been making. Esperanza tried to probe and Memo offered encouraging words, but their efforts seemed to have no effect on Ruben's gloomy state. He said he didn't want to talk anymore. At the end of the one-hour session, we all held hands and Esperanza lead a prayer from Numbers 6:24, "May the lord bless you." But Ruben remained somber.

Reformed Barrio Masculinity
Reshaping Gang Embodiment

Gang recovery leaders played a key role in negotiating masculine gang embodiment through bodily practices (see figure 6.1).[2] Concealed gang tattoos, the use of Caló or an East Los Angeles cadence, aggressive body language or fearful stares were almost as rigid and fixed as more permanent features of gang embodiment. However, recovering gang members were often unaware of these practices or their meaning until a leader in gang recovery pointed it out to them. Advanced members at both sites eschewed embodiment strongly associated with gang masculinity, such as visible tattoos, oversized jeans, shaved heads, and aggressive body language.

According to Jeremy, recovering gang members' bodies had habituated gang life, and this was expressed through posture and clothes. At a Criminals and Gang Members Anonymous meeting, Jeremy compared alcoholism with the fixation that Chicano gang members often have with ironing clothes. He said, "The problem with drinking is the same as shaving your head or ironing *ropa*. It's an addiction." As he said this, he stood up and did a *cholo*, a Chicano gang member, stance; he was slightly bent at the knees with hands in pockets, looking forward with a serious demeanor. He then remarked, "We don't even know why we do it, we do it so much now." Men in the class laughed light-heartedly at Jeremy's keen observation, validating his claim that the urge for gang life had become symbiotic with clothes and posture.

Pastor Raul made a similar remark concerning posture and gang embodiment during one Victory Outreach sermon. He demonstrated how active gang members posture by leaning back and critiqued them

Chicano Gang Masculinity	Gang Recovery	Reformed Barrio Masculinity
Gang Tattoos	Tattoo Removal	Removed Gang Tattoos
Drug Addiction	Drug Abstinence	Religious Asceticism
Emaciated Weight	Eating Abundantly	Being Overweight
Oversized Clothes	Following Dress Code	Dress Clothes
Shaved Head	Growing Hair Out	Long Hair Style
Aggressive Body Language		Affectionate Body Language

Figure 6.1. Masculine Gang Embodiment and Recovery

for having an exaggerated sense of importance. He said, "Some of you think you're all bad, all *aqua*. You think you're God's gift to the world." He then stood up straight and scolded, "Well, you need him more than he needs you." Members of Victory Outreach looked at each other, laughed, and clapped when they heard this. Pastor Raul's observation, though of a different posture than the one demonstrated by Jeremy, also underscored the symbiotic nature of gang poses and gang behavior. Both leaders claimed that, for recovery from gang life to be achieved, masculine gang embodiment had to be reshaped. However, some forms of gang embodiment, such as standing in a certain posture, are easier to reshape than others, such as overcoming cravings for drugs. Gang recovery leaders thus mocked the more malleable types of gang embodiment because they were perceived to be much easier to change than rigid types.

In lieu of masculine gang embodiment, recovery leaders promoted removal of gang tattoos, drug abstinence, wearing formfitting or dress clothes, grooming a long hairstyle, and practicing anger management during emotionally upsetting moments. Leaders claimed that engaging in embodied practices and performances facilitated the construction of reformed barrio masculinity. At both sites, men were expected to engage in the process of recovery from gang life, including working and providing for a family, and it was assumed that recovery from gang life would follow reform of dress. Due to leaders' strong advocacy for changes in attire as part of the process of recovery, members who were serious about leaving gang life welcomed such changes. Recovering gang members who embraced the path of recovery wore slightly oversized polo shirts or plaid shirts and formfitting khakis or slightly baggy jeans to give the impression that they once had a gang background, but were now fulfilling the duties of conventional manhood.

The link between dress and recovery was made very explicit by some gang recovery leaders. At a Sunday service, Pastor Raul growled, "I was bound to drugs and gang violence, and I cursed my family. Some people got their children Nike Cortezes and shaved heads and miniskirts before they're even four years old. They're putting a curse on their family." He blamed his own children's exposure to gangs and drugs on his previous style of dress, and referenced the Christian notion of a "generational curse" in suggesting that parents might "bind" their children to an undesirable life by exposing them to elements that countered the message of the church. Thus, wearing gang clothing deepened one's involvement—or that of one's children—in gangs, whereas shedding gang clothing distanced one—or one's children—from gang life.

At Homeboy Industries, I once saw one "senior navigator," a member from a crew of three men responsible for general supervision, exclaim, "He can't be doing that, I gotta go stop him," after he saw a newer member hitch his pants up and adjust his belt—with gestures very similar to gang posturing—in the lobby of Homeboy Industries' nonprofit wing. In addition, at the Homeboy Industries reception desk, Father Greg once noticed an old gang tattoo exposed on a Homeboy's freshly shaven head. Father Greg kindly asked the Homeboy if he really wanted to be at Homeboy Industries, shaming him and implying his behavior suggested otherwise.

Homeboy Industries had a relatively lax, but strictly enforced dress code. All employees were to wear a Homeboy Industries shirt: either a T-shirt, polo shirt, or collar shirt. Oversized clothes were permitted, although "sagging," the practice of wearing pants below the waistline, was not. Because oversized hooded sweatshirts were associated with gangs, on rainy days, Homeboys were told that they had to wear a hooded sweatshirt with the Homeboys logo, or their hooded sweatshirt under their T-shirt. Men at Victory Outreach usually dressed more formally than men at Homeboy Industries; older male members attended Sunday service dressed in slacks, shirt, and a tie. However, there was also greater flexibility in dress codes at Victory Outreach. Newer members were permitted to attend church in any attire, even in the most

Figure 6.2. Homeboys after taking a How to Tie a Tie class (courtesy of Homeboy Industries)

oversized clothes. Most attended weekday services or "fellowship" events wearing slightly oversized barrio clothes, such as khakis, blue jeans, plaid shirts, white shirts, hooded sweatshirts, and sports jerseys, although higher-ranking members wore clothes that were more form-fitting. This was part of the church's evangelizing mission, to accept any person—no matter how much of a misfit to mainstream society.

Leaders enforced dress codes at each site. Dress codes gave gang recovery leaders the ability to praise or stigmatize members for their progress, or lack of progress, in recovery. As an extreme example, if Homeboys or Homegirls wore clothes to work that did not have the Homeboys/girls logo, or if they wore their pants below the waistline, they would be "clocked out" and sent home. However, short of this one type of violation, most individuals who violated dress codes were not reprimanded so harshly. Rather, dress code violations at Victory Outreach and Homeboy Industries were addressed through gang recovery leaders' sharp rebukes during sermons or in group therapy classes.

At both organizations, reform of dress led to opportunities for advancement within the group's hierarchy. At Homeboy Industries, ex–gang members who were senior staff members, such as case managers and supervisors, were higher paid and more likely to wear form-fitting and business-casual clothes. Such dress allowed recovered gang members to more easily blend in and interact with professional senior staffers, most of them female white-collar workers with college education and high pay. However, these distinctions between senior staffers and newer members enflamed tensions. When newer members flunked drug tests, they often deflected blame by accusing recovered gang members in senior staff positions of being just as imperfect, but dishonestly pretending to be recovered.

Homeboy Industries men were inspired to recover from gang life by reshaping soft gang embodiment along with hard gang embodiment. Sergio's struggle with gang recovery illustrated that embodied gang life was, in some forms, malleable, and that men could reform Chicano gang masculinity through attire and the body. Over a couple of Heinekens, as we sat on the front stoop of his home, Sergio confessed that he had been experiencing cravings for crystal meth. Sergio was trying to stop using the drug, because it had been pulling him back into old gang friendships and compromising his ability to be a good father. Sergio said he didn't see that hanging out with his old homeboys was going to lead him "anywhere good," and added, "Part of me wants to be more than what I am . . . so that I can provide for my son."

Sergio's notions of manhood were shaped in this context, and he addressed the masculine struggle between gang life and recovery by reshaping his bodily practices. Every morning, Sergio woke up to practice yoga meditations he learned from his therapist at Homeboy Industries. He sat cross-legged and cleared his mind. In addition, before every meal, even in public, Sergio closed his eyes and placed his hands together for about a minute to give thanks. Lastly, Sergio was growing his hair out as part of his commitment to quit meth use. This struck me as significant; a shaved head represents gang life, and men in recovery were often encouraged to grow their hair out. Sergio said that he had not used meth in a week. Touching his hair with a prideful grin, he said it was a reminder that he had made a commitment.

In Victory Outreach, the ascribed meanings of attire were far less contested than at Homeboy Industries. Leaders often dressed in full suits for church events, embodying the "health and wealth gospel" of the Protestant church, and members were eager to partake in such embodied displays. As newer members became more involved with the church, they received formfitting and dressy clothes, some from

Goodwill and others from fellow members. These fine clothes were considered "blessings," which allowed newer members opportunities to imitate the pastor when giving their testimony, or when leading a sermon during Bible study or another small group setting. Newer members enjoyed mild forms of patriarchal status as they began to embody the changes seen in leaders.

However, newer Victory Outreach members were often embarrassed to experiment with new types of appearance. As a result, Victory Outreach leaders stressed their advice to "grow your hair out." At a Sunday service, Brother Alex encouraged members to change the way both they and their kids dressed to facilitate the process of exit from gang life. As he stood at the pulpit and gave his testimony of gang involvement and exit, Brother Alex told the congregation, "I had that gang mentality. I was challenged years ago to grow my hair. I had a shaved head for so many years I didn't know what to do with it. . . . I'd comb it to the side, I'd comb it back, I'd put it in a pompadour—I didn't know what to do with it. I threw out my baggy clothes." Victory Outreach leaders aggressively encouraged recovering gang members to throw out their gang clothes, reform their gang behavior, and see themselves as future pastors and leaders of the church. This was never more clear than when Pastor Raul passionately exclaimed to men in the congregation, "God wants to raise you up!"

Redirecting Gang Embodiment

Victory Outreach and Homeboy Industries leaders did not attempt to discard all facets of gang masculinity, or masculine gang embodiment. Reforming all facets of embodied gang masculinity was unlikely. As described earlier, most male recovering gang members had habituated gang masculinity through having spent years practicing particular ways of walking, speaking, greeting others, or observing their surroundings. Recovering gang members had been exposed to violence in the home, on neighborhood streets, and with the police; they had a way of quickly shifting from laughing with peers to nervously looking around. Sometimes they stared at strangers for longer than one might expect.

Recovering gang members blended masculine gang embodiment with the nurturing characteristics of reformed barrio masculinity through complex handshakes. Men exchanged elaborate handshakes to greet each other, to say goodbye, or to facilitate conversation. At each site, at the beginning of fieldwork, men exchanged handshakes, then turned in my direction as I took notes and jokingly asked, "Did you get that?" In lieu of saying "goodbye," men shook hands with a loud clasp, or by a soft slapping of palms. The typical goodbye handshake ended with a fist bump, although this could also be used in the middle of a conversation, such as in confirming a later meeting. There were variations even within this fist bump handshake; some men used closed fists, and others open hands, to accept the fist bump. These handshakes were also a rough indicator of social location. Good friends shook hands and also gave a half-embrace, staying in that position while talking privately and resting a hand on each other's back or shoulder. Older men, those in their forties, sometimes exchanged handshakes involving hand and thumb movements with which I wasn't familiar. Handshakes bonded recovering male gang members across different classes, ages, and neighborhoods into a new male fraternal order: recovery.

Another embodied feature from gang life that carried over into recovery was weight gain. Men at both sites esteemed large bodies; this was a key feature of reformed barrio masculinity. The pastor, a towering figure at six feet tall and well over two hundred pounds, told stories of having entered the home on drugs and "all sucked up." Many men had crystal meth addiction in their past and had entered recovery emaciated. The weight they put on in recovery was prized. Once, a couple of respondents from Homeboy Industries commented on how a member of Victory Outreach they knew from the streets was "doing good, all Christian" and was "healthy and fat" now. The meals at Victory Outreach helped men put on weight. Fattening foods were served at or after most church events, such as Sunday services or fellowship barbecues at local parks. Aside from traditional Mexican food, such as rice and beans, low-cost foods such as chips, punch, and soda were frequently available in excess. In addition, meals in the Victory Outreach men's home were similar to jail food. Although the home distributed food for a food bank and got a variety of products, dinners often resembled a "jailhouse spread"—ramen or pasta noodles, with or without tuna, Fritos, Louisiana Hot Sauce, and beans or any other food that could be mixed in. This was eaten with a large white roll of bread.

The weight men gained in recovery was a symbol of manhood that elevated their status. Sergio became employed in the Homeboys Bakery after quitting crystal meth use. During their fifteen-minute-long work breaks, the men at the bakery ate from jailhouse spreads mixed in large plastic trash bags. Bouncing with joy as he got in my car, Sergio said that he was eating a lot and was going to "get big." This was surprising considering he was a healthy weight, at about six feet tall and 160 pounds. He asked me, "About how much you think I can throw on in a month? Like twenty pounds?" Excited, he said he would be eating well and working out, "hitting pull-ups" on a bar outside before going into work. Sergio, anticipating the attention he would receive from women, exclaimed, "All the *honeys* are gonna be up on me! Women like that sort of shit!" Accordingly, slimness was shunned. Although I weighed 145 pounds, Alvaro from Victory Outreach teased me, saying I reminded him of photos he'd seen of Jewish prisoners during the Holocaust.

Victory Outreach members constructed reformed barrio masculinity through soft embodiment by eating large meals after worship and performing strenuous physical labor for the church. Once, after Francisco's Bible study ended, I walked over to the kitchen and an older, overweight woman offered me food. When I asked her for a small plate, she laughed and said, "Oh you want a small plate? That's too bad, because I only make large plates." I responded, "It's because I just ate before coming here, but I wanted to try the food." She seemed to disregard this comment and proceeded to serve me a substantial amount of food, chuckling, "Well here you go, here's a large plate."

As I ate standing, Rick pinched my shirt above the shoulder and tugged it slightly, asking me, loud enough for everyone to hear, "Dang bro! How much do you weigh?" I replied, "140 pounds." He howled, "What? Each of my legs weighs like that much!" Rick exaggerated, because although he had a very wide frame, he also had an athletic build—he was neither obese nor a bodybuilder. As we continued talking, he said, "I gave my youth to the lord. . . . Really, I did. I gave my early twenties." Our conversation ended as Rick walked back to the living room, and Victor told me, motioning with his right shoulder as if it was stiff, "He sacrificed his youth, but I sacrificed my body." A tall, thin, young Native American recovered alcoholic, Victor went on to give me a list of his ailments, including his right shoulder, which he hurt lifting trees to raise money for the men's home. He commented that he thought I couldn't do such work. Without saying it, he implied that I lacked his physical tenacity, which was shaped through addiction and then recovery. In the sphere of recovery, reformed barrio masculinity held a higher social status than other masculinities.

In addition to handshakes, dance was another stylized gesture reappropriated from gang life to reformed barrio masculinity. After a Bible study at Ivan's house, Ivan put on a Christian "oldies" CD, with soft music in the style of Otis Redding's "Remember Me." I said I liked the music. I spoke with Brother Ivan and listened to the Christian words sounding gently against the backdrop of horns and melodic guitar. Brother Ivan turned it up, only to be confronted by his wife, who walked into the living room and told him to turn it down. It was too loud and the women in the kitchen couldn't talk. Ivan playfully responded to his wife, "C'mon, it's a Holy Ghost party," as he lifted his arms up, leaned on one foot, then pivoted. He said these words with a groove common to dance parties among older crowds in East Los Angeles barrios. Although Brother Ivan's wife seemed annoyed by his comical gesture, his dance and masculine expressions were grounded within the Christian theme of fellowship. In contrast to his normally serious demeanor, Brother Ivan was grinning from beneath his thick *brocha*; he was able to enjoy music he grew up with and dance in a way that was natural, adding to the religious gathering. Even his defiance when told to turn his music down carried a spiritual connotation.

In sum, embodied practices in gang recovery positioned gang identities as pathological manifestations of gender and constructed reformed barrio masculinity as an expression that was conventional, dominant, and privileged. Thus, at times, the accomplishment of conventional masculinity in recovery was contingent upon masculine gang embodiment. Recovery allowed men to appropriate facets of gang embodiment in order to facilitate recovery from gang life and progress toward conventional manhood. This was shaped by the theological foundations and religious practices of each organization. The next section explores how leaders at Homeboy Industries used a Jesuit-based social justice approach to facilitate recovery through the body, while Victory Outreach leaders drew from evangelical-Pentecostal practices. Homeboy Industries leaders used therapy and meditation to teach members to monitor their bodies, whereas members of Victory Outreach largely redirected embodiment from gang life to worship and evangelism.

Faith and Embodied Recovery
Integrative Redemption: Therapy and Meditation

When Homeboy Industry leaders sought to facilitate recovery through reformed gang embodiment, they blended masculine gang embodiment with the notion of the "family man." Recovering gang members at Homeboy Industries facilitated gang recovery through embodied practices rooted in eclectic spirituality and group therapy (see figure 6.1). For example, the art show held by Antonio at Homeboy Industries, described in chapter 3, blended the lay spirituality of group therapy culture with some aspects of syncretic Mexican Catholicism. In group therapy classes, members learned to deal with situations that could lead to physical confrontations in part by monitoring their body language. Discussions in these settings taught men how to reappropriate facets of gang embodiment. Construction of reformed gang embodiment occurred by *reshaping* the body into reformed barrio masculinity, through eclectic spirituality, monitoring behavior, and meditation. In addition, construction of reformed gang embodiment occurred through *redirecting* the body to activities away from gangs, such as group therapy, AA-style testimonies, and performances of underground hip-hop (see figure 6.1). At Homeboy Industries, the strategies for avoiding gang violence were crucial as, outside of work, recovering gang members were often surrounded by gang members in their neighborhoods on evenings and weekends.

Alfredo, moderator of the Anger Management class, taught members how to avoid fights. Typically, he covered a different topic each week with distributed readings. In one Anger Management class, Alfredo taught the importance of eye contact in communication. At the end of the class, he asked members to list one thing they had learned about nonverbal communication. When it was one woman's turn, she neither answered nor looked up, and he kindly reminded her that one of the classes' lessons was about eye contact in communication. She eventually answered. In another class, Alfredo distributed readings concerning facial expressions and body language. He said, "Alright. It's like, if I

Table 6.1. Reformed Barrio Masculinity and Embodiment

	Segregated Redemption	Integrative Redemption
Reshaping Embodiment	Pentecostal Worship	Eclectic Spirituality
	Altar Calls	Monitoring Behavior
	Laying Hands on Others to Pray	Meditation
Redirecting Embodiment	Evangelism	Group Therapy
	"Holy Ghost" Testimonies	AA-Styled Testimonies
	Christian Rap	Underground Hip-Hop

come at someone all hot . . ." Someone interrupted and asked, "All mad-dogging?" Alfredo replied, "Yeah, right, all mad-dogging," acting out the movement of getting up from his chair quickly as if to assault someone. He stopped in midstride and said, "The way you come at somebody is gonna make them react before anything is necessarily said."

In Criminals and Gang Members Anonymous, Jeremy taught members how to hold on to certain aspects of gang embodiment that protect one's self-esteem and prevent transgressions into gang activity, while desisting from those aspects that could lead to such transgressions. In one class, a member made a comment about having to put on the façade of being a "real man." Jeremy turned on him and said, "I just wanna correct you. I don't think that it should matter whether someone thinks you're a man." Jeremy got up and went to one end of the room, then walked across to the other, strutting with "cool pose."[3] As he finished his short walk, he looked at the Homeboy and asked, "You don't think I'm a man? I'll be like 'So?'" As he reappropriated the cool pose aspect of his gang embodiment to reformed barrio masculinity, the other member countered by relating heartfelt experiences with his cell mate,

> Just to clarify, I'm not saying that. There's been times when I see my *celly* crying and I'll give 'em time alone and say, "Yo, I'm gonna go for a walk around the yard. You need anything? Naw? Well you need anything, just let me know, I'm here for you."

At that moment, a third member sought clarification between the two stances, and asked, "But J, you know you still gotta keep that mask on, right?" Jeremy conceded the point, exclaiming, "Oh yeah, dawg, the mask is mandatory."

At the end of one Spreading Seeds class, its leader, Evo, asked everyone to stand around in a circle. He said, "When I was twenty-three, I was angry. . . . I don't want you to be angry. . . . This is ending . . . it's natural for it to come to an end. . . . So don't give the wrong vibe with police officers." Felipe, a newer member of Homeboys in his late teens, replied, "I get angry, like I see them and I just wanna . . ." Felipe looked out from the corner of his eye with a frown, turning around and walking with exaggerated movements toward an imaginary figure. Evo remained standing in the circle and responded, "No!" As he looked down, barely moving his hands, Evo peacefully said, "I'll be like, 'They don't know what I'm about.'" Felipe said, "Well we gotta take another breath." As we took a deep breath, I relaxed and thought to myself that Felipe had learned a valuable lesson.

Segregated Redemption: Worship and Evangelism

Victory Outreach leaders sought to facilitate recovery by blending masculine gang embodiment into the notion of the "man of God" and the Christian mission of evangelization. In contrast to the way men at Homeboy Industries used eclectic spirituality and group therapy to reshape and redirect gang embodiment, men at Victory Outreach used Pentecostal worship and evangelism (see figure 6.3). These strategies helped build social cohesion, as ex–gang members in Victory Outreach experienced recovery by distancing themselves from "the world" through "the sanctuary."

During worship, recovering gang members experienced reformed gang embodiment through the intimacy of "brotherly love." At the end of a Victory Outreach sermon, the pastor would exclaim that congregants needed to accept Jesus in order to be "set free" from gang life. Pastor Raul once recounted in a sermon, "I was a gang member, drug addict, wanting to die in a shootout, living that lifestyle 24/7 for ten years." Screaming, he proclaimed, "I was bitter! Angry! Hateful!" Then he softly sighed, "But Jesus set me free." The congregation cheered and applauded in delight, and the man next to me raised his hands high. Pastor Raul proclaimed, "Confess to God. We're making an altar call.

Figure 6.3. Victory Outreach leaders baptizing a member (courtesy of Victory Outreach)

Come on, break through your stronghold, surrender." As the band played the popular Christian song "Surround Me," most of the congregation headed toward the altar. Members tightly crowded into small spaces, closed their eyes, raised their arms, and sang along. Leaders took turns walking around, placing their hands upon members, and praying for them in stream-of-thought invocations.

Men with reformed gang embodiment, those who were able to filter gang embodiment through reformed barrio masculinity and teach Scripture, often led Victory Outreach ministries. At his weekly Bible study in his backyard, Brother Ivan walked like a prisoner to illustrate a sermon concerning Proverbs 29:18. He explained that "without a vision people parish" and mentioned that he had done time in several state prisons. Describing it as being led into a "pit of hell," he walked away from the pulpit with his hands down and in front of him, taking small steps. However, he declared, God "broke his shackles." Adalberto, who had just gotten out of jail, proclaimed, "Amen!" In this way, Brother Ivan used his body to illustrate a lesson from the Bible as it applied to

Chicano gang members. His embodied sermon noticeably appealed to members' faith in God, as well as faith in Victory Outreach as an organization that could help them with recovery. Adalberto was impressed by Brother Ivan's gang background and recovery. After the Bible study, on our car ride home, he said he noticed the weights in Brother Ivan's backyard and asked if I thought Brother Ivan would let him start working out at his place. Through his Bible study, Brother Ivan carefully redirected gang embodiment away from the streets and toward recovery.

Victory Outreach members tried to spread the "good news" of the Gospel through masculine gang embodiment: performance of urban male rapper "cool pose." They performed evangelical rap on street corners, at public rallies, and on church stages to reach urban gang members in a way in which other Christian groups had failed—through what members referred to as "common ground." Victory Outreach members performed rap songs about Jesus and living life positively, dressing with baggy clothes and waving their hands and gesturing like typical rap artists. They used their own personal testimonies to try to draw the attention of gang members who were in and out of jail, and warn them that living gang life would lead only to ill health and violence.

Victory Outreach members' use of worship and evangelism demonstrates what Dwight Conquergood conceptualized as "the politics of performance" (1991, 190). By engaging in embodied gang recovery, Victory Outreach men rejected the ideas embedded in the Latino crime threat and earned legitimacy as Christians and reformed gang members; however, they also reinforced the dominance of hegemonic masculine expressions.

One hot, smoggy Fourth of July holiday, at a strip mall parking lot on Los Angeles's lower east side, Victory Outreach set up a firework stand as a fundraiser. Members worked at the booth, taking breaks to eat with their families on folding chairs under the shade of table umbrellas. Prerecorded Christian rap music spilled out from the speakers until Rick, a four-year member of Victory Outreach in his twenties, and David, an adolescent member of Victory Outreach's teen group G.A.N.G. (God's Annointed Now Generation), took microphones and faced the street. Together, they rapped for the public in what Rick had told me was "radical evangelism." Rick then introduced a slightly overweight teen standing next to him, who was wearing a backward baseball cap. Rick said,

"G.A.N.G.-affiliated Lil' G, 2008, doin' it for Jesus Christ." An electronic beat of bass and a snare drum blasted through two large speakers just as an SUV police cruiser rolled by with two white officers inside. They looked out their windows, which were rolled down, in the direction of the booming speakers. After the police vehicle rolled by and Lil' G's song ended, Rick took the microphone again. Whereas Lil' G was not an ex–gang member and was new to rap, Rick had been gang affiliated and addicted to crystal meth, and his movements embodied the cool pose of a rapper. He wore-loose fitting jeans, dropped low at the knees, and wove one hand around as he rapidly rhymed into a microphone. His rap lyrics ended with the words "One chance in life, and you better live it right." In this instance, redirected masculine gang embodiment, in the form of rapper-styled dress, gestures, and body movements, aligned reformed barrio masculinity with the dominant "man of God."

Conclusion

Victory Outreach and Homeboy Industries drew upon faith-based practices to facilitate gang recovery through the body. Embodied masculine practices and performances facilitated recovery, as the body symbolically and concretely represented the struggle between gang life and recovery. Previous chapters covered how addictions to gang violence and drugs prevented men from fulfilling the functions of conventional manhood (e.g., working and being affectionate with family). Reforming gang life required reforming rigid, embodied habits. In addition, leaders in recovery shunned masculine gang embodiment, in order to elevate reformed barrio masculinity over gang masculinity.

Gang masculinity existed along a spectrum of embodiment. Embodiment included the rigid, fixed aspects of embodied gang life, such as addictions to drugs or violence, habituated mannerisms, and physical disabilities. Men had difficulty reforming these. However, embodiment also included superficial facets of gang life, such as oversized clothes, shaved heads, and gang tattoos. Men more easily reformed these.

Recovery reformed facets of masculine gang embodiment, reorienting men away from gang life. Men redirected the meanings and use of handshakes, dances, clothes, pain, and weight gain. They used the handshake to blend the cool pose of gang embodiment with the nurturing characteristic of reformed barrio masculinity. They tempered their barrio-styled clothing and removed or covered tattoos to give the impression that they had a gang background, but were now working and providing for a family. They endured physical pain and esteemed large bodies in ways that emasculated gang life and masculinized gang recovery.

The embodied religious practices at each site helped to rearticulate Chicano gang masculinity into reformed barrio masculinity. Men at Homeboy Industries used eclectic spirituality to reshape their own bodies and group therapy to avoid violence. On the other hand, Victory Outreach leaders used Pentecostal practices to reshape the body and evangelism to redirect embodiment away from gang life. Through the body and bodily practices, reformed barrio masculinity resisted the dominant racist and sexist images of Latinos produced by the Latino crime threat. Although reformed barrio masculinity was aligned with conventional expressions of masculinity, and positioned as superior to Chicano gang masculinity, it was made accessible to recovering gang members through the adoption of bodily practices.

Conclusion

We're from the world's largest prison colony.... We're from
Rampart, poverty pimps and broken promises. From trade
in your public housing for section 8 to plead guilty and
we won't strike you out . . . (this time). We're the children
that rose from the ashes of Watts in '65 and South Central
in '92. The children that fled from American-made bullets
and bombs in Nicaragua, El Salvador, Guatemala, and Laos.
We're from the blood of Sandino, Zapata, Malcolm and Ché.
From the East LA High School Blow Outs, the Black Pan-
thers, and the FMLN.

Jones, Watkins, and McGill 2002, cited in Narváez Gutiérrez
2007, 117

In *Ruta Transnacional*, Mexican scholar Juan Carlos Narváez Gutiérrez (2007) used the cases of Mara Salvatrucha 13 (MS-13, a transnational gang) and Homies Unidos (a nonprofit dedicated to serving El
Salvadoran exiting gang members) to grapple with the issues of gangs,
transnationalism, and social activism. Narváez Gutiérrez suggested that
at the root of the gang problem in the twenty-first century were the
problems of late modernity: unease, marginality, and exclusion. Where
the old state used to be primarily concerned with spreading its domain
over new populations, the new state has engaged in projects of margin-
alizing and casting out populations—most notably through mass incarceration and immigrant deportation (Bauman 2004).

The first chapter of this book documented how racist tensions under-
lay the broad sweep of changes across the nation during the twentieth
century, and how this was particularly true in Los Angeles. Racial paternalism structured social reform efforts in the city during the Roosevelt
era, as reformers characterized Mexican communities not only as poor,

but socially disorganized and prone to crime (Lewthwaite 2009). Conservative white backlash against the Civil Rights Movement later recast racial stereotypes of blacks and Latinos as marked by cultural pathologies, exacerbated by government aid (Omi and Winant 1994[1986]). This set the stage for a retreat from overt, state-sanctioned structures of racist domination to covert, neoliberal racist expressions that blame the individual and promote a retreat of big government. Colorblind racism is the new racial hegemony of the post–Civil Rights Movement era (Bonilla-Silva 2009), while late-modern projects of marginalization and exclusion have cast out subaltern populations, such as blacks and Latinos, under the auspices of crime control (Garland 2001).

It has been said that Los Angeles is paradigmatic of changes in postmodern geographies (Soja 2011[1989]). Los Angeles is deeply characteristic of processes Jock Young (2011) has identified as fueling the unease of dominant responses to crime: immigration, urban hyperpluralism, manufacturing decline, and feminization of the public sphere. He has argued, however, that scholars' view of late-modern penality is blurred by ethnocentric myopia, when focused too narrowly on viewing the American case. Understanding the Los Angeles school of new urbanism, or Guliani's "New York Miracle," does not help to explain the parallel rise in mass arrests across various parts of the industrialized world. As Loic Wacquant elegantly argued in *Prisons of Poverty*, mass incarceration is "not just a consequence of neoliberalism . . . but an integral component of the neoliberal state" (2009[1999], 174). The rise of neoliberalism, and mass incarceration, has infected not just America; it has spread internationally through the various tropes of crime control: zero tolerance, *zero tolerancia, mano dura*, and so forth.

Gutiérrez claims that a spirit haunts the world: resistance. Jones, Watkins, and McGill's (2002) moving prose, cited in Narváez Gutiérrez's conclusion, suggests that amid the shadow cast upon us by the "new world order," and the mounting gloom of discontent, exclusion, and marginality, there is still a faint glimmer of hope visible. To this end, organizations that have facilitated recovery from gang life—such as Homies Unidos—might just have the capacity to organize a social movement, set forth clear demands, and achieve inclusion, justice, and equality. The theme of hope in Narváez Gutiérrez's work resonates throughout the Los Angeles–based organizations described in this book, and very likely similar programs across the nation and around the world.

However, the findings discussed herein indicate that the gang recovery movement's resistance and activism do not yet target the institutional apparatus upholding neoliberalism, mass incarceration, and colorblind racism. Rather, as Omi and Winant suggest, when excluded "*outward*, away from political engagement with the hegemonic racial state," racial groups are "forced *inward* upon themselves, as individuals, families, and communities" (1994[1986], 80–81). It is within this "war of maneuver," to borrow from Omi and Winant's use of Antonio Gramsci's theory of hegemony, that "institutional and cultural terrains" are mounted, allowing the development of racial projects and political struggle that then form a "war of position." The story of recovering gang members, therefore, is a story about Latinos who have turned inward to cope with and resist the processes of racialized exclusion and marginality; an analysis of neoliberal penality and counter-hegemonic resistance, as relevant as it is, should follow from—rather than proceed before—this study.

This book has endeavored to demonstrate how in everyday inner-city Los Angeles, adult Latino men simultaneously resist racialized notions of Latino criminality while also attempting to leave gang life behind. They go to work, attend drug treatment, and fill pews on Sunday mornings. They try to assist with parents' medical bills, take their children grocery shopping, and learn to cook for their families. They work on redeeming themselves in the eyes of their mothers, partners, and children, and try to "give back" to their communities by counseling younger men.

Recovering gang members use new expressions of manhood, shaped through images such as the "family man" or the "man of God," to craft reformed identities. Contrary to popular Chicago School–influenced debates that portray gang life as marked by lack of social mobility, I found that—even in areas with high concentrations of poverty and gangs—ambitions to move up and out of the neighborhood were typical among recovering gang members.

Latino recovery from gang life is set amid a context of very modest socioeconomic and geographic mobility, which is often thwarted by the exclusionary currents of late modernity. As a result, recovery from gang

Figure C.1. A Homeboy Industries member visits Light of the Village, a Christian ministry founded by John and Dolores Eads in lower Alabama (courtesy of Los Angeles Times)

life is not rapid or linear. Recovering gang members experienced the push and pull of gang life and conventional life. While some recovering gang members successfully left gangs, others had trouble cutting their ties. They still talked to old gang associates, used drugs, and continued to experience poverty, violence, and incarceration.

Immigrant Assimilation in the Twenty-First Century

Chapter 2 discussed how Los Angeles is a paradigmatic case for the study of segmented assimilation theory's concept of downward assimilation. Los Angeles entered the twenty-first century with a high percentage of immigrants and nonwhite residents, and a manufacturing sector that underwent a steep decline following the postwar economic boom. The city was also characterized by high rates of poverty, a large gang population, and the highest rate of gang homicide among large U.S. cities. In this sort of hostile context, segmented assimilation theory has predicted cyclical and intergenerational racism and poverty for new immigrants and their offspring: a trajectory of downward assimilation.

In contrast to the grim predictions that arose from snapshot statistics on immigration, poverty, and gangs, census data employed in chapter 2 revealed a counterintuitive finding: residents of inner-city Los Angeles continued to experience some economic progress. They experienced lower levels of poverty as they grew older, and many moved out of the inner city. Among immigrants, economic progress has been masked by the simultaneous exodus of some settled immigrants and the recent entrance of new, younger ones. Although immigrants have settled in racially segregated neighborhoods with high rates of poverty and gangs, these neighborhoods are not characterized by entrenched, isolated poverty, but rather modest socioeconomic mobility—up and out of the neighborhood.

The demographic trends highlighted above resonated with the hopes and ambitions that motivated many of the recovering gang members described in this book. Despite some downward mobility in late adolescence, many Latino recovering gang members continued to experience (or aspire to) modest socioeconomic mobility: working, advancing above the poverty line, and becoming homeowners. In addition, recovering gang members experienced some geographic mobility, such as relocating out of the inner city, or moving within it but out of the neighborhood associated with their gang.

Religious Reintegration

It has been suggested that it is misleading to assume that federal funding can create effective ex-offender reentry initiatives through inner-city churches. Departing from a sociology of religion perspective that has highlighted the limits of religious voluntarism and congregations, namely the ethnocentric tendencies of religious particularism (Ammerman 1997; Warner 1993), Omar McRoberts (2002; 2003) pointed out that churches were not necessarily part of the physical, surrounding neighborhoods in schemas for federally funded ex-offender reentry initiatives, and that, as a result, churches lacked meaningful relationships with community members that would make such initiatives effective. However, whereas the sociology of religion has highlighted religious particularism in studies of congregations and warned that social cleavages only deepen through religiosity, my findings suggest that federally funded faith-based gang recovery would not necessarily be incongruous with social reintegration.

Contrary to the position taken by McRoberts (2002), ex-offender reintegration does not have to hinge upon a faith-based organization's ties with the immediate physical neighborhood. Gang recovery is a good example of social reintegration into the church and the household that does not rely upon strong community ties with the surrounding area. As mentioned earlier, gang recovery reformulated Chicano masculinity, engaging recovering gang members with conventional expressions of manhood that facilitated the transition from street life to church, home, and the workplace. This reorientation of the focus of Chicano masculinity softened what would have ordinarily been hard social boundaries between the streets and the household. The site of social reintegration can thus be marked by open boundaries with the broader local community, or by closed boundaries while it still provides a community for faith worshippers and their families.

Faith-based gang recovery operates in the context of America's free religious marketplace, in which urban ministries such as Victory Outreach and Homeboy Industries offer contrasting models based on differing theological foundations and religious practices. Victory Outreach's model of gang recovery reflected the Protestant-influenced dialectic imagination, in which God is largely absent but sometimes transcendent, and members are to be "in the world, but not of the world." This model, segregated redemption, was further rooted in the decentralizing and ascetic theologies of Pentecostal evangelism. In Victory Outreach, recovering gang members experienced recovery through activities meant to shelter them from the broader local community. Recovering gang members attended church activities, such as services and evangelizing events, and abstained from drug and alcohol use or nonchurch activities.

On the other hand, Homeboy Industries' model of gang recovery reflected the Catholic-inspired analogical imagination, in which God is omnipresent and His grace is to be discovered in all that is in the world. This model, integrative redemption, was rooted in the centralizing and ecumenical theologies of Roman Catholicism. In Homeboy Industries' model, recovering gang members experienced recovery through activities meant to integrate them with the broader local community. Recovering gang members were encouraged to work and participate in spiritually inclusive prayers and meditations, although they left this setting and returned to their local neighborhoods when they were not working.

Irrespective of theological foundations, recovering gang members construct rich cultural memory, resonating with the gang experience, to facilitate social reintegration. Recovery from gang life was not linear, and recovering gang members drew from vast symbolic resources to facilitate a continuous process of redemption and reintegration. They drew upon parables and protest to distance themselves from gang life. They used prayer to experience social cohesion with each other and to consolidate their new social ties. It was through the specific theologies and religious practices of each site that cultural memory was constructed.

Recovery was a sacrilizing experience. Recovering gang members imagined themselves on a morally higher ground than the dominant institutions from which they were marginalized. They had experienced racism, poverty, violence, drug addiction, incarceration, and some were undocumented immigrants. These experiences were understood through parables of Christians as religiously persecuted, or through stories of minority groups as oppressed due to racism and colonization. They used such understandings of urban life to participate in Sunday morning church services, street evangelism, prayer, and meditations.

In terms of immigrant religious practice, Latino gang recovery was a form of reactive religion; it contrasted with religious practices originating in members' (or their parents or grandparents') countries of origin. Gang recovery models did not present Latino immigrant gang members with cultural memory of hardships situated in their country of origin. Rather, the construction of cultural memory resonated with members' experiences in and out of gangs.

Recovering gang members resisted downward assimilation by practicing faith and spirituality, fostering a sense of belonging, and building communities. These findings on gang recovery and religious practices extend the segmented assimilation canon, which up to this point has focused only on the role of peer group associations, the coethnic community (or church), and the educational system in shaping outcomes.

Segmented assimilation theory has dealt largely with how immigrant families infuse a blend of immigrant and American values with traditional immigrant practices to create trajectories of high educational attainment and upward socioeconomic mobility. Within this framework, the church has been deemed most prominent in anchoring the coethnic community. As most recovering gang members described herein are of immigrant origin, this study suggests that processes of acculturation and assimilation may yet continue in adulthood, beyond the period on which most segmented assimilation research has focused. This book concludes with two implications for segmented assimilation theory's analysis of religion, delinquency, and immigrant integration.

First, gang recovery does not fit the immigrant-centered model of social integration posited by segmented assimilation theory. As shown in this study, recovering gang members drew from faith practices at Mexican American–dominant urban ministries that were founded by outsiders to the Mexican community; it is notable that both organizations in this study were leading models of gang recovery in the United States. At both of these sites, recovering gang members drew upon cultural memories of hardship rooted in urban Los Angeles neighborhoods, rather than cultural memories of hardship in a foreign country.

Homeboy Industries members primarily identified with an understanding of the Mexican American experience, rooted in racial oppression, and their recovery from gang life was subtly constructed upon the legacies of the 1960s Chicano and Black Power movements. Members wanted to learn about "our history," which meant Chicano and colonial Mexican history, and they practiced indigenous and non-Western spirituality, and critiqued the deep inequalities of a postcolonial nation. Victory Outreach members primarily identified with their Christian faith, and their recovery from gang life was facilitated by evangelical practices. Members learned about the persecution of the Jews during biblical times and made parallels with their experiences as recovered gang members and Christian converts. They engaged in ecstatic forms of Christian worship, which promised the health and wealth promises of the Protestant social gospel, but simultaneously denounced the materialism rampant in mainstream America.

Second, through gang recovery, male adult Latinos with gang backgrounds integrated into the broader local community and resisted downward assimilation. Whereas segmented assimilation has posited that the coethnic community is the only shelter for urban immigrants from cyclical poverty, recovering gang members did make significant strides in resisting long-term poverty without significantly drawing upon traditional coethnic religious practices (namely Catholicism). This resonates with recent research finding that second-generation immigrants may experience socioeconomic trajectory shifts in adulthood; "downwardly assimilated" second-generation immigrants may experience higher rates of religiosity in adulthood than their counterparts, and religious conversion to nonmainline faiths is common among previously delinquent second-generation immigrant adults. As shown in this study, recovering gang members used parable, prayer, and protest through eclectic spirituality at Homeboy Industries and evangelical-Pentecostalism at Victory Outreach to upstage traditional coethnic religious practices.

The Chicano Patriarchal Bargain

Chapter 4 explored how recovery from gang life offered male privileges of status and respect that came with integration into the domestic and public spheres. Recovering gang members had experienced violence, poverty, drug addiction, incarceration, and strained family relationships. As a result, men entered recovery poor, marginalized, and remorseful. Having incurred the many costs of gang masculinity, recovering gang members sought to exit gang life.

Gang scholarship has suggested that gang members generally commit little crime, and that most mature out of gang lifestyle through employment and parenthood as they reach adulthood. However, growing obstacles to labor market participation have prevented men from cutting ties with gangs. Although the answer to the gang problem seems as straightforward as Homeboy Industries' slogan, "Jobs Not Jails," this study has reaffirmed that exit from gang life requires much more than simply obtaining work. Gang members can hold down jobs while remaining active in gang life (Jankowski 1991; Hagedorn 1994).

Some men had histories of being involved in gang life while maintaining stable employment. Although substance abuse was a factor in some cases, respondents still talked of the fear of being emasculated for leaving gang life. Gerardo, for example, wanted to seek revenge on a rival gang member after almost being killed in an ambush. The data in these cases resonate with previous research, which has suggested that core gang members have a violent "macho syndrome" and cannot be socially integrated into dominant society without therapeutic intervention (Yablonsky 1997, 18). This research has suggested that gang members' process of maturing out might be muddled with social marginality, jobs, drugs, violence and therapy. The question of how recovering gang members navigate difficulties, such as cutting ties with gang life and socially reintegrating into the household or community, is key to understanding how they progress along a path of recovery, which sometimes requires multiple attempts.

Chapter 4 revealed that recovery from gang life offered a localized type of the patriarchal bargain: the Chicano patriarchal bargain. As they progressed through the process of recovery and shifted their masculine orientations from the street to the household, recovering gang members gained status within the patriarchal hierarchies of recovery and the household. They became staff leaders, group therapy moderators, and Bible study leaders. At the same time, they become affectionate family men and breadwinners, gaining status and respect within their families. Thus, they traded the costs of gang masculinity for the privileges of reformed barrio masculinity.

Historically, religion has been a site where women have contested men's authority, but it has also been a site where men have rolled back gains in women's autonomy (George 2005; Heath 2003; Kurien 2003). As mentioned in chapter 4, at the turn of the twentieth century, industrialization, modernization, and the gendered division of labor expanded American women's influence within the home, schools, churches, and civic groups (Kimmel 1996). Fearing women's increasing influence in these spheres and trying to retain their privileges, men reacted by advancing hegemonic masculinity through "muscular Christianity" (Messner 1997, 24–25). Many Chicano gang members had low educational attainment, little job experience, criminal records, and substance abuse problems. These problems created obstacles for recovering gang members seeking employment and a Chicano patriarchal bargain to trade in the costs of gang life (substance abuse, violence, incarceration) for the privileges of conventional manhood (working and offering economic and social support to partners, mothers, and children).

Looking-Glass Reform

Chapter 5 investigated how recovering gang members experienced themselves as "reformed" through the space for public talk that gang recovery provided: the podium. Men constructed reformed barrio masculinity at the podium, by sharing details about their relationships with women and children, and by nurturing each other throughout the process of recovery. Public talk allowed recovering gang members to construct a "redemption script" (Maruna 2001, 87) through the negotiation of Chicano gang masculinity. First, reform from gang life involved distancing one's self from previous gang behaviors, such as drug use, violence, or extramarital affairs. Second, when recovering gang members reflected on their past behavior, they claimed that they hadn't known what it meant to be a "real man." Reform from gang life was a reorientation of what it meant to be a "real man," and this was framed through the discourse of being a "man of God" or a "family man." Recovering gang members demonstrated care for family formation and socioeconomic advancement when they spoke about marriage and children, employment, and homeownership. Third, recovering gang members experienced reform through the construction of narratives that emphasized helping others who now experienced drugs and gangs—even if it meant only making a difference in one person's life. Men at Homeboy Industries expressed wanting to "give back to the community," whereas men at Victory Outreach more often expressed wanting to be "where the Lord takes me"—which they hoped meant to lead a new church in a different city.

Recovery was a site where reformed barrio masculinity held a higher social status than gang masculinity. When asked who they admired or tried to be like, some respondents spoke of family members who had given to or provided for other family members—and usually these were women. But, by and large, men admired other men who were leaders in their organization and who had "given back to the community." Several recovering gang members at Homeboy Industries mentioned that they admired Father Greg for demonstrating unconditional love and helping inner-city residents, and these men talked about wanting to follow in his footsteps. Recovering gang members at Victory Outreach often talked about wanting to be like Pastor Raul and becoming a pastor at a new church. When asked where they wanted to be in five years, or who they admired or looked up to, not one respondent made reference to any member of his gang, or any aspect of gang life—even though some were often still tangled in gang life through violence or substance abuse.

Finally, chapter 6 examined how recovering gang members faced significant obstacles in experiencing reform from gang life, in part due to masculine gang embodiment. Although some facets of masculine gang embodiment were difficult to reshape, such as physical disabilities and addictions, other facets were reshaped through the incorporation of new bodily practices. Men tempered their barrio-styled clothing and removed or covered tattoos, giving the impression that they had a gang past, but were now working and providing for a family. They used handshakes to blend the cool pose of gang embodiment with the nurturing characteristic of reformed barrio masculinity. And they celebrated physical pain and esteemed large bodies in ways that emasculated gang life and masculinized recovery.

Gang recovery did help men cope with some of the rigid embodied habits of gang masculinity, such as cravings for drugs or gang violence. The theologically influenced activities at each site structured bodily practices and performances that reshaped and redirected gang embodiment toward the construction of reformed barrio masculinity. Homeboy Industries' model used talk therapy to teach men to monitor their own bodies for aggression. Members also moderated cravings for drugs and violence through meditation, and used cool pose to avoid violence. Victory Outreach's model drew from very sheltered embodied worship and evangelism. During worship, the pastor would lash out at gang masculinity. Recovering gang members redirected drug addictions toward ecstatic social cohesion through the embodied intimacy of "brotherly love." They redirected gang embodiment, especially rapper style, at evangelizing events, for instance by performing Christian rap.

In sum, it is extremely tempting to try to essentialize the experience of Latino immigrant integration in the post-1965 period as following in the historical trajectory of one of two major groups. From one such perspective, Latinos appear to follow in the tradition of early-twentieth-century Southern and Eastern European immigrants. Latinos do indeed often self-classify as "white," have had experiences with juvenile delinquency and street gangs similar to those of earlier

Italian immigrants, and have experienced some of the socioeconomic advancement between the first and second generation that other immigrant groups experienced. However, the enactment of oppressive policing approaches, the stiffening of sentencing laws targeting street crime, the steep rise in incarceration, and the rearticulation of gang activity as a threat to the nation almost guarantee that low-income Latinos—especially gang members—will not be seamlessly integrated into the American mainstream anytime soon. Instead, it becomes equally tempting to analyze contemporary Latino immigrant integration through the perspective of the African American experience, which has been marred by hypersegregation, low educational attainment, joblessness, and high levels of victimization and crime. Overall, however, Latino-dense neighborhoods are not characterized by these dynamics to the same severe extent as neighborhoods with dense African American populations. Rather, modest socioeconomic mobility and geographic mobility can be expected even in the most disadvantaged Latino neighborhoods. This suggests that, although marginal Latino men may not come to fulfill the promise of the American Dream, they still witness it happen to others in their daily lives—and they still hold out hope for a sliver of it.

Understanding the fate of marginal, inner-city Latino men today requires grappling with the complexity of their lived experiences. On the one hand, they are easily characterized as hypermasculine threats. On the other hand, they live in neighborhoods where waves of previous immigrants have, to some degree, achieved the American Dream: well-paying employment, home ownership, and the ability to provide for family. How marginal, inner-city Latino men experience the push and pull of these experiences depends, in part, upon how successfully they are able to turn inward, amid a racializing and exclusionary climate, and redeem themselves in the eyes of their family members, fellow church members, and their communities at large.

A major contradiction appears when one looks closely at the lived experiences of marginal Latino men. Contemporary Latino immigrant integration does not fit the trajectory of classical assimilation, but neither does it succumb to cyclical, entrenched poverty as suggested by the Chicago School or segmented assimilation theory. Rather, the Latino experience of drifting between these two major currents is navigated in great part through the sacralizing forces of urban American ministries and by their ability to harness social reintegration by drawing upon theologies, religious practices, and models of gang recovery in the competitive American religious marketplace. In Los Angeles's inner-city, recovering gang members hope to resist a racializing and exclusionary climate by reintegrating into their households and communities—leaving street life, shedding their reputations as gang members, and becoming "family men" or "men of God" in the process.

NOTES

NOTES TO THE INTRODUCTION

1. "Chicano" refers to a person of American origin and Mexican descent. Due to
   the fact that all respondents had joined Chicano street gangs by adolescence,
   respondents are referred to as Chicano, Mexican American, or Latino. However,
   I also use Chicano interchangeably with the synonymous category Mexican
   American and the broader racial category Latino to situate these findings within
   the broader field of sociological research.

   Use of the word "gang," whether in academic or public discourse, has been
   plagued by unclear or contradictory definitions (Ferrell et al. 2008). I use the
   word as follows: Respondents were, or had been, members of the fundamental
   unit of Chicano street gangs: *klikas*, or "age-graded cohorts" (Moore 1978; Vigil
   1988). In addition, respondents shared several key characteristics of Chicano
   street gangs: names, colors, hand signs, rituals, writing graffiti, selling and using
   drugs, and violence. These gangs were distinct from "drug gangs," which function as efficient, criminal enterprises (e.g., Klein 1995).

2. Although the introduction mentioned that Sergio's girlfriend was in the house,
   this was not the father of his son. At the time of my visit, his son's mother had
   not called or visited Sergio for months.

3. Businesses at Homeboy Industries (i.e., Homeboy Bakery, Homegirls Café,
   Homeboys Silkscreen, etc.) generated $2.5 million of Homeboys' $9.8 million
   budget in 2010.

4. Controversy followed when the City of Los Angeles, with a $25 million gang
   intervention budget, wouldn't approve Homeboy Industries' contracts for 2010.
   Homeboy Industries fell five million dollars short of its annual budget, and 330
   of Homeboy Industries' 427 employees—including all senior staff members—
   were laid off (Rutten 2010). (A week later, however, senior staff members were
   rehired.)

5. It should be noted that prosocial outreach programs make important contribu-
   tions to gang desistance, but that they are not the only ways out of the gang life.
   Many gang members do not have access to outreach programs or choose not
   to take advantage of them, but nevertheless make a successful (though perhaps
   more difficult) exit from gang life.

6. Segmented assimilation predicts three paths of assimilation for post-1965
   immigrants. The first is classical assimilation into a white mainstream. This
   occurs through "consonant acculturation," or the same rate acculturation for

first-generation immigrants and their children. The second path is downward assimilation into the urban underclass. This occurs through "dissonant accul- turation," or the more rapid acculturation of second-generation immigrant chil- dren than their first-generation parents. As black and Latino immigrants realize their grim prospects in a racially stratified society, they may acculturate into "oppositional groups" such as gangs that resist education and formal employ- ment as avenues of upward mobility. In the third path, the immigrant coethnic community provides a protective influence. This occurs through "selective acculturation," which involves drawing on social capital from the immigrant community to protect against the negative influences of street life (Portes and Rumbaut 2001).

7. As one example, John and Dolores Eads, founders of the lower Alabama gang prevention program Light of the Village, periodically have two members of Homeboy Industries visit and contribute to their work. This was beautifully showcased in a short *Los Angeles Times* online video documentary that received substantial attention (see Baylen 2009).

8. See Victory Outreach's (2010a) website. Following a handful of stories in the 1990s, coverage of Victory Outreach in the *Los Angeles Times* was virtually extinct by the time I conducted fieldwork. Earlier stories glorified Victory Outreach's success at turning around gang members and drug addicts' lives (e.g., Smith 1989; Tagami 1994; Johnson 1994; Simon 1994). After this honey- moon period, the press tended to paint a negative picture of Victory Outreach leadership as corrupt and questioned the officially reported rates of rehab success (e.g., Glover 1999; Chawkins 1999; Luna 2005). Victory Outreach was criticized for having no formal board of directors and claims were made that it was riddled with financial corruption and took advantage of members. A *Los Angeles Magazine* story depicted Victory Outreach members as having ties with the Mexican mafia. Pastor Sonny Arguinzoni replied with a letter accus- ing the magazine of having lied in claiming Victory Outreach had offered "no comment" (Grant 1997; Arguinzoni 1997). *Los Angeles Magazine* responded two months later with another story on the supposed Victory Outreach–Mexican mafia connection (Mathison 1997).

9. A similar parallel might be found among children of Southeast Asian refu- gees who convert to Mormonism; Aihwa Ong (2003) found that Mormon conversion paradoxically tied second-generation immigrants back to their ethnic origins, due to the faith's emphasis on ancestor worship. Maria Patricia Fernandez-Kelly (2007) has conceptualized the process by which religious practices transcend conversion to facilitate social reintegration as "dialogical acculturation."

10. Dissonant acculturation refers to second-generation immigrants' cultural integration into American society at a faster rate than their parents' integration; downward assimilation is the trajectory that is presumed, in most cases, to fol- low from dissonant acculturation (Portes and Rumbaut 2001).

Kasinitz et al. (2004) have critiqued segmented assimilation theory, claiming that dissonant acculturation is largely superficial. However, Portes and Rumbaut (2006) have argued that the most convincing evidence of downward assimilation is incarceration rates: about one in five second-generation Latinos and West Indians have been incarcerated by age twenty-four.

11. Victory Outreach was evenly split between male and female members. Homeboy Industries had an all-male bakery, an all-female café, and a nonprofit division that was roughly three-fourths male. A very small minority of members at each site were black. However, I focused on cases of adult male Latinos for conceptual clarity.

12. The design of this research project included only males. However, women also participate in gangs, in which they often play important roles. Scholars find that women who participate in men's gangs often seek protection from abusive relationships with men, but recreate such relationships through male-centered gang hierarchies (i.e., Miller 2001; Vigil 2007). Thus, the issue of women's exit from gangs—and this book's focus on gendered dynamics in the process of gang exit—is especially relevant for the study of female gangs. Research investigating women's experiences with gang exit would yield rich findings to complement the ones discussed herein.

13. Christian Base Communities originally gained popularity through the Liberation Theology movement in Latin America, specifically after the meeting of the Latin American Council of Bishops in 1968. Viewed by some as a product of the radical left, the model of Christian Base Communities emphasized solidarity with a community, as well as evangelization and class consciousness.

14. VETI offered semester-long three-credit evening courses in every region for men planning careers in ministry. Each course cost $50 and took place at a local Victory Outreach church. Students chose between two curricula, leading either to an Associate of Religious Studies Certificate, or a Ministerial Studies Diploma. The classes were also transferrable as college-level credit to two four-year Christian colleges, Azusa Pacific University and Fuller Theological Seminary.

NOTES TO CHAPTER 1

1. Including adults on probation or parole, an estimated 7.3 million adults were in the corrections system in 2008, translating into one in thirty-one American adults (Bureau of Justice Statistics 2010).

2. In Bratton's tenure as New York's top cop, officer-involved shootings resulting in death almost doubled, and damage settlements went from $13 million per year to $26 million per year (Jones and Wiseman 2003).

3. Moreover, any conviction for an offense prior to the passage of the law counted toward "three strikes," and multiple strikes could be given in the same case.

4. Community policing consists of a five-pronged approach: (1) mobilizing community leaders; (2) engaging gang youth through outreach workers; (3)

facilitating access to educational, economic, and social opportunities; (4) suppressing gang activities; and (5) helping community agencies address gang problems through a team problem-solving approach (Jones and Wiseman 2003).

NOTES TO CHAPTER 2

1. See Ruggles et al. (2010) for more information on IPUMS data.
2. As mentioned in the introduction, the Victory Outreach chapter described in this book is an anonymous chapter located in Los Angeles's Eastside area. This falls within the "inner-city Los Angeles" geographies described in the next paragraph.
3. In general, gang statistics should be viewed with skepticism. Changes in gang membership are, much like any official statistics, shaped by changes in classification schemes (Kitsuse and Cicourel 1963). The purpose of providing gang statistics here is precisely to show that the LAPD socially constructed tens of thousands of blacks and Latinos as gang members (and far fewer whites and Asians).

NOTES TO CHAPTER 3

1. A 2001 presidential executive order established the White House Office of Faith-Based and Community Initiatives (OFBCI) and allotted federal funds for faith-based and community organizations to provide social services.
2. Victory Outreach's website proclaimed, "To maximize its potential for growth around the globe, Victory Outreach has in place a structure that decentralizes the decision-making processes, empowering local churches to meet the needs of their communities, utilizing their own distinctive approach. . . . By operating ministries independently, new leadership will develop to propel this fellowship into the new millennium" (Victory Outreach 2010b).
3. Although the pastor gave brief theological lessons to members during worship services—explaining, for instance, how Victory Outreach is a Foursquare Pentecostal church—members rarely spoke in tongues. For this reason, I analytically frame Victory Outreach not within research on Pentecostal churches and glossolalia (e.g., Marina n.d.), but rather under the broader umbrella of Pentecostalism and evangelical Christianity.

NOTES TO CHAPTER 5

1. Rios's work is an important analytic contribution, as he was once a gang member and his fieldwork was carried out in the community where he had been active as a gang member.

NOTES TO CHAPTER 6

1. Educational attainment is gendered and classed. Low-income students enter school disadvantaged from their class background, and as a form of

self-protection adolescent males perform a tough masculinity that degrades those who perform well in school (Willis 1977; Macleod 1995[1987]).

2. The critical criminology school suggests agency is expressed through the body and embodiment (e.g., Brotherton 2008; Ferrell et al. 2008; Garot 2010).

3. Walking with a swagger is a common form of "cool pose" for urban men. Geoffrey Canada, in his autobiographical memoir of street life in Brooklyn, similarly described "bopping"—a walk with "a slight dip on one leg"—as a performance of "street tough" masculinity (1995, 71).

REFERENCES

Alba, Richard. 2003. *Remaking the American Mainstream: Assimilation and Contemporary Immigration*. Cambridge, MA: Harvard University Press.

Alexander, Michelle. 2010. *The New Jim Crow: Mass Incarceration in the Age of Colorblindness*. New York: New Press.

Ammerman, Nancy T. 1997. *Congregation and Community*. New Brunswick, NJ: Rutgers University Press.

Anderson, Elijah. 1976. *A Place on the Corner*. Chicago: University of Chicago Press.

———. 1990. *Streetwise: Race, Class, and Change in an Urban Community*. Chicago: University of Chicago Press.

Arguinzoni, Sonny. 1991. *Treasures Out of Darkness*. Green Forest, AR: New Leaf Press.

———. 1997. Letters. *Los Angeles Magazine*, September 1997, 42(9):24.

Baca Zinn, Maxine. 1982. "Chicano Men and Masculinity." *Journal of Ethnic Studies* 10(2):29–44.

Badillo, David A. 2006. *Latinos and the New Immigrant Church*. Baltimore: John Hopkins University Press.

Barber, Kristen. 2008. "The Well-Coiffed Man: Class, Race, and Heterosexual Masculinity in the Hair Salon." *Gender & Society* 22:455–476.

Baylen, Liz O. 2009. "Former L.A. Gang Members Take Their Message to Alabama." *Los Angeles Times*, December 30, 2009. Retrieved from http://articles.latimes.com/2009/dec/30/local/la-me-web-alabama30-2009dec30 on February 26, 2010.

Becerra, Hector. 2010. "Homeboy Industries Lays Off Most Employees as Financial Woes Worsen." *Los Angeles Times*, May 13, 2010.

Benedetti, Mario. 1974. "Te Quiero." *Poemas De Otros*. Buenos Aires: Editorial Alfa Argentina.

Bettie, Julie. 2003. *Women Without Class: Girls, Race, and Identity*. Berkeley: University of California Press.

Bonczar, Thomas P. 2003. "Prevalence of Imprisonment in the U.S. Population, 1974–2001." Special Report. Washington, DC: Bureau of Justice Statistics.

Bonilla-Silva, Eduardo. 2003. *Racism without Racists: Color-Blind Racism and the Persistence of Racial Inequality*. Lanham, MD: Rowman & Littlefield.

Bourgois, Philippe. 1995. *In Search of Respect: Selling Crack in El Barrio*. Cambridge, MA: Cambridge University Press.

Bourgois, Philippe, and Jeff Schonberg. 2009. *Righteous Dopefiend*. Berkeley: University of California Press.

Boyle, Gregory. 1990. "Self-Esteem: A Matter of Life, Death." *Los Angeles Times,* January 28, 1990.

———. 2010. *Tattoos on the Heart: The Power of Boundless Compassion.* New York: Free Press.

Boyle Heights Historical Society. 2011. Story from Audrey Mcnab. Retrieved from http://boyleheightshistoricalsociety.org/page3.php on February 19, 2012.

Braithwaite, John. 1989. *Crime, Shame and Reintegration.* New York: Cambridge University Press.

Brandes, Stanley. 2002. *Staying Sober in Mexico City.* Austin: University of Texas Press.

———. 2003. "Drink, Abstinence, and Male Identity in Mexico City." In Matthew C. Guttman (ed.), *Changing Men and Masculinities in Latin America.* Durham, NC: Duke University Press.

Bratton, William. 2009. "The LAPD Fights Crime, Not Illegal Immigration." *Los Angeles Times,* October 27, 2009. Retrieved from http://articles.latimes.com/2009/oct/27/opinion/oe-bratton27 on February 26, 2010.

Brenneman, Robert. 2009. "From Homie to Hermano: Conversion and Gang Exit in Central America." Ph.D. thesis. Department of Sociology, University of Notre Dame.

———. 2011. *Homies and Hermanos: God and Gangs in Central America.* New York: Oxford University Press.

Brotherton, David C. 2008. "Youth Subcultures, Resistance, and the Street Organization in Late Modern New York." In Michael Flynn and David C. Brotherton (eds.), *Globalizing the Streets: Cross-Cultural Perspectives on Youth, Social Control and Empowerment.* New York: Columbia University Press.

Brotherton, David C., and Luis Barrios. 2004. *The Almighty Latin King and Queen Nation: Street Politics and the Transformation of a New York City Gang.* New York: Columbia University Press.

Brusco, Elizabeth. 1995. *The Reformation of Machismo: Evangelical Conversion and Gender in Colombia.* Austin: University of Texas Press.

Burawoy, Michael, Alice Burton, Ann Arnett Ferguson, Kathryn J. Fox, Joshua Gamson, Nadine Gartrell, Leslie Hurst, Charles Kurzman, Leslie Salzinger, Josepha Schiffman, and Shiori Ui. 1991. *Ethnography Unbound: Power and Resistance in the Modern Metropolis.* Berkeley: University of California Press.

Bureau of Justice Statistics. 2010. "Total Correctional Population." Retrieved from http://bjs.ojp.usdoj.gov/index.cfm?ty=tp&tid=11 on June 1, 2010.

Cahalan, Margaret Werner. 1986. *Historical Corrections Statistics in the United States, 1850–1984.* Rockville, MD: Westat/U.S. Department of Justice, Bureau of Justice Statistics.

Canada, Geoffrey. 1995. *Fist Stick Knife Gun: A Personal History of Violence in America.* Boston: Beacon Press.

Cao, Nanlai. 2005. "The Church as a Surrogate Family for Working-Class Immigrant Chinese Youth: An Ethnography of Segmented Assimilation." *Sociology of Religion* 66(2):183–200.

Carr, E. Summerson. 2010. *Scripting Addiction: The Politics of Therapeutic Talk and American Sobriety*. Princeton, NJ: Princeton University Press.

Center for Labor Market Studies. 2009. "The Consequences of Dropping Out of High School." Boston: Center for Labor Market Studies, Northeastern University. April 2009.

Chafetz, Janet Saltzman, and Helen Rose Ebaugh. 2002. "Introduction." In Helen Rose Ebaugh and Janet Saltzman Chafetz (eds.), *Religion Across Borders: Transnational Immigrant Networks*. Walnut Creek, CA: AltaMira Press.

Chavez, Leo R. 2008. *The Latino Threat: Constructing Immigrants, Citizens, and the Nation*. Palo Alto, CA: Stanford University Press.

Chawkins, Steve. 1999. "Reaching Out—to the Very End." *Los Angeles Times*, July 16, 1999.

Chen, Carolyn. 2008. *Getting Saved in America: Taiwanese Immigration and Religious Experience*. Princeton, NJ: Princeton University Press.

Chong, Kelly H. 1998. "What It Means to Be Christian: The Role of Religion in the Construction of Ethnic Identity and Boundary among Second-Generation Korean Americans." *Sociology of Religion* 59(3):259–286.

Collins, Patricia Hill. 1990. *Black Feminist Thought: Knowledge, Consciousness, and the Politics of Empowerment*. Boston: Unwin Hyman.

Connell, R. W. 1987. *Gender and Power: Society, the Person, and Sexual Politics*. Stanford, CA: Stanford University Press.

———. 1995. *Masculinities*. Berkeley: University of California Press.

———. 2002. *Gender*. Malden, MA: Polity.

Connell, R.W., and James Messerschmidt. 2005. "Hegemonic Masculinity: Rethinking the Concept." *Gender & Society* 19(6):829–859.

Conquergood, Dwight. 1991. "Rethinking Ethnography: Towards a Critical Cultural Politics." *Communication Monographs* 58:179–194.

———. 1994. "Homeboys and Hoods: Gang Communication and Cultural Space." In Lawrence R. Frey (ed.), *Group Communication in Context: Studies of Natural Groups*. Hillsdale, NJ: Lawrence Erlbaum.

Coulton, Claudia, Brett Theodos, and Margery A. Turner. 2009. *Family Mobility and Neighborhood Change: New Evidence and Implications for Community Initiatives*. Washington, DC: Urban Institute.

Davalos, Karen May. 2002. "The Real Way of Praying: The Via Crucis, Mexicano Sacred Space, and the Architecture of Domination." In Timothy Matovina and Gary Riebe-Estrella (eds.), *Horizons of the Sacred: Mexican Traditions in U.S. Catholicism*. Ithaca, NY: Cornell University Press.

Davis, Mike. 1990. *City of Quartz: Excavating the Future in Los Angeles*. London: Verso Press.

Dawsey, Darrell. 1989. "Many People Want Police 'Hammer' to Hit Gangs Harder." *Los Angeles Times*, July 4, 1989.

Decker, Scott H., and Janet L. Lauritsen. 1996. "Breaking the Bonds of Membership: Leaving the Gang." In C. Ronald Huff (ed.), *Gangs in America*. Thousand Oaks, CA: Sage.

Delgado, Melvin, and Keva Barton. 1998. "Murals in Latino Communities: Social Indicators of Community Strengths." *Social Work* 43(4):346–356.

Dellinger, Kirsten. 2004. "Masculinities in 'Safe' and 'Embattled' Organizations: Accounting for Pornographic and Feminist Magazines." *Gender & Society* 18:545–566.

Ebaugh, Helen Rose, and Janet Saltzman Chafetz. 2000. *Religion and the New Immigrants: Continuities and Adaptations in Immigrant Congregations.* Walnut Creek, CA: AltaMira Press.

Edin, Kathryn, Timothy J. Nelson, and Rechelle Paranal. 2004. "Fatherhood and Incarceration as Potential Turning Points in the Criminal Careers of Unskilled Men." In Mary Pattillo and David Weiman (eds.), *Imprisoning America: The Social Effects of Mass Incarceration.* New York: Russell Sage.

Enriquez, Sam. 1989. "Held in Sweep; Violence Continues." *Los Angeles Times,* August 20, 1989.

———. 1990. "Arrested in S.F. Valley Gang Sweeps: Crime: Police Call It Most Successful Operation Ever. But Violence Plagues Southland as at Least 15 People Are Reported Slain." *Los Angeles Times,* February 26, 1990.

Espinosa, Gastón. 2006. "Methodological Reflections on Social Science Research on Religions." In Miguel A. De La Torre and Gastón Espinosa (eds.), *Rethinking Latino(a) Religion and Identity.* Cleveland: Pilgrim Press.

Espinosa, Gastón, Virgilio Elizondo, and Jesse Miranda. 2005. "Introduction: U.S. Latino Religions and Faith-Based Political, Civic, and Social Action." In Gastón Espinosa, Virgilio Elizondo, and Jesse Miranda (eds.), *Latino Religions and Civic Activism in the United States.* New York: Oxford University Press.

Espiritu, Yen Le. 1997. *Asian American Women and Men: Labor, Laws, and Love.* Thousand Oaks, CA: Sage.

Fagan, Jeffrey. 1996. "Gangs, Drugs and Neighborhood Change." In C. R. Huff (ed.), *Gangs in America,* 2d ed. Thousand Oaks, CA: Sage.

Fairbanks, Robert P. 2009. *How it Works: Recovering Citizens in a Post-Welfare Philadelphia.* Chicago: University of Chicago Press.

Ferguson, Ann Arnett. 2000. *Bad Boys: Public School in the Making of Black Masculinity.* Ann Arbor: University of Michigan Press.

Fernandez-Kelly, Maria Patricia. 2007. "The Moral Universe of Fabian Garamon: Religion and the Divided Self among Second-Generation Immigrants in the United States." Paper presented at the 77th Annual Meetings of the Eastern Sociological Society, Philadelphia, PA, March 16.

Ferrell, Jeff, Keith Hayward, and Jock Young. 2008. *Cultural Criminology.* Thousand Oaks, CA: Sage.

Flores, Edward. 2009. "'I Am Somebody': Barrio Pentecostalism and Gendered Acculturation among Chicano Ex-Gang Members." *Ethnic and Racial Studies* 32(6):996–1016.

———. 2012. "Latinos and Faith-based Recovery from Gangs." In Carolyn Chen and Russell Jeung (eds.), *Sustaining Faith Traditions: Race, Ethnicity, and Religion among the Latino and Asian American Second Generation.* New York: New York University Press.

Fremon, Celeste. 2004[1995]. *G-Dog and the Homeboys: Father Greg Boyle and the Gangs of East Los Angeles*. Albuquerque: University of New Mexico Press.

Gans, Herbert J. 1962. *The Urban Villagers: Group and Class in the Life of Italian-Americans*. New York: Free Press.

———. 1992. "Second Generation Decline: Scenarios for the Economic and Ethnic Futures of the Post-1965 American Immigrants." *Ethnic and Racial Studies* 15(2):173–193.

———. 2007. "Acculturation, Assimilation and Mobility." *Ethnic and Racial Studies* 30(1):152–164.

Garland, David. 2001. *The Culture of Control: Crime and Social Order in Contemporary Society*. Chicago: University of Chicago Press.

Garot, Robert. 2003. "Where You From: Gang Identity as Performance." *Journal of Contemporary Ethnography* 36(1):50–84.

———. 2010. *Who You Claim: Performing Gang Identity in School and on the Streets*. New York: New York University Press.

Garot, Robert, and Jack Katz. 2003. "Provocative Looks: Gang Appearance and Dress Codes in an Inner-City Alternative School." *Ethnography* 4(3):421–454.

Garvey, Megan, and Richard Winton. 2002. "City Declares War on Gangs: Hahn and Bratton Say They'll Go After Leaders and Members with the Same Aggressive Tactics that Worked against the Mafia on the East Coast." *Los Angeles Times*, December 4, 2002.

Gates, Daryl F. 1991. "LAPD's Efforts to Stop Gangs." *Los Angeles Times*, October 28, 1991.

George, Sheba. 2005. *When Women Come First: Gender and Class in Transnational Migration*. Berkeley: University of California Press.

Gilmore, Ruth Wilson. 2007. *Golden Gulag: Prisons, Surplus, Crisis, and Opposition in Globalizing California*. Berkeley: University of California Press.

Glover, Scott. 1999. "Column One: Casting a Critical Eye on Church of Castoffs." *Los Angeles Times*, February 1, 1999.

Gonzales, Roberto G. 2011. "Learning to Be Illegal: Undocumented Youth and Shifting Legal Contexts in the Transition to Adulthood." *American Sociological Review* 76(4):602–619.

Gorman, Anna. 2009. "Tougher Rules on Policing Immigrants." *Los Angeles Times*, October 14, 2009. Retrieved from http://articles.latimes.com/2009/oct/14/local/me-immig-law14 on February 26, 2010.

Grant, Richard. 1997. "Dial Eme for Murder." *Los Angeles Magazine*, May 1997, 42(5): 34.

Greeley, Andrew. 1990. *The Catholic Myth: The Behavior and Beliefs of American Catholics*. New York: Charles Scribner's Sons/Macmillan.

———. 2001. *The Catholic Imagination*. Berkeley: University of California Press.

Gustafson, Cloyd. 1940. "An Ecological Analysis of the Hollenbeck Area of Los Angeles." Master's thesis, Department of Sociology, University of Southern California.

Hadaway, C. Kirk, and Penny Long Marler. 1991. "The Unchurching of America: An Exploration and Interpretation of Post-War Religious Identification and

Involvement Trends." Unpublished paper. Cleveland: United Church Board for Homeland Ministries.

Hagan, John. 2010. *Who Are the Criminals? The Politics of Crime Policy from the Age of Roosevelt to the Age of Reagan.* Princeton, NJ: Princeton University Press.

Hagan, John, and Bill McCarthy. 1997. *Mean Streets: Youth Crime and the Homeless.* New York: Cambridge University Press.

Hagedorn, John M. 1994. "Homeboys, Dope Fiends, Legits, and New Jacks." *Criminology* 32(2):197–219.

———. 1998. *People and Folks: Gangs, Crime and the Underclass in a Rustbelt City.* Chicago: Lake View Press.

———. 2008. *A World of Gangs: Armed Young Men and Gangsta Culture.* Minneapolis: University of Minnesota Press.

Hallsworth, Simon, and John Lea. 2011. "Reconstructing Leviathan: Emerging Contours of the Security State." *Theoretical Criminology* 15:141–157.

Haney, Lynne. 2010. *Offending Women: Power, Punishment, and the Regulation of Desire.* Berkeley: University of California Press.

Hays, Sharon. 2004. *Flat Broke with Children: Women in the Age of Welfare Reform.* New York: Oxford University Press.

Heath, Melanie. 2005. "Soft-Boiled Masculinity: Renegotiating Gender and Racial Ideologies in the Promise Keepers Movement." *Gender & Society* 17(3):423–444.

Hernández, Francisco. 1996. "El hallazgo del cuerpo." *Poesía Reunida: 1974–1994.* Mexico City: Universidad Nacional Autónoma de México, Coordinación de Humanidades.

Himmel, Nieson. 1988. "L.A. Gang Killings Put at 236—Up 15% From "87." *Los Angeles Times,* December 16, 1988.

Hirschman, Charles. 2004. "The Role of Religion in the Origins and Adaptation of Immigrant Groups in the United States." *International Migration Review* 38:1206–1233.

Hoffmann, Heath C. 2006. "Criticism as Deviance and Social Control in Alcoholics Anonymous." *Journal of Contemporary Ethnography* 35(6):669–695.

Homeboy Industries. 2008. "About Us: Past Events." Retrieved from http://www.homeboy-industries.org/events-01.php on June 1, 2010.

———. 2010. "About Us: Father Greg Boyle, S.J." Retrieved from http://www.homeboy-industries.org/father-greg.php on January 1, 2010.

Hondagneu-Sotelo, Pierrette. 1994. *Gendered Transitions: Mexican Experiences of Immigration.* Berkeley: University of California Press.

———, ed. 2007. *Religion and Social Justice for Immigrants.* New Brunswick, NJ: Rutgers University Press.

———. 2008. *God's Heart Has No Borders: Religious Activism for Immigrant Rights.* Berkeley: University of California Press.

Hondagneu-Sotelo, Pierrette, and Michael Messner. 1994. "Gender Displays and Men's Power: The New Man and the Mexican Immigrant Man." In Harry Brod and Michael Kaufman (eds.), *Theorizing Masculinities.* Thousand Oaks, CA: Sage.

Horowitz, Ruth. 1983. *Honor and the American Dream: Culture and Identity in a Chicano Community*. New Brunswick, NJ: Rutgers University Press.

Howell, James C., Arlen Egley Jr., George E. Tita, and Elizabeth Griffiths. 2011. "U.S. Gang Problem Trends and Seriousness 1996–2009." *National Gang Center Bulletin*. Tallahassee, FL: Institute for Intergovernmental Research.

Hunt, Geoffrey P., and Karen Joe-Laidler. 2001. "Alcohol and Violence in the Lives of Gang Members." *Alcohol Research and Health* 25(1):66–71.

Hunt, Geoffrey P., Karen Joe-Laidler, and Kathleen MacKenzie. 2005. "Moving Into Motherhood: Gang Girls and Controlled Risk." *Youth & Society* 36(3):333–373.

Jacobson, Matthew Frye. 1999. *Whiteness of a Different Color: European Immigrants and the Alchemy of Race*. Cambridge, MA: Harvard University Press.

Jankowski, Martin Sanchez. 1991. *Islands in the Street: Gangs and American Urban Society*. Berkeley: University of California Press.

Jiménez, Tomás R. 2009. *Replenished Ethnicity: Mexican Americans, Immigration, and Identity*. Berkeley: University of California Press.

Johnson, John. 1989. "Night of the 'Hammer': Retaking the Streets of South L.A." *Los Angeles Times*, July 3, 1989.

———. 1994. "A Fighting Chance: Gang Members Learn the Art of Discipline at Van Nuys Gym." *Los Angeles Times*, June 20, 1994.

Jones, Arthur A., and Robin Wiseman. 2003. "Bratton's Drumbeat: How Does the Chief Really Intend to Fight the Gang War?" *Los Angeles Daily News*, January 12, 2003.

Jones, Shawnta, Tameka Watkins, and Kim McGill. 2002. "Youth Justice Coalition Members' Poem." Los Angeles: Youth Justice Coalition.

Kandiyoti, Deniz. 1987. "Bargaining with Patriarchy." *Gender & Society* 23:274–290.

Kasinitz, Philip, John H. Mollenkopf, and Mary C. Waters. 2004. "Worlds of the Second Generation." In Philip Kasinitz, John H. Mollenkopf, and Mary C. Waters (eds.), *Becoming New Yorkers: Ethnographies of the New Second Generation*. New York: Russell Sage.

Kasinitz, Philip, John H. Mollenkopf, Mary C. Waters, and Jennifer Holdaway. 2008. *Inheriting the City: The Children of Immigrants Come of Age*. New York: Russell Sage.

Katz, Jesse. 1990. "Gang Sweeps Earn Low Marks." *Los Angeles Times*, June 18, 1990.

Kennedy, David. 2011. *Don't Shoot: One Man, a Street Fellowship, and the End of Violence in Inner-City America*. New York: Bloomsbury.

Kim, Claire Jean. 1999. "The Racial Triangulation of Asian Americans." *Politics & Society* 27(1):105–138.

Kim, Rebecca Y. 2004. "Second Generation Korean American Evangelicals: Ethnic, Multiethnic, or White Campus Ministries?" *Sociology of Religion* 65(1):19–34.

Kimmel, Michael. 1996. *Manhood in America: A Cultural History*. New York: Free Press.

Kitsuse, John I., and Aaron V. Cicourel. 1963. "A Note on the Uses of Official Statistics." *Social Problems*. 11(2):131–139.

Klein, Malcolm. 1971. *Street Gangs and Street Workers*. Englewood Cliffs, NJ: Prentice Hall.

———. 1995. *The American Street Gang: Its Nature, Prevalence and Control*. New York: Oxford University Press.

———. 2004. *Gang Cop: The Words and Ways of Officer Paco Domingo*. Walnut Creek, CA: AltaMira Press.

Kurien, Prema. 2003. "Gendered Ethnicity: Creating a Hindu Indian Identity in the United States." In Pierrette Hondagneu-Sotelo (ed.), *Gender and U.S. Immigration: Contemporary Trends*. Berkeley and Los Angeles: University of California Press.

Laub, John, and Robert J. Sampson. 2003. *Shared Beginnings, Divergent Lives: Delinquent Boys Until Age 70*. Cambridge, MA: Harvard University Press.

Lay, Soda. 2004. "Lost in the Fray: Cambodian American Youth in Providence, Rhode Island." In Jennifer Lee and Min Zhou (eds.), *Asian American Youth: Culture, Identity, and Ethnicity*. New York: Routledge.

Lee, John H. 1989. "Police Arrive—and This Time They'll Stay." *Los Angeles Times*, July 21, 1989.

León, Luis D. 1998. "Born Again in East LA: The Congregation as Border Space." In R. S. Warner and Judith G. Wittner (eds.), *Gatherings in Diaspora*. Philadelphia: Temple University Press.

———. 2004. *La Llorona's Children: Religion, Life and Death in the U.S.-Mexican Borderlands*. Berkeley: University of California Press.

Leonard, Karen I. 2005. "Introduction." In Karen I. Leonard, Alex Stepick, Manuel Vásquez, and Jennifer Holdaway (eds.), *Immigrant Faiths: Transforming Religious Life in America*. Walnut Creek, CA: AltaMira Press.

Levitt, Peggy. 2001. *The Transnational Villagers*. Berkeley: University of California Press.

———. 2008. "Religion as a Path to Civic Engagement." *Ethnic and Racial Studies* 31(4):766–791.

Lewthwaite, Stephanie. 2009. *Race, Place, and Reform in Mexican Los Angeles: A Transnational Perspective, 1890–1940*. Tucson: University of Arizona Press.

Lieberson, Stanley. 1980. *A Piece of the Pie: Blacks and White Immigrants Since 1880*. Berkeley: University of California Press.

Light, Ivan. 2008. *Deflecting Immigration: Networks, Markets, and Regulation in Los Angeles*. New York: Russell Sage.

Lipsitz, George. 1998. *The Possessive Investment in Whiteness: How White People Profit from Identity Politics*. Philadelphia: Temple University Press.

Lopez, David. 2009. "Whither the Flock? The Catholic Church and the Success of Mexicans in America." In Richard Alba, Albert J. Raboteau, and Josh DeWind (eds.), *Immigration and Religion in America: Comparative and Historical Perspectives*. New York: New York University Press.

Lopez, Nancy. 2003. *Hopeful Girls, Troubled Boys: Race and Gender Disparity in Urban Education*. New York: Routledge.

Los Angeles County Department of Public Health—Injury & Violence Prevention Program. 2011. "Gang Homicide Chart, April 21, 2011." Gang Awareness Prevention.

Retrieved from http://www.publichealth.lacounty.gov/ivpp/injury_topics/GangA-warenessPrevention/Gang%20Homicide%20Chart%20Apr%2021%202011%20chart.pdf on January 1, 2012.

Los Angeles Municipal Housing Commission. 1910. Annual Report. Los Angeles.

Los Angeles Police Department. 2012. Citywide Gang Crime Summary, 1993–2008. Gang Statistics Archives. Retrieved from http://www.lapdonline.org/crime_mapping_and_compstat/content_basic_view/31590 on January 1, 2012.

Luna, Claire. 2005. "Facing Tragedy, Pastors Put Their Faith on Hold." *Los Angeles Times,* July 18, 2005.

Macleod, Jay. 1995[1987]. *Ain't No Makin' It: Aspirations and Attainment in a Low-Income Neighborhood,* 2d ed. Boulder, CO: Westview Press.

Maguire, Kathleen. 1995. *Sourcebook of Criminal Justice Statistics: 1995.* Darby, PA: Diane Publishing.

Majors, Richard, and Janet Mancini Billson. 1992. *Cool Pose: The Dilemmas of Black Manhood in America.* New York: Simon & Schuster.

Marina, Peter. n.d. *Getting the Holy Ghost: Experiences in a American Tongue-Speaking Church.* New York: Lexington Books (under contract).

Marrow, Helen. 2009. "Immigrant Bureaucratic Incorporation: The Dual Roles of Professional Missions and Government Policies." *American Sociological Review* 74:756–776.

Maruna, Shadd. 2001. *Making Good: How Ex-Convicts Reform and Rebuild Their Lives.* Washington, DC: American Psychological Association.

Mathison, Dirk. 1997. "Gunning for God?" *Los Angeles Magazine,* November 1997, 42(11):72.

Matza, David. 1964. *Delinquency and Drift.* New York: John Wiley & Sons.

McCarthy, Terry. 2004. "The Gang Buster." *Time,* January 14, 2004.

McDonald, Kevin. 2003. "Marginal Youth, Personal Identity, and the Contemporary Gang: Reconstructing the Social World?" In Louis Kontos, David C. Brotherton, and Luis Barrios (eds.), *Gangs and Society: Alternative Perspectives.* New York: Columbia University Press.

McRoberts, Omar M. 2002. "Religion, Reform, Community: Examining the Idea of Church-based Prisoner Reentry." *Reentry Roundtable: Prisoner Reentry and the Institutions of Civil Society: Bridges and Barriers to Successful Reintegration.* March 20–21, 2002. Washington, DC: Urban Institute.

———. 2003. *Streets of Glory: Church and Community in a Black Urban Neighborhood.* Chicago: University of Chicago Press.

Menjivar, Cecilia. 2003. "Religion and Immigration in Comparative Perspective: Catholic Evangelical El Salvadorans in San Francisco, Washington, D.C., and Phoenix." *Sociology of Religion* 64(1):21–45.

Messerschmidt, James. 2000. *Nine Lives: Adolescent Masculinities, the Body, and Violence.* Boulder, CO: Westview Press.

———. 2004. *Flesh and Blood: Adolescent Gender Diversity and Violence.* Lanham, MD: Rowman & Littlefield.

Messner, Michael A. 1997. *Politics of Masculinities: Men in Movements*. Thousand Oaks, CA: Sage.

Metro Digest. 1990. "'Hammer' Falls on 74 Possible Gang Members." *Los Angeles Times*, November 17, 1990.

Milkman, Ruth. 2006. *L.A. Story: Immigrant Workers and the Future of the U.S. Labor Movement*. New York: Russell Sage.

Miller, Donald E., and Tetsunao Yamamori. 2007. *Global Pentecostalism: The New Face of Christian Social Engagement*. Berkeley: University of California Press.

Miller, Jody. 2001. *One of the Guys: Girls, Gangs and Gender*. New York: Oxford University Press.

———. 2002. "The Strengths and Limits of 'Doing Gender' for Understanding Street Crime." *Theoretical Criminology* 6:433–460.

Mirandé, Alfredo. 1997. *Hombres y Machos: Masculinity and Latino Cultura*. Boulder, CO: Westview Press.

Mitchell, John L. 1989. "The Raid that Still Haunts L.A." *Los Angeles Times*, March 14, 2001.

Moloney, Deirdre M. 2002. *American Catholic Lay Groups and Transatlantic Social Reform in the Progressive Era*. Chapel Hill: University of North Carolina Press.

Moloney, Molly, Kathleen Mackenzie, Geoffrey P. Hunt, and Karen Joe-Laidler. 2009. "The Path and Promise of Fatherhood for Gang Members." *British Journal of Criminology* 49:305–325.

Moore, Joan W. 1978. *Homeboys: Gangs, Drugs and Prison in the Barrios of Los Angeles*. Philadelphia: Temple University Press.

———. 1991. *Going Down to the Barrio: Homeboys and Homegirls in Change*. Philadelphia: Temple University Press.

Morrison, Patt. 2010. "Father Greg Boyle: Life among the Homies. Patt Morrison Asks." *Los Angeles Times*, April 10, 2010.

Myers, Dowell, Janna Goldberg, Sarah Mawhorter, and Seong Hee Min. 2010. "Los Angeles 2010: State of the City." Los Angeles: Pat Brown Institute.

Myers, Dowell, Linda Lou, Edward Flores, Hyojung Lee, Anthony Guardado, and Stephanie Young. 2012. "Community Profile for Los Angeles County in 2010." Los Angeles County Census Report for 2010. Los Angeles: First 5 LA.

Myers, Dowell, and John Pitkin. 2010. "Assimilation Today: New Evidence Shows the Latest Immigrants to America Are Following in Our History's Footsteps." Washington, DC: Center for American Progress.

Narváez Gutiérrez, Juan Carlos. 2007. *Ruta transnacional: a San Salvador por los Ángeles. Espacio de interacción juvenil en un contexto migratorio*. Mexico City: Instituto Mexicano de la Juventud.

National Drug Intelligence Center. 2000. "National Drug Threat Assessment 2001—The Domestic Perspective." U.S. Department of Justice. Retrieved from http://www.usdoj.gov/ndic/ on January 31, 2008.

National Public Radio. 2012. "Falling Crime Rates Challenge Long-Held Beliefs." Talk of the Nation. National Public Radio. Retrieved from http://www.npr.

org/2012/01/03/144627627/falling-crime-rates-challenge-long-held-beliefs on January 3, 2012.

Ng, Kwai Hang. 2002. "Seeking the Christian Tutelage: Agency and Culture in Chinese Immigrants' Conversion to Christianity." *Sociology of Religion* 63(2):195–214.

Omi, Michael, and Howard Winant. 1994[1986]. *Racial Formation in the United States: From the 1960s to the 1990s.* New York: Routledge.

Ong, Aihwa. 2003. *Buddha is Hiding: Refugees, Citizenship, the New America.* Berkeley: University of California Press.

Padilla, Felix. 1992. *The Gang as an American Enterprise.* New Brunswick, NJ: Rutgers University Press.

Pardo, Mary. 2005. "Mexican American Women, Grassroots Community Activists: Mothers of East Los Angeles." In Maxine Baca-Zinn, Pierrette Hondagneu-Sotelo, and Michael A. Messner (eds.), *Gender through the Prism of Difference.* Oxford: Oxford University Press.

Park, Julie, and Dowell Myers. 2010. "Intergenerational Mobility in the Post-1965 Immigration Era: Estimates by an Immigrant Generation Cohort Method." *Demography* 47(2):369–392.

Park, Robert E., Ernest Burgess, and Roderic McKenzie. 1925. *The City.* Chicago: University of Chicago Press.

Perlmann, Joel. 2005. *Italians Then, Mexicans Now: Immigrant Origins and Second-Generation Progress, 1890 to 2000.* New York: Russell Sage.

PEW Center on the States. 2008. "One in 100: Behind Bars in America." Retrieved from http://www.pewcenteronthestates.org/uploadedFiles/One%20in percent20100.pdf on June 1, 2010.

Portes, Alejandro, and Rubén G. Rumbaut. 2001. *Legacies: The Story of the Immigrant Second Generation.* Berkeley: University of California Press.

———. 2006[1990]. *Immigrant America: A Portrait.* Berkeley: University of California Press.

Portes, Alejandro, and Min Zhou. 1993. "The New Second Generation: Segmented Assimilation and Its Variants." *Annals of the American Academy of Political and Social Science* 530(1):74–96.

Pyke, Karen D. 1996. "Class-Based Masculinities: The Interdependence of Gender, Class, and Interpersonal Power." *Gender & Society* 10:527–549.

Ramirez, Hernan, and Edward Orozco Flores. 2010. "Latino Masculinities in the Post 9/11 Era." In Maxine Baca Zinn, Pierrette Hondagneu-Sotelo, and Michael A. Messner (eds.), *Gender Through the Prism of Difference,* 4th ed. New York: Oxford University Press.

Rios, Victor M. 2009. "The Consequences of the Criminal Justice Pipeline on Black and Latino Masculinity." *Annals of the Academy of Political and Social Science* 623(1):150–162.

———. 2011. *Punished: Policing the Lives of Black and Latino Boys.* New York: New York University Press.

Roberts, Dorothy. 2012. "Beyond the Picket Fence: The Impact of Traditional Laws on Changing Families." Panelist at the Loyola University Chicago School of Law's annual Race and the Law Symposium, Chicago, IL March 30.

Rodríguez, Luis J. 2005[1993]. *Always Running: La Vida Loca: Gang Days in L.A.* New York: Simon & Schuster.

Roof, Wade Clark, and William McKinney 1987. *American Mainline Religion: Its Changing Shape and Future.* New Brunswick, NJ: Rutgers University Press.

Roy, Kevin M., and Omari Dyson. 2010. "Making Daddies into Fathers: Community-based Fatherhood Programs and the Construction of Masculinities for Low-income African American Men." *American Journal of Community Psychology* 45:139–154.

Rubin, Joel. 2009. "Massive Police Raid Targets Brutal L.A. Gang." *Los Angeles Times,* September 23, 2009. Retrieved from http://articles.latimes.com/2009/sep/23/local/me-avenues-gang23 on February 26, 2010.

Rudy, David R., and Arthur L. Greil. 1989. "Is Alcoholics Anonymous a Religious Organization?: Meditations on Marginality." *Sociology of Religion* 50:41–51.

Ruggles, Steven, J. Trent Alexander, Katie Genadek, Ronald Goeken, Matthew B. Schroeder, and Matthew Sobek. 2010. "Integrated Public Use Microdata Series: Version 5.0 [Machine-readable database]." Minneapolis: University of Minnesota.

Rutten, Tim. 2010. "What Price Hope?" *Los Angeles Times,* May 15, 2010.

Sahagun, Louis. 1989. "The Mothers of East L.A. Transform Themselves and Their Neighborhood." *Los Angeles Times,* August 13, 1989.

Sanchez, George. 2004. "What's Good for Boyle Heights is Good for the Jews: Creating Multiracialism on the Eastside during the 1950s." *American Quarterly* 56(3):633–661.

Sanchez-Walsh, Arlene. 2003. *Latino Pentecostal Identity: Evangelical Faith, Self, and Society.* New York: Columbia University Press.

Sassen, Saskia. 1998. *Globalization and Its Discontents: Essays on the New Mobility of People and Money.* New York: New Press.

Simon, Stephanie. 1994. "Rehab Program Plants Organic Seeds of Hope Therapy: Ventura Branch of Victory Outreach Helps Recovering Addicts and Criminals Weed Out Their Lives Through a Regimen of Prayer and Farming." *Los Angeles Times,* January 7, 1994.

Skolnick, Jerome H. 1988. "The Social Structure of Street Drug Dealing." Bureau of Criminal Statistics and Special Services. Sacramento: Office of the Attorney General, State of California.

Smilde, David. 2008. *Reason to Believe: Cultural Agency in Latin American Evangelicalism.* Berkeley: University of California Press.

Smith, Christian. 1998. *American Evangelicalism: Embattled and Thriving.* Chicago: University of Chicago Press.

Smith, Robert C. 2006. *Mexican New York: Transnational Lives of New Immigrants.* Berkeley: University of California Press.

Smith, Shawn Maree. 1989. "Faith Helps Ex-Addicts Reach Out." *Los Angeles Times,* April 22, 1989.

Soja, Edward W. 2011[1989]. *Postmodern Geographies: The Reassertion of Space in Critical Social Theory.* London: Verso Press.

Spaulding, Sophie. 1992. "The Myth of the Classic Slum: Contradictory Perceptions of Boyle Heights Flats, 1900–1991." *Journal of Architectural Education* 45(2):107–119.

Stacey, Judith. 1990. *Brave New Families: Stories of Domestic Upheaval in Late Twentieth Century*. New York: Basic Books.

Steffensmeier, Darrell, and Stephen Demuth 2000. "Ethnicity and Sentencing Outcomes in U.S. Federal Courts: Who is Punished More Harshly?" *American Sociological Review* 65(5):705–729.

Stohlman, Sarah. 2007. "At Yesenia's House . . . : Central American Immigrant Pentecostalism, Congregational Homophily, and Religious Innovation in Los Angeles." *Qualitative Sociology* 30(1):61–80.

Tagami, Ty. 1994. "Body and Soul: Victory Outreach Travels the Mean Streets, Offering Spiritual Refuge to Those Who Have Lost It All." *Los Angeles Times,* November 30, 1994.

Taylor, Carl S. 1990. "Gang Imperialism." In C. Ronald Huff (ed.), *Gangs in America*. 1st ed. Newbury Park, CA: Sage.

Thomas, William Isaac, and Florian Znaniecki. 1918. *The Polish Peasant in Europe and America: Monograph of an Immigrant Group*. Chicago: University of Chicago Press.

Thrasher, Frederic. 1927. *The Gang: A Study of 1,313 Gangs in Chicago*. Chicago: University of Chicago Press.

Tracy, David. 1982. *The Analogical Imagination: Christian Theology and the Culture of Pluralism*. New York: Crossroad Press.

Vásquez, Manuel A., Marie Friedmann Marquardt, and Ileana Gómez. 2003. "Saving Souls Transnationally: Pentecostalism and Youth Gangs in El Salvador and the United States." In Manuel A. Vásquez and Marie F. Marquardt (eds.), *Globalizing the Sacred*. New Brunswick, NJ: Rutgers University Press.

Venkatesh, Sudhir Alladi. 1996. "The Gang and the Community." In C. Ronald Huff (ed.), *Gangs in America*, 2d ed. Newbury Park, CA: Sage.

———. 1997. "The Social Organization of Street Gang Activity in an Urban Ghetto." *American Journal of Sociology* 103(1):82–111.

———. 2008. *Gang Leader for a Day: A Rogue Sociologist Takes to the Streets*. New York: Penguin.

Vernon, Robert L. 1990. "Social Solutions to Gang Problem." *Los Angeles Times,* November 23, 1990.

Victory Outreach. 2010a. "History of Victory Outreach International." Victory Outreach.org. Retrieved from http://www.victoryoutreach.org/aboutus/victory-outreach-history.asp on June 1, 2010.

———. 2010b. "Structure of Victory Outreach." Victory Outreach.org. Retrieved from http://www.victoryoutreach.org/aboutus/victory-outreach-structure.asp on June 1, 2010.

Vigil, James Diego. 1982. "Human Revitalization: The Six Tasks of Victory Outreach." *The Drew Gateway* 52(3):49–59.

———. 1988. *Barrio Gangs: Street Life and Identity in Southern California*. Austin: University of Texas Press.

———. 2007. *The Projects: Gang and Non-Gang Families in East Los Angeles*. Austin: University of Texas Press.

Vigil, James Diego, Steve C. Yun, and Jesse Cheng. 2004. "A Shortcut to the American Dream?: Vietnamese Youth Gangs in Little Saigon." In Jennifer Lee and Min Zhou (eds.), *Asian American Youth: Culture, Identity, and Ethnicity*. New York: Routledge.

Wacquant, Loic. 2009[1999]. *Prisons of Poverty*. Minneapolis: University of Minnesota Press.

Waldinger, Roger. 2001. *Strangers at the Gates: New Immigrants in Urban America*. Berkeley: University of California Press.

Warner, R. Stephen. 1993. "Work in Progress Toward a New Paradigm for the Sociological Study of Religion in the United States." *American Journal of Sociology* 98(5):1044–1093.

———. 2007. "The Role of Religion in the Process of Segmented Assimilation." *Annals of the American Academy of Political and Social Science*. 612(1):102–115.

Warner, R. Stephen, and Judith G. Wittner, eds. 1998. *Gatherings in Diaspora*. Philadelphia: Temple University Press.

Waters, Mary C. 1999. *Black Identities: West Indian Immigrant Dreams and American Realities*. Cambridge, MA: Harvard University Press.

Watson, Carol. 1989. "Police Arrest 1,092 in Weekend Sweeps; Gang Killings Continue." *Los Angeles Times*, October 2, 1989.

Welkos, Robert. 1988. "700 Seized in Gang Sweep; 2 More Die in Shootings." *Los Angeles Times*, September 19, 1988.

West, Candace, and Don H. Zimmerman. 1987. "Doing Gender." *Gender & Society* 1:125–151.

Western, Bruce. 2007. *Punishment and Inequality in America*. New York: Russell Sage.

Whyte, William F. 1943. *Street Corner Society: The Social Structure of an Italian Slum*. Boulder, CO: Westview Press.

Wilson, William J. 1987. *The Truly Disadvantaged*. Chicago: University of Chicago Press.

Wolseth, Jon. 2010. "Safety and Sanctuary: Pentecostalism and Youth Gang Violence in Honduras." *Latin American Perspectives* 35(4):96–111.

Yablonsky, Lewis. 1997. *Gangsters: Fifty Years of Madness, Drugs, and Death on the Streets of America*. New York: New York University Press.

Young, Jock. 2011. *The Criminological Imagination*. Cambridge, UK: Polity.

Young, Pauline V. 1929. "The Russian Molokan Community in Los Angeles." *American Journal of Sociology* 35(3):393–402.

Zhou, Min, and Carl L. Bankston. 1998. *Growing Up American: How Vietnamese Children Adapt to Life in the United States*. New York: Russell Sage

Zhou, Min, Carl L. Bankston, and Rebecca Y. Kim. 2002. "Rebuilding Spiritual Lives in the New Land: Religious Practices among Southeast Asian Refugees in the United States." In Pyong Gap Min and Jung Ha Kim (eds.), *Religions in Asian America: Building Faith Communities*. New York: AltaMira Press.

Zhou, Min, Jennifer Lee, Jody Agius Vallejo, Rosaura Tafoya-Estrada, and Yang Sao Xiong. 2008. "Success Attained, Deterred, and Denied: Divergent Pathways to Social Mobility in Los Angeles' New Second Generation." *Annals of the American Academy of Political and Social Science* 620(1):37–61.

crime policy (*continued*): Summer Night Lights, 6, 60; suppression, 3, 6, 52, 56, 60; surveillance, 52; "New Jim Crow," 48; Three Strikes, 6, 51, 207n3; "tough on crime," 47, 51; War on Crime, 51, 52; War on Drugs, 47, 51; War on Terror, 36, 51, 56, 61; zero tolerance, 192, 49, 61

Criminals and Gang Members Anonymous, 99

Cruz, Nicky, 21

cultural memory, 89–91, 108, 197–98

Debora, Fabian, 58

desistance from crime, 111

discourse: altar call, 157, 186–187; Anger Management class, 99, 145–146; Antonio on desistance from crime, 111; Antonio's testimony, 110, 162; call-and-response, 152; "check-ins," 146–148, 159; Chicano gang masculinity (*see* Chicano gang masculinity); Christian soldiers, 125; church services, 152, 156; colorblind discourse, 35, 45–46; as communication phenomenon, 148; Criminals and Gang Members Anonymous class, 99; failing at masculine performance, 163; family man, 162; fatherhood, 156; gang masculinity (*see* Chicano gang masculinity); gang recovery as discourse, 28, 163–165; gangs, 148; "generativity," 111; group therapy, 99, 151–152, 158–161; "looking-glass rehabilitation," 147, 201; man of God, 188–189; masculine negotiations, 151; morning meeting daily prayer, 158; neoliberalism, 51; "politics of performance," 28, 187–188; public talk, 28; Ramon, 125; rap music, 188–189; real man, 165, 201; rearticulation of masculinity, 190; "redemption script," 28, 111, 146, 158, 201; "reformed barrio masculinity," 150, 163, 187–188; regret as strength, 151; religion in performance, 164–165; resistance to the "Latino crime threat," 188; self-help workshops, 99; sermons, 153, 156–158; shaming, 149, 150, 153, 161, 165, 202; social integration, 111; social reintegration, 149–150; street evangelism rallies, 107, 188–189; "stronghold of the devil," 155; testimonies, 153, 162; the podium, 150–152, 156, 158, 160, 162–165, 201; "thought of the day," 101; "tragic optimism," 146–148; twelve-step model, 160; yoga, 99

"disintegrative shaming," 150

eagle feather, 128

embodiment; blending masculine styles, 180–182, 189–190, 202; bodily practices, 190; bopping, 209n3; Canada, Geoffrey, 209n3; Chicano gangs, 171 to 172; conventional manhood, 177; cool pose, 158, 185, 189–190, 202, 209n3; disabled men, 174–175; dress clothes from goodwill, 180; embodied displays, 170, 171, 179–180; embodiment, hard, 170; embodiment, soft, 170; family man, 184; gang attire, 171–172; growing hair out, 180; handshakes, 181; "health and wealth gospel," 179–180; manhood, 181–182; masculine gang embodiment (*see* Chicano gang masculinity); masculine negotiations, 175, 181; nurturing, 158, 180–81; Pastor Raul on embodiment, 175–177; recovering gang members, 143; in recovery, 202; recovery through dress, 177; redirecting the body, 184–185, 202; reform of dress, 178–179; reformation of masculine expressions, 143; "reformed barrio masculinity," 169, 184, 189–190, 202; reshaping the body, 179, 181–182, 184, 202; social hierarchies, 178–179; swagger, 209n3; weight, 181–182

entrée-ism, 43

ethnic nationalists, 44

eugenics, 15, 35, 38, 44, 60

"family man": Antonio as, 162; gang recovery, 165; giving back to the community, 201; at Homeboy Industries, 160–161; Mario as, 117; men of God, 26, 29, 153, 186, 188–189, 193, 201, 204; the "podium," 162, 165; as a "real man," 165, 201; religion in the performance of the, 165; at Victory Outreach, 153, 186–189

Fenstermaker, Sarah, 163

Fernandez Kelly, Maria Patricia, 94

Fremon, Celeste, 5

gang masculinity. *See* Chicano gang masculinity

gang recovery, 2, 10, 14, 28, 92, 113, 143–144, 163–165, 198, 202; Brenneman, Robert, 150; Chicano gang masculinity and (*see* Chicano gang masculinity); conventional manhood, 177, 200; legitimacy, 165; men's recovery home, 24; models of gang recovery, 107, 196; as a movement, 193; as a performance, 163–65; "the podium," 163–165; redemption, 92, 107, 196; religious theologies, 92, 107;

Edward Orozco Flores is Assistant Professor of Sociology at Loyola University Chicago. He received his Ph.D. in sociology from the University of Southern California.